A Bandit Called Derby

By
Oliver Franklin Jones

**Lightly revised and edited by
Derby F and Sheryl Jones**

authorHOUSE

1663 LIBERTY DRIVE, SUITE 200
BLOOMINGTON, INDIANA 47403
(800) 839-8640
www.authorhouse.com

First published by AuthorHouse 06/29/04

ISBN: 1-4184-3450-7 (sc)

Printed in the United States of America
Bloomington, Indiana

This book is printed on acid-free paper.

FOREWORD

By Derby F. Jones, the son of a bandit

In my mind my father was always bigger than life. I was always trying to please him, make him as proud of me as I was of him. He'd had a hard life, fifteen years in two state penitentiaries back when Hard Time really was hard. When released the third time he decided to go straight. He was forty years old, it was then that he got married, started a family and raised three kids, all of whom turned out to be outstanding people. He taught me that to make it in this world, I had to work hard. And no matter what I did in life always do it to the best of my ability.

I remember being about five when some neighborhood boys were throwing rocks at my older sister, I was scared, so I ran home and left her to fend for herself, after all she was older and bigger than I. When Dad found out he beat my ass good. He said he was ashamed of me, that no son of his should run simply because he was scared, leaving a female to fend for herself. After that, no matter how scared I was deep down inside, no one ever knew it. I would always stand my ground and never, ever leave someone who was defenseless. That is why I was awarded the Silver Star while in Vietnam, I would not turn and leave my wounded buddies, even though we were outnumbered ten to one, and I had the chance to save myself.

I also remember Dad telling my sisters and me about his life outside the law. He told us that he had robbed a store, and been put in jail, that he had robbed a bank and been put in jail, and that he had robbed a gambling establishment and been put in jail. He told us what it was like being put in The Hole for eighteen months, how nothing was worth living without freedom. He said that crime did not pay, but that no matter what I did in life always reley on myself, that he was always caught because his partners turned him in. I listened, but only half listened like most kids do when their parents tell them tales of the past.

In 1968 I was in the Army and home on leave, staying at Dads with my two-year-old son. The day I was leaving he wheeled over to me (he was in a wheelchair by then) and told me good-bye, he also said that it would be our final good-bye, that we would not see each other again. In all my self-indulgent ignorance I said "Oh Dad, don't worry, I'll make it back from Vietnam again, just like the last two times." He said "I know son, but I won't be here." A few months later I was out on a mission in Vietnam and was ordered back to base, to go home for a family emergency. I knew as soon as I got the message that it was Dad. When I got back to base and called home my sisters told me Dad was in the hospital and would not last much longer, but that he was trying to hold on until I got there. I caught the next plane to the states. When I landed in the good old USA, I called the hospital and found out that he had passed away just 2 hours before, and that he had been asking for me right up to the end. When I did finally arrive home I took his ashes and buried him. As I dug his final resting-place I would take a drink of Early Times, his favorite drink, and then pour a drink on his urn. Together we said our last goodbyes.

Years later, after my mother died my sisters and I were going through her personal effects, we came across the original manuscript that Dad had written about his early life. He had it published, but had only printed 250 copies for his friends and family. I took the manuscript home and started reading it; I could hear him telling me these stories, he wrote just like he spoke. It was then that I decided to share my father with the rest of the world and try and get his book republished. I approached Kenn Miller, a friend and old Vietnam buddy of mine, who knew the ins and out of publishing a book. He read the manuscript and said that with some additional material he thought it would make a great book. And so it all started.

My wife, Sheryl, and I went to Boise to try and do some research, hopefully to find some small article in the Boise newspaper (if they kept papers back that far) that might give us some names and dates that my father had left completely out of his book. All we had were copies of his pardons; they showed the date of his incarceration and release. When we arrived in Boise we found out that the old Idaho State Penitentiary had been made into a museum, and that the library carried all the old *Idaho Statesman* newspapers on microfilm. We first went to the library, and since we knew that date he was incarcerated, January 19, 1925, we decided to start with the October 1, 1924 microfilm. After a very discouraging hour and a half the October 17, 1924 front page appeared with my father staring back at me. We had found the article on his jailbreak, and from there on the most amazing story unfolded right in front of our eyes. My father's book was only a half-truth, not that he had told any lies, he had just left out half the story. Later that afternoon we visited the Old Idaho Penitentiary, and started receiving more information.

What an incredible journey, none of which would have been possible without the overwhelming response and help we received from some very wonderful people who live and work in Idaho and Nevada. Our sincere thanks to:
Kenn Miller, for getting us started
Rey Martinez, for all his moral support
The Document and Periodical Staff from the Boise Library
Barb Christian and Ronda Smoot from the Idaho Penitentiary Documents Office
The Idaho Historical Society
Chris Brady and Stephan McMaines from the Old Idaho State Penitentiary

Glenna Traylor, Phyllis Kaufman, and Lt. Batt from the Ada County Sheriffs Office

Lorriane Willams from the Ada County Records Office

Cheryl Lamb from the Jerome County Court Records Office

Lois from the Jerome Library

Brenda from the Jerome Northside News

Laura Johns from the West Charleston Library in Las Vegas

Bennie McGuiness from the Nevada State Penitentiary

Jeff Kintop and Guy Rocha from the Nevada State Archives

Ron James from the Nevada Historical Preservation Office

Beverly Clugg, M. Attwood and young Jerald Matter from the Jerome Historical Society

Stephen Greenberg from the National Library of Medicine for his E-Mail telling us what CC Pills were

Fred Hallberg from the Canyon County Historical Society for sharing with us his wealth of knowledge on trains and the railroads in southern Idaho

and all the other people we have spoken with that are to numerous to mention.

A very special thanks to Ron Marshall from Eagle, Idaho for inviting us to a 50th year Eagle High School reunion, and for getting us in touch with Marie Maines, who actually remembered the Bank robbery and for introducing us to her good friend, Lester Sommers. Ron also put us in contact with Jim Calbus who informed us that Margaret Fikkan was now Margaret Gillam and put us in touch with this very gracious lady.

I would also like to thank the following writers from whose published works I unabashedly stole pertinent information:

William C. Anderson, "Lady Bluebeard"
J. Campbell Bruce, "Escape From Alcatraz"
G. Russell Girardin, "Dillinger, The Untold Story"
Matt R. Penrose, "Pots 'O Gold"
Lee Thomas, "Sheriffs, Twin Falls County 1907-1996"
Jill M. Sevy, "Old Idaho Penitentiary 1870-1973, A Walking Tour Guide"
Sister M. Alfreda Elsensohn, "Idaho Chinese Lore"
Arthur A. Hart, "Life In Old Boise"
Merle Wells, "Boise, An Illustrated History"
Robert G. Grimmett, "Cabal of Death"
The Idaho Statesman
The Boise Evening Capital News
The Elko Daily Free Press
The Elko Independent
The Twin Falls Daily News.

My father was not a prejudiced man; he had many friends throughout his lifetime that were of many different ethnic backgrounds. However, in reading the original manuscript, we found a lot of slang words that in today's society would be considered offensive. We decided to leave these words in the story because they were the slang of the day and add to the flavor of the book. As you read, please remember that these words were slang, and not meant to be offensive.

So here, in his own words, is the story of a Bandit called Derby...

INTRODUCTION

My name is Oliver Franklin Jones, and I have frequently been asked by my friends to write the story of my life. They have told me it would be a wonderful lesson to the younger generation. I have lived an unusual life, and if I can stand as a bad example, then maybe some good will come from my many mistakes and my many crimes. I have been in more jails than I can remember. I have been accused of almost every crime on the statutes. I have done fifteen calendar years in different prisons. I had the first gun moll in the Northwest. I broke jail with a wooden gun in 1924, the same year John Dillinger was sent up for his first grocery store robbery. I was locked in one dungeon for eighteen months. I have served my time, and received official pardons for my crimes. As far as the law is concerned, I have paid my debt to society. As far as I am concerned, I still owe a debt to society. And that's why I have written this book.

Hello Stranger

Hello, hello stranger,
I won't spit into your eye.
So come on over to the bar,
And have a drink, I'll buy.

I have a little story,
I'd like very much to tell
I've just returned from a trip,
I made down into hell.

I just got out of the big house,
After doing six years flat.
Don't let the lousy bums.
Say they can't do that!

I was doing some hijacking,
With a great big tommy gun.
A gambling in the cabbage green,
And having lots of fun.

Had a partner in there with me,
He was yellow down his spine.
His squealing to the bulls
Got me all that time.

Fill them up again bartender,
And all the drinks I'll pay.
I'm still out looking for that rat,
I must be on my way.

Oliver F. Jones

I

The Wrong Side of The Law

I was born March 22 in the year 1896 to Alice Elizabeth and Issac Norman Jones, in the Ozark Mountains near Eureka Springs, Arkansas. When I was a very small boy my father bought a general store in the small railroad town of Urbanette. There he established a business that he kept until his death. I had two twin brothers, Onnie and Lonnie, and two sisters, Ina and Ella. My father was noted for his kindness and honesty. He was always willing to help anyone who was in trouble. When any of the boys got in a jam, they would call on my father for help. I never knew him to turn anyone down. But I guess I was born to have trouble, not to help people out of it.

I well remember the first time I got arrested. Another boy and I got in a fight at a church picnic with half the town there, and we created quite a disturbance, knocking over tables of food, bloodying each other's noses, and spattering people with blood. The town constable pinched us, and Dad had to go to the Justice of the Peace to pay my fine, which amounted to three dollars. Back then, three dollars was a lot of money. Dad whipped me good, and then he warned me that this had better be the last time I got in trouble.

It wasn't the last; it was just the first. I don't recall how many fines Dad paid for me, but I do remember the last one. On our ride home, Dad gave me a lecture that hurt more than a thrashing. He ended up by saying, "Son, if you don't change your ways, you will be hung, or in the state pen before you're twenty-one!"

Dad never lived to know how near the truth those words were. On October 7, 1913 he passed away. At his death, he left us with the store and the depot agency. My mother was already the local Postmaster, or "Postmistress" in today's terms, one of the few women to hold that title in the whole country. She managed to get me appointed the depot agent, and I was all set to settle down, take responsibility, and turn into a law-abiding citizen. Unfortunately, I never got the chance. One of my Dad's brothers, John B. Jones, tried to take over Dad's estate by getting himself appointed guardian for my seven-year-old twin brothers, Onnie and Lonnie, and me. He failed in that, but he didn't give up. The next thing he tried to do was get me and my brothers sent to reform school. He failed in that too, but he still didn't give up. By this time, he had it in for me on a personal basis. I knew he was trying to get me canned from my job as depot agent, and I knew that sooner or later we were going to mix. I was determined not to let him win. Uncle John was a "good Christian man", at least that is what he claimed, but in my opinion if he was an example of a "good Christian", I wanted nothing to do with religion, and stayed away from any form of religion for the rest of my life. One night, railroad lantern in hand, I went down to meet a train, and there was Uncle John. I knew my chance had come so I let him have it with my railroad lantern, right between the eyes. I'd hoped to knock him out, and if the truth be told, I didn't much care if I killed him. But all I did was knock him to his knees, and before I knew it, he'd hopped up, grabbed me, and started choking me. If two of my friends hadn't shown up and pulled him off me, I might have been a goner. As it was, he had a warrant sworn out against me, and I had to pay another fine. But at least I had the satisfaction of seeing him pay one too.

After that, my uncle devoted himself to slandering me every chance he got. Whenever anything bad was done in the whole community, I got the rap for it. I almost broke my mother financially, and I almost broke her heart, with all the fines she had to pay for me. What made it worse was that I was getting bum raps, but wasn't seeing any justice. Finally things came to a head between my uncle and me. We passed some words between us, and next thing I knew, he had a warrant sworn out for my arrest, on the grounds that I was threatening his life, which by this point, I probably was.

Two bulls came out to serve the warrant, and even though I was plenty sore about it, I went with them to fix up a bond. While I was talking to some men about signing my bond, I suddenly saw a chance that looked too good to pass up. I grabbed one of the bulls' six-gun, shot it over his head until it was empty, then handed it back to him. You should have seen the look on that bull's face. He was too embarrassed to reload his six-gun, and for a long moment, he and everyone else were too shocked to do anything. Seeing them just standing there, I saw my second chance, and took off.

I ran and ran and ran until I gave out, then I found a place to hide. Before long, those first two bulls, and another bull they brought along, came beating the bush for me. If I'd stood up, or tried to run, chances were they might have just shot me. And if they didn't shoot me, I knew I was in for a pistol-whipping, at the very least. There wasn't much I could do except stay hidden, and that's what I did. Fortunately, I'd picked a good hiding place, and although they passed just a few feet from me, they didn't find me. When they were gone, I stayed there for a while, thinking to myself, and that's when I realized that I had now become an outlaw.

When it got dark, I ventured out and found a friend of mine. I had him buy me some chuck, then we went out and found a better hiding place. The place we found was a tumbled down old shack back in a thicket, and except for the spiders and bugs and maybe some snakes that were more afraid of me than I was of them, I was all alone. Every couple of days, my friend would come around with some supplies and news about what the bulls who were looking for me were up to. Those first few days I got a thrill out of being an outlaw, and it seemed a fine life. But before long, it started to get tiresome. Every time anyone came anywhere near, I'd have to go back into deep hiding. I could see I wasn't accomplishing anything this way, and so, one night after the heat had died down a little, I came in and gave myself up.

Thanks to the fact that everyone had had time to cool down a little, and thanks to the fact that there were some people in the community who had good words to say about me, all I had to do was pay another fine. But while I was hiding out, I'd done a lot of thinking. As long as I stayed around home I was going to have nothing but trouble, and I'd never get ahead. I talked things over with Mother, and we finally came to the conclusion that it would be best for me to go to some other state and try to get a job.

The further I could get from Uncle John and my bad reputation back home, the better off I was going to be. So I set off for the Great Northwest, and eventually washed up in Twin Falls, Idaho, which was about as big a town as Eureka Springs, Arkansas, but looked a lot more exciting to me.

Trouble was, I couldn't eat excitement. I needed work, but I was just a kid, and small for my age and the people doing the hiring preferred to hire the big ones. I finally landed a job in a hotel as a cook's helper, and set out to make good. The cook seemed to think I had the makings of a cook. I liked the work, and got along well with the cook, and if it hadn't been that Twin Falls was still pretty much the Wild West, I might have stayed out of trouble and kept to the kitchen for life. But as I said, there was plenty of excitement around here, and the excitement that struck my fancy first was all the poker games that seemed to be going on all over town. Being a kid, I must've looked like an easy mark, and I was, at first. The first few times I sat in on a poker game, I didn't sit in for long, because I was playing with a cook's helper's wages, and I didn't know how to play with the big boys. But I learned fast, and I seemed to hold the best of luck. Before long, I had made a few good winnings, and I started thinking that it was a lot easier to sit in on the games and beat the boys for their dough, than it was to work in the hotel kitchen, peeling their spuds and mixing their dough.

One night, after making a good winning, I decided to quit my cook's helper job, and set out to see more of the world, taking gambling as my profession. Heading out west from home, I had already learned how to beat my way on the trains, riding for free, if not always in the height of comfort and safety, and being as how I was a little homesick, I thought about heading back to Arkansas. However, on second thought, I could see that that wasn't in the cards! I could just see the law back home riding up and saying, "Jones, I have a warrant for your arrest." That picture didn't please me, and so when I left Twin Falls, I left without any particular destination in mind. I'd just go where the trains took me, and I was sure I could get by.

After leaving Twin Falls I made a stop in the first good town I came to. I jumped off the train when it slowed outside town, and walked in looking for a game. Almost immediately, I ran into a fellow that I had met on the bum when I had bummed my way West. At first I didn't make him, for he had got over well, and was dressed up and holding a bankroll. But he recognized me, and he was as glad to see me as I was glad to see him. We talked for a while, then went to a cafe for something to eat. It turned out that he was a gambler too, and a good one. He said he would always win if the boys let him play and the way he was dressed up and flashing that bankroll, I believed him.

We went to the town's one hotel, and got us a room, and there he showed me how to mark cards. This was a skill I was very glad to be learning, and the two of us decided to team up, on the grounds that two guys can get a sucker's dough better than one.

I soon got to where I could read the cards from the back as well as most people could from the face. My friend was going by the name "Kelly", which might even have been his real name, and he seemed pleased at how quick I caught on. He had it in his mind that we ought to head back East, and this pleased me. I was thinking I might be able to slip home some night and see Mother and the boys, but I soon realized that "back East" was a big place, and we weren't headed near my home.

Where we were headed, and where we went, was just about everywhere else. We had some good luck for a spell, but it wasn't long before I discovered that Kelly liked Ol' John Barleycorn just a little too much. Almost every saloon town we would stop in, first thing he'd do is start drinking. Now, drinking didn't seem to affect his playing, but it did affect his disposition, and when Kelly got a few drinks in him, he'd usually turn quarrelsome, whether we were winning or not. I can't begin to remember how many times I just barely managed to save him from jail, nor how many towns we had to leave in a hurry.

One night, we were in a rough little no-name town that wasn't really much of a town, just a muddy street of unpainted shacks, populated by miners and lumberjacks, railroaders, and other such people, with a couple of the shacks containing women that kept those men warm at night. Our specialty was poker, but this night we got ourselves in a crap game. The other players were a tough bunch of mean looking men, and I could only figure that those who weren't wearing their guns and knives out where everyone could see, were still wearing them, just wearing them concealed. Because I was a kid and Kelly was wearing dirty but fancy clothes, and since we drifted in separately like we didn't know each other, we looked like a couple of marks, and so we didn't have much trouble getting into the game. We didn't have much trouble staying in it, either, and Kelly didn't have much trouble raking in most of the dough. This made a few of the boys suspicious and before too long, someone accused Kelly of cheating. I was sitting with my back to the window, and I saw Kelly give me a wink. His eyelid had hardly recovered from the wink when he shot out of his chair, and punched the fellow in the nose who'd accused him of cheating. Just then, someone turned out the lights, so I kicked out the window and went out with it. I hit the bricks just as all those fellows back in that shack were fumbling around for their guns and knives. Almost as soon as I hit the bricks, Kelly was right beside me, yelling, "Let's go!"

We took off running, splashing and slipping in the mud. Behind us, we could hear the ruckus of those fellows cursing us and arming themselves. They were pouring out of the door and the window to come after us. But it was dark and they couldn't get a shot off, and we were faster than they were, even though we were slipping and laughing like a couple of loonies. We made our getaway, then after walking all night, we came to the rail yards in the next town, and caught the first freight train East.

Kelly and I traveled for some time, stopping only when we got hungry. When we got into Missouri, we decided to stop a few days and rest up. Kelly always seemed to have a scheme to clean up a good stake, and he had one now. He knew a guy who had a large bank account and most any business house would cash his checks. The guy was a heavy drinker, so we looked him up and bought him plenty of drinks. Kelly gave him a line about beating a big game in town, told him he wanted to make a flash. He got the mark to sign some blank checks, telling him he wouldn't use them. Then we kept giving him whiskey, until he fell asleep. We knew he wasn't going to bother us for a few hours. Kelly filled out the checks, giving them all to me, except the one he was going to cash. He was lucky. When he got back, he gave me the money, and took another check. He did this until he'd cashed all the checks, and I had all the money, then we headed for the depot to get out of town.

On the way to the depot, Kelly told me he might get thrown in jail, but told me not to worry; there was no danger of them bothering me. I was carrying the money, but he was the one they'd pinch, since he'd cashed the checks. Kelly told me that if he got pinched, he wanted me to slip him a good saw in jail. By this time, I was beginning to think that my friend, "Kelly," was something besides just a gambler.

We made it out of that town, and on to the next, where we stayed in a hotel. When we went to the depot to leave that town, two bulls pinched us just as we were getting on the train. Kelly knew one of the bulls and was friendly with him. When we heard what the rap was, Kelly said there was nothing to it, and told the bulls I had nothing to do with it anyway. They turned me loose, but held him. Telling them he'd cover their expenses, Kelly talked the bulls into waiting until the next day to take him back to the other town, and then he proceeded to charm the bulls, and buy them drinks until he had a chance to have a private word with me.

Kelly always had a plan, and this time his plan worked. He had told me to meet him in the alley beside the towns' only drug store, and then he talked the two bulls into going to the drug store with him that night. He gave them the slip, and met me in the alley behind the drug store, and we hightailed on out of town. Of course, we couldn't take the train, so we walked. It was cold and raining, but we had to make a soft getaway, so we walked all night. If we hadn't kept walking, one of two things would have happened to us. Maybe we would have got pinched again. And if that didn't happen, we would have frozen to death. Our clothes, our matches, and our new money were all soaking wet and we were shivering till our teeth almost broke from rattling, but we made our getaway.

About noon the next day, we spotted a small town. There was only one store. We had to have something to eat and we had to dry out, so we took a chance and headed for that store. It was warm in the store, and we thought it would be a good place to eat. It was a big mistake. While we were eating, a bull rode up, slipped into the store, covered Kelly with his gun, put him under arrest, and handcuffed him. He didn't arrest me, and he didn't really want me around, but he let us finish our meals, and then he let me tag along when he took us to a bunkhouse, with a big, warm, potbellied stove. I told the bull I wanted to go back with Kelly after we dried out, and after a while the three of us walked outside. Kelly and the bull were talking, but I couldn't hear what they were saying, and I didn't see Kelly slip the bull any dough.

Suddenly, Kelly started yelling, "Let's go!" Go I did, but I got a bad start, I slipped and fell in a hole full of water. Kelly already had the store building between himself and the bulls. Me, I was expecting a bullet in the back any moment, so I wasn't going to let a hole full of water slow me down long. I was up and out and running right quick, and I soon caught up with Kelly.

We worked our way into the bush, and kept running all the way until we hit the swamp. We didn't let the swamp stop

9

us, either. We were already about as wet as we could get, and so we plunged on in, Kelly reassuring me that they didn't have any alligators in Missouri anymore and hadn't had any since back when the Indians were running things. Kelly told me he knew Missouri because his own daddy had spent the war in Missouri, most of it riding with Mr. Quantrill. Kelly told me his daddy used to ride with the James brothers, Frank and Jesse, back in the war, but hadn't been all that impressed with them until after the war, when they robbed the Glendale train.

It wasn't until we were a couple hours, at least, into the swamps, when we took a rest on a little spot of drier ground., I told Kelly it wasn't alligators I was worried about, it was snakes, and the fact that working with him was beginning to look like it was going to get me shot, or hung, or drowned in a swamp, if I wasn't careful.

"Another thing that has me worried is those bracelets you're wearing," I said. "How do you propose we're going to get you out of those handcuffs?" Kelly frowned and looked down at his handcuffs, then he jiggled the chain, and frowned some more.

"I want you to forget what you're going to have to be witness to now," said Kelly, looking real serious. "It's not proper for a good Christian white man like me to be even using such powers, much less to be exposing them to the young. You got to promise you'll forget this spell when it's over. If you promise me that, maybe I can find a way out of these handcuffs. Do you promise?" I promised, and as soon as I did, Kelly began chanting and singing like a half-colored Indian medicine man, and then he blew on his wrists and the handcuffs fell away. I was in awe, and wondering if I was in the presence of a Houdini, but then Kelly started to laugh. "Money's magical stuff," he said. "I slipped that bull back there a sawbuck, and had him unlock the cuffs. He let me run."

He folded the handcuffs, and put them in his pocket, then patted the pocket where he put them, and smiled to himself in a way that made me a little nervous, though I tried not to show it. Kelly said, "Stick with me just a little longer, kid, and I'll make your fortune."

Kelly got to his feet and I did too, and we headed on into the swamp for the next spit of land. The next time we stopped to rest, the mosquitoes were driving me crazy, and all Kelly could talk about was how much he wanted a drink, how much he loved whiskey. "Whiskey... " he said it like he was homesick, talking about home.

"You just leave the whiskey drinking to me, kid. You keep your palate clean for all the French wines and champagne you'll be drinking after I help you make your fortune. Just leave the whiskey to me..."

Oliver and twins Onnie and Lonnie - 1907

Oliver and the Girls From Urbanette - 1913

II

Gambling Man

It turned out that Kelly had been through this general area before, and knew of a place where he bummed a feed once. Luck was with us, and sometime after dark we found the place. It was a little house, out in the middle of nowhere, and that was just what we needed. Instead of bumming them he asked them to cook us a feed and let us dry our clothes. He said he would pay them for their trouble. Kelly told them he was an officer of the law. He took out the handcuffs and laid them on the table, causing them to believe what he had told them. They had us undress and hang our clothes around the fire to dry them. Kelly told the lady that when he was through there before and bummed her for a feed he had been looking for a guy he had finally located. When he told the lady that the guy was on the run from the law, her eyes lit up like candles. She began naming names, and I bet she named every man in that whole district, hoping we'd tell her when she said the right name. Kelly told her that he couldn't tell her who we were looking for, because nobody knew we were looking for him. He told her she'd know who it was after we pinched him, and she finally shut up. That lady was ready to snitch on everyone, just to be in the know. But I do have to say she was a good cook and fed us well. Kelly gave the woman and her husband two bucks for the feed, and promised to let them know who the party was after we made the pinch. As soon as we were fed and our clothes were dry, we took off.

After we got back to the railroad track, Kelly pitched the handcuffs into the swamp, and we headed for the next town. There was another railroad that crossed the one we were on. We planned to catch a train on it, which we did. The next day, we got off the train at the end of the division. Kelly told me to go up to the town and get us something to eat. He would wait there. I asked him why he wouldn't go along. He said that if they caught him in that town, they would hang him.

That crack caused me to do a little thinking on the road up to town. Murder was about the only crime I knew of that they could hang a fellow for, and I couldn't help wondering if they could hang a fellow if they caught him running around with a murderer. When I got back with lunch, I asked Kelly what he meant by that crack. He smiled real easy, and explained that he had been in this town several times and beat a lot of fellows out of a lot of their dough, and they had accused him of cheating. Because of this, he'd had to knock a guy in the head, but he hadn't killed him.

I felt a little better hearing this, but I did do some thinking, I decided that when we got to where we were safe, it was going to be time to split up the bankroll, and go my way while he went his. Three days later, we stopped in a saloon town, where Kelly spent most of his time at the bar. Gambling was good in this town, and even though Kelly was full drunk the whole time, he could still play, and we made some good winnings. Nobody accused us of cheating, which was a relief to me. But before we left, Kelly got in a drunken fight with the guy who owned the local tailor shop. The night we left town, Kelly wanted to set fire to the guy's shop and burn him. This is where I balked. I told Kelly I'd help him beat the guy up, but no dice on the fire racket, and we left town without harming the tailor.

We crossed the Mississippi River into Illinois, stopping in the town of Cairo. Here, Kelly met an old acquaintance. He was a tough looking egg, and I found out he was as tough and mean as he looked. I overheard him and Kelly making plans to rob a saloonkeeper who wore some good-sized diamonds. I didn't like their plans, and when we got alone, I told Kelly so. He tried to talk me out of splitting, saying he was going to make my fortune, but finally he gave in. We split our bankroll, and I left Kelly with his old friend, and headed west.

I landed in Kansas City, with no particular place to go. One day, I passed an employment office. I noticed they wanted men to ship into Wyoming. It seemed like a good way to get back to Idaho, as it was still a little cold to bum my way. The man in the office said he was sending out a shipment that night. The office fee was two dollars, but I couldn't go unless I had some baggage. That clued me in about a few things. If I had to have baggage, that meant they were going to hold the baggage until after they put us to work. The work involved was working on a steel gang, and I had no intention of doing that, on the grounds it was too much work for too little money. And besides, I had my profession of gambling. Still, I found a second hand store, bought me an old suitcase and some old clothes that I wouldn't care about them keeping, and the man signed me up. There were two coach loads of us when we left Kansas City.

When I quit the train about fifty miles from the job, there wasn't much more than one coach load of boys left. I caught the next train west, and the next day as I passed through the town I had shipped to, I saw a number of gangs at work, and thought how lucky I was to escape from that work. Steel gangs weren't all that different from chain gangs, the difference being that you got a chain gang for doing a crime, but you got a steel gang for being a fool.

Before long, I landed back in Twin Falls, Idaho. I knew quite a few boys there who were drinking men, and they had a problem. At that time, Idaho had a local option, and Twin Falls was dry. I was still a kid, but I wasn't a dumb kid---or at least I didn't figure I was a dumb kid, even if I probably was. I could see that Twin Falls needed another bootlegger, so I decided to enter that business. It wasn't hard. The adjoining county was wet. I would go across the Snake River into Jerome, get a load of booze, bring it to Twin Falls, and peddle it. I soon worked up a good business for myself.

I made good, and everything was going dandy---until I started drinking too much myself. Old Kelly had told me to stay off the whiskey, and it was maybe the one good thing he told me all the time we were running together, but it was about the one thing he told me I ignored. I was drinking my own goods, and trying to run my business drunk. My business began to suffer, and I must have been drawing attention to myself, because the bulls began to watch me. Fortunately, before the bulls could pinch me for bootlegging, I got sick drunk on some rotgut whiskey, and after that I sobered up long enough to get my bearings. I decided it was time to take a vacation.

I left town, stopping in Pocatello, where I rented me a room and ended up in a poker game. I had no trouble finding players, for my take-off didn't amount to much. I was using marked cards, and I didn't need a take-off at all. I ran the game for about two months, and then the law raided me. I escaped, but had to close my game. I felt it was time for me to leave Pocatello.

I hopped a freight train, and when I landed, I was in Wyoming, where they weren't so strict on gambling. I stopped in Cokeville, a mining town. There was a large payroll there, and money seemed plentiful. I got a long "Okay" until a bunch of us guys bought some booze and went out to a creek at the edge of town to play cards. I was exceedingly lucky, but one of the players began to think it was something besides luck. He was drinking pretty heavily, and holding plenty of dough. I ignored the cracks he started to make and I started in to break

him. He stayed in the game, and he kept on drinking, and kept on losing his bankroll. After I broke him he stayed with us and kept drinking. When the game finally broke up he said, "I believe you cheated me out of my money."
"You think so? Well, what're you going to do about it?" I asked.

He showed me what he was going to do about it. He pulled a rod and stuck it in my stomach, and then he mentioned the money he'd lost. "I'm going to get it back," is what he said.

I didn't think he would shoot me, but he was pretty damn drunk, and you can never tell what a drunken man might do. I do know I felt damned uncomfortable.

I argued with the guy for a while, and then I took a chance, I grabbed the rod, stepped to one side, and it exploded, the bullet striking me in the lower part of the leg and powder burning my hand. Through fear and pain, I hung on to that rod. I finally wrenched it out of his hand, and then I hit him over the head with it. I don't know how many times I hit him, but I do know that when it was over, the doctor had to do a sewing job on him. I had my leg dressed. Some of the boys suggested I have him pinched, but I'd found out by this time that what the law didn't know wouldn't hurt them. I left town soon after the doctor got through with me, and that was one time John Law didn't get to play his hand,

I didn't stop until I got to Denver, where I stayed until my leg got better. Then I bought a ticket to Tulsa, Oklahoma, where I had made some easy money once before. My bankroll was getting thin. I had to do something soon. As much as I hated to, it looked like I was going to have to hit the heavy once again. There was a company hiring men to work building a telephone line. I knew by the size of the crew that there would be gambling on the job, so I decided to go to work and make a payday any way I could. Since I was small, I got a job as trucker's helper. Payday was every Tuesday, and they paid off with cash instead of checks. Some of the boys never opened their pay envelopes until they got to the room where the poker game was running, and when they left the room, they didn't have any money left.

The timekeeper seemed to think a lot of me. He knew I gambled with the boys. Me being just a kid, he figured they beat me out of my dough. He was wrong. I was boozing pretty heavy, and that's where most of my dough went. The timekeeper went to holding my pay, just giving me cigarette money, and banking the rest for me.

Because the boys had a rule that you couldn't sit in the game without ten dollars or more, this kept me out. One day, I asked the timekeeper for all of my pay. He asked me if I wanted to gamble, and I told him I needed some clothes. The timekeeper's wife was sitting there, and she spoke up, "Why don't you give the kid his money? It's his isn't it?" That's where she made a friend, the timekeeper didn't like it, but he gave me my dough anyway.

I had given the boys one of my decks I had marked, and they were using it. I could hardly wait until I got into the game. It was my favorite game, five-card stud, that way I only had one hole card to make. In about one hour, I had won over a hundred dollars. Then somebody knocked on the door, and one of the boys asked who was there. It was the timekeeper. He came over to my chair, and looked at my bankroll. I hadn't even opened my pay envelope. The timekeeper looked for a moment, then he said, "When you get through, Jones, come up to my office."

I thought he was going to fire me, and some of the boys thought the same thing. There was one guy in the game who didn't like me. He said, "It must be nice to have a guardian." I asked him who the hell had a guardian, but he didn't say anything. I couldn't case his hole card very well where I was sitting, but one of the guys had earlier asked me to change seats with him. He was sitting by this guy. After a short while, I asked if he still wanted to change seats, and he did. We changed seats, and then I started in to break the guy who had wisecracked.

We played for some time before I got my chance. He wired with a pair of nines back to back. I was dealing, and I had a queen in the hole when the fourth card was dealt. The highest card I had showing was an eight spot. He was high, with a jack showing. He bet a good-sized bet, causing the other players to throw in their hands. I had cased the second card, it being a queen. The top card was a five spot, not helping my "friend" any. When the bet got to me, I set in enough to top him. His nines being a cinch, he called what he had. I was afraid he'd ask for the cards to be cut, but he didn't. All he said was, "Deal." I gave him the five spot, taking the queen for myself. When I raked in the pot, he grabbed the queen and began looking it over, looking for a mark. I didn't think he would find any, but I couldn't take any chances. After my game in Wyoming, I had bought me a good rod and I wore it all the time I was in Denver. I kept my hand on my rod until he threw the queen down, pushed back his chair, and left the room. He was a hard loser and none of the boys liked him very much. After a few more hands, I quit, telling the boys I would go see the timekeeper.

Thinking I was going to be fired, I walked into the office feeling pretty good about my winnings. The timekeeper told me to sit down. He asked how I made out in the poker game. When I told him I had over two hundred dollars, he wouldn't

19

believe me until I showed him the dough. He told me he was going to stop the game, thinking it was crooked, but if a kid like me could win, then it must be on the square. I almost laughed when I thought of the marks on the cards.

The timekeeper asked me how far I had gone in school, asked me about my folks, and how old I was when I left home. He then told me they had had one boy, who died when he was two years old. He offered to adopt me, and said he would send me to school and see that I got a good education, and teach me a trade. It was such a shock; all I could think to say was that I'd think it over. Instead of going out and getting drunk, like I usually did, I got something to eat, and went to my room, but I couldn't sleep from thinking about the timekeeper and his wife. Outside of the cook I had worked for in Idaho, they were the only people who had ever showed an interest in me since I left home.

I worked until the job was completed. From there, the timekeeper and his wife were going to Texas. The timekeeper tried to get me to go with them, but I had been still too long. The wanderlust and the love of whiskey had got hold of me. Through the timekeeper's help, I had a nice bankroll saved up, and I was grateful for the kindness he and his wife showed me. But I just couldn't go with them.

My next stop was one of the best oil towns in Oklahoma. You could do almost anything you wanted in this town, and I decided it was a good place for me to rest up. Without really meaning to, I got in with a pretty fast mob, and got to drinking again. It wasn't long before my bankroll was gone. Gambling was open in this town, and so I got a job as a dealer in one of the joints. They paid eight dollars a shift and a buck to eat on. I was the youngest dealer in town, working a stud poker spread. One day, the dealer at the blackjack table was being taken. The boss came to me and asked if I ever dealt blackjack.

I told him I had dealt some, so he took over my stud spread, and sent me to relieve the blackjack dealer. My luck ran good. I got the bank back and then won some dough for the house.

That night, the boss asked me how I would like to deal blackjack steady. He gave me so much a shift and a commission on winnings. This way, I made a lot more than dealing poker. Everything was going fine, until one night I went to work after having a few drinks too many. The boss wanted to see me. He told me I was drunk, and I was drunk enough to deny it. We took to arguing, and I demanded he pay me off, which he did. I then told him of a place he could go. I walked out and got drunk, and I stayed drunk for three weeks. During those weeks, I went through my bankroll, and then I discovered nobody was hiring dealers, so I headed for the rail yards and caught a freight headed north.

I soon picked up a buddy who was like me, going nowhere particular. We rode until we got hungry, and then we got off. We found we were in Coffeyville, Kansas. We ate, and then that night we went to the train station. There weren't any freights due out until the next morning so we caught the blinds of a passenger train. We traveled for some time, and then the train stopped at a small town. When the train started again another man grabbed my buddy, trying to pull him off the train. Thinking he was another bum, my buddy kicked him loose. The engineer stopped that train. The man pulled a rod and made us unload. He was a railroad bull. He shook us down, then took us to jail. We had a trial the next morning. We were charged with vagrancy. The judge gave us twenty days on a chain gang. That afternoon they put us to work on the street. We were going to lam if we got the chance. That night, my buddy picked the lock on our cell, and we left town, giving them back nineteen and a half days.

We split, him going one way, and me another, thinking it was the safest. I unloaded off a freight train, broke and hungry, one morning in northern Oklahoma. I had made up my mind that some good citizen was going to give me something to eat. I started out to find this good-hearted citizen. I spotted a big cafe and went into the kitchen and tried to bum off the chef. He put me to peeling spuds, and I had begun to think he had forgotten I was there when he finally came to me and said "O.K. kid, that's enough. Get that stool and sit down over there." He must have been a mind reader for he sure fixed me up with just what I wanted, a good hot meal. I thanked him and headed out for the rail yards.

I was sitting in the jungles near the yard waiting for a train to pull out. I looked over and saw another bum coming down the track. He spotted me and came over and sat down. He asked me which way I was going and I said I guessed it didn't make much difference. I was going to catch the first train out. After we talked awhile, he took out a pair of dice, began shaking them and throwing them on the ground. I was watching him, and noticed he could make those dice do anything he wanted them to. I asked him what he was doing on the bum. He laughed and said he had just got through tossing his bankroll off in Kansas City. He was a friend of Ol' John Barleycorn too. I told him I was fairly good with cards, then he propositioned me to go with him up into the Kansas harvest fields. His name was Blackie and he said we could follow the harvest up through Nebraska and North and South Dakota. We could gamble together and make us a good stake off the harvest workers. Not having anything better in mind to do I said that that sounded good, and besides, I kind of liked this bum.

We caught the next train for the harvest fields. There were a lot of boys heading up that way. Most of the shacks would let the boys ride their trains, but we happened to catch a hard-boiled crew. About fifteen or twenty of us were riding in a boxcar partially loaded with railroad ties. We had taken a siding to let another freight train pass when I looked out and saw a shack coming. He looked tough and when he got to our car he told us to unload and do it quick. Nobody made a move to unload, I told him we were riding his train unless he had the balls to throw each and every one of us out of that boxcar. Then he changed, he began begging us to get off, saying if the road master saw us on his train, he would lose his job, and he had a wife and two kids to support. I told him he didn't have a damn thing on me, I had a wife and six kids and no job. He told us that there was another train following us. He said we were crowded in that box car like a bunch of cattle, so why didn't some of us unload and catch the next train. I said, "Hell, if we get to crowded we would just unload some of the ties. " I really believe that shack got mad, but we still rode his train.

We unloaded in the wheat belt. Blackie had a few dollars so we went and got something to eat. While we were eating I suggested that we go out and work a few days in the field so we could get a bankroll together. Blackie thought that sounded like a plan. When we went out to the fields we found that the harvest had just started and there were no jobs in the fields, but we did get a job working in a header barge. I guess that was really the first time in my life that I had done manual labor. I do know that was one of the toughest jobs I've ever done. I can still feel those wheat beards scratching my neck. We hung tough for a week, drew our pay and headed for town. After we cleaned up, I went to the drug store, bought some cards, and Blackie and I walked out of town. I found a nice shady spot, marked the cards and taught Blackie the combination. It didn't take him long to learn to read them. We went back to town to see if we could find a game.

It didn't take long to get a game arranged. I took one of the boys down to the drug store and bought two decks of cards

identical to the deck I had bought earlier. I slipped him the
marked deck, telling him to go on, as some of the boys wanted
to get the game started. I let them play for a while before I
joined the game, which was in a livery barn. After I played a
few hands, I asked if there was any danger of getting pinched.
Some of the boys started laughing, when the guy sitting on my
left said, "Well, that might be a possibility since I am the
sheriff." Blackie and I made a nice winning, and the sheriff
was real good-natured about it, of course we had let him win
about every third hand. After a couple of days we decided to
move on and see the sights in Kansas City.

By the time we got to Kansas City, we had us a nice
bankroll, but our luck didn't hold and soon we had dropped
most of it. At that time, the International Workers of the World
union was pretty strong, and if you didn't have a union card,
you couldn't mix with them.   As the majority were card
carrying union members, we decided to take out union cards so
we could gamble with the boys. When we got off in Omaha,
Nebraska we went to the union hall and got cards.   It was a
good thing we had bought that card, for there were over one
hundred bums on that train and all of them were "Wobblies,"
and they didn't like people who weren't.   We went on into
South Dakota, stayed there for a while, and then moved on to
North Dakota. Blackie and I were a good team, and the whole
world seemed open to us.

We went to Montana, and from there we decided to go
back to Kansas City. We had made some good winnings
bumming on the train so we decided to rest up in Kansas City
and then go on to Oklahoma. I had tried bootlegging and had
made good for a while, so I asked Blackie how it would suit
him to run some booze. He said anything to get the cabbage.
We made it fine for three trips, then we figured we were hot, so
we decided to cool off awhile.

We made a big mistake in that instead of cooling off, we went up North to the saloon town, where we had been buying our booze by the case, and began buying it by the drink. We made lots of friends, at least we thought they were friends, but they would later turn out to be chiselers. One day, Blackie and I were standing at a bar drinking beer. I felt someone frisking me. I glanced around and saw a bull. I grabbed my bottle of beer, and let him have it between the eyes. My pal then let him have it upside the head. The bull yelled for the bartender to help him. By the time the bartender got over the bar, we had that bull down on the floor, giving him what he deserved. The bartender drew a sap on us, making us get up. The bull then took us to jail, where we gave phony names. I wasn't feeling any too well when they booked us in that jail.

After I got to feeling better, I climbed up where I could look out one of the windows. Some girls came by, and I began to talk to them. Some man hollered and told me to get out of the window and stop talking. I told him to go to hell, which caused me to get in trouble, because the man hollering at me turned out to be the Chief of Police. He ordered me to the dungeon, and one of the bulls started beating me up. He knocked me down, I got up, and he knocked me down again, and then I got wise and stayed down. That bull kicked me in the ribs, then went out, locking the door. My face and hair were bloody. I started crawling around, thinking I might find some water. I found another man on the floor who had been beaten also. They had done a real job on him, for he was still out.

The next morning, they came and got me, and took me to the courtroom, which was full of guys waiting to be kangarooed. The judge called the name I had given him. I stood up. He read off two or three charges against me, asking, "Guilty or not guilty?" I said, "Guilty." The judge sang out,

"One hundred dollars fine and sixty days. Next case" He sure was wearing a grouch.

The bulls took me to the bullpen where I finally saw Blackie. He had made a plea of not guilty, and the judge set his trail for a week later. The next day, they transferred a load of prisoners out to a park to work out their fines. Instead of letting me go with the others, they put me in a cell on bread and water. The guard in charge told me it was orders from headquarters. A colored boy who was a flunky in the kitchen slipped me in some food and some tobacco and matches.

A few days later, they picked up a fellow who had lammed, and threw him in with me on the same rations. He had put in most of his time. He told me a lot about the place, and said he would help me lam, but he didn't want to go, as he wanted to finish his time. They turned me out into the yard after ten days, and I was so weak and hungry I could hardly stand. They put me to cutting weeds. I worked for some time, and when the guard turned his back, I took off. I was almost at the top of the hill when he started firing, but he missed me. I was out of wind when I topped the hill. I laid down and rolled, the bullets from the guard's gun passing over me. Presently, I saw a switch track and made for it. I started running for it, thinking it would lead me to town. I soon decided, however, that they would beat me to town, so I took to the underbrush. When I started to cross a highway, I nearly ran smack into a car full of bulls. I stayed in the underbrush, making my way back to the town where I had been pinched, but I didn't hang around long. I headed for the railroad yards, where I caught a freight for parts unknown.

The next day I unloaded in Joplin, Missouri, bummed some money, bought some food, and went down to the jungles to cook me a feed. There were some bums there, and I heard them talking about registering. When I asked them what was the registering for, they looked at me sort of funny. One bum asked if I knew there was a war. I looked at him for a long moment, then told him hell yes, I knew there was a war, and if he wanted to get funny, there would be another one. Then they went on to explain about the draft, and how everybody between the ages of twenty-one and thirty had to register. It had been some time since I had read a newspaper. I didn't know what date it was until those bums told me. I had just passed the age of twenty-one, and the draft would include me. That surprised me almost as much as the fact that America was now in the war going on over in Europe, the war President Wilson had bragged about keeping us out of.

"Derby" and friends, this picture was made into a postcard and send to his mother, postmark 1918

"Derby" and friend, Dent Hankson about 1914

III

I'm In the Army Now

At that time, I didn't feel very patriotic, but I didn't want to be a slacker. Later that evening, I decided to go up town and join the Army, for I still had that hundred-dollar fine and that time hanging over me. I would rather have faced the whole German army than be taken back to do that time. When I got to town, I found out I could register, but they wouldn't let me enlist. They gave me a registration card, which I quickly, almost wore out showing to bulls, because there were bulls all over, looking for slackers. When I registered, I told them I was going to leave town. They told me to leave a forwarding address. Then I headed west. I stopped and stayed in a number of small towns. In the first town I sent a forwarding address to the registrar's office. In each of the following towns I left a forward to General Delivery in the next town I was headed to. I was in Idaho when I got a letter from Uncle Sam directing me to come to the town in Missouri where I had registered, and be examined. The letter had been forwarded so many times they had used both the front and back of the envelope. It looked something like the map of Mexico. Thinking I was going to join the Army, I bid several of my friends good-bye, and bought a railroad ticket, which cost me half a C-note. When I arrived in Joplin, I went to the registration office and handed my letter to the girl at the grill. She began to laugh, and said, "Boy, if you fight like you travel, the war will soon be over!"

After the doctor examined me, I found out I would have to wait; they would get in touch with me when it was time to go. I walked out of the office, not caring where I went. I took a

29

coin out of my pocket, and named Oklahoma heads, and Kansas City tails. I flipped the coin, and it fell heads.

I headed for Oklahoma, but stopped in a mining town where I had been once before. I knew gambling was good there, and before long I found something else good there. I met a nice looking hasher. I thought she was too pretty to sling hash, and I told her so---and to prove it, I rented an apartment, and we moved in. I told her I was just killing time until I got my call to go into the Army. She told me she hoped I wouldn't have to go. One day, I received my classification card, and I was marked in class five. I didn't know what to think. Class five was for preachers, and the like. I wasn't any preacher. My girlfriend seemed to be pleased, thinking I wouldn't have to go. We enjoyed life for some time.

I began to think I wouldn't have to go into the service. But one day I went to the Post Office, and they handed me another letter from Uncle Sam. That letter really tore our playhouse down. I was in class one and they wanted me to report for duty. My girlfriend had a good cry, then she told me to go on and win the war, she knew I could, and she'd be waiting for me when I got back. That helped.

I had two days to get there. I decided I would stop in the town where I owed the fines and have a farewell party, and a party it was. I ran into some old friends, and we started to drink liquor and get into trouble. I recall a fight or two. Eventually, I got separated from my friends after a free-for-all in a saloon, during which I lost my hat.

The fight was in the north part of town, and I ended up in the south part. When I got my bearings, I headed north. I was walking along a street where there were some Jewish clothing stores. I spotted a large box filled with caps in front of one of the stores. I took an armload and started trying them on until I found one that fit. Then I tossed the rest of them into the gutter. About then, the owner spotted me. I took off, with most of the Jewish shopkeepers chasing me. I ducked into a saloon, went out the side door, and gave them the slip. I tried to find my friends but couldn't locate them.

The next morning, I woke up in jail with one hell of a headache. In a short time the door of my cell was unlocked, and a bull stuck his head in and called, "Jones!" I got up and went to the door. The bull took me to the office. The desk sergeant and another bull were sitting there. They both spoke to me. The bull asked how I felt. I told him to be honest, I felt like hell. They both laughed. Then the bull explained that he had pinched me the night before. He said he had followed me for a couple hours, and he could tell by the way I was talking that I was going into the Army. He said he didn't want to pinch me, but he didn't know what I might do next. He got quite a laugh out of my race with the shopkeepers, and he said, "If you fight like you did last night when you get across, the war will be over soon. "

Then the desk sergeant gave me back the letters and what money he had taken from me. They both shook hands with me, wishing me the best of luck. They told me I could go, which was a big shock. I reflected that there might be a few good bulls, after all. I went out, got a feed, then bought a ticket to Joplin, where I was to report.

There was about a coach load of us on that call. Most the other boys were local boys, and I didn't know any of them. We wouldn't be leaving until that night, and I had a hard time killing time. I was walking along one of the streets when who did I run into but the girl from the registration office. She stopped and spoke to me--asked what I was doing in town. I told her I'd decided it was up to me to go settle that argument across the pond. She laughed, and we got to talking. She was off duty, and she kept me company until it was time to go. I left Joplin liking it better than I did when I got there.

At Jefferson City, Missouri, we went through medical examinations. I got a kick out of watching some of the boys. They seemed so serious. When I came to the doctor with the rubber hammer, who asked you a lot of foolish questions, he hit me on the knee and asked, "Who is President of the United States?" I knew it was Woodrow Wilson, who got re-elected for keeping us out of the war I was now headed off to, but I said "Why it's Paul Bunyan." The doctor laughed and said, "You'll do", slapped me on the back and told me to go on. After we were outfitted, we were shipped to a training camp in Texas, where I would run into more grief. On July 15, 1918 I was twenty-two years old. For the last five years I had made a living as a gambler, roaming from town to town, living just outside of the law. Now I was an honest American citizen, a soldier in the United States Army.

I couldn't get used to the idea of having superior officers over me, and it wasn't long before I was in bad again. One day, we were on the drill grounds, doing bayonet drill with that old Texas sun was broiling down. We were standing at ready position. The second louie in charge did not like me any better than I liked him. He stopped in front of me and told me to move my foot. I raised my foot and put it down in the same spot. Trying to sound real hard-boiled, he said, "I told you to move your foot." I told him that I did move my foot. He thought for a moment about being an officer, and then he said "Don't talk back to me, I'm an officer." I had to laugh, but he didn't find it funny. He called the sergeant, and the sergeant asked my name. I told him I was Jones. He asked which Jones, and I told him I was the only Jones in the outfit, and he could just put it down as "Jones." Boy, did he put it down!

I got handed enough K.P. for a whole squad of Jones's. In fact, I was given so much K.P.; they started calling me "K.P. Jones." This was fine with me, because it made it easy for me to make friends with the boys when I wasn't on K.P. Making friends made it easy to get some gambling going, and it was easy pickings, for a lot of those boys had never had a pair of dice or a deck of cards in their hands before. What little time I didn't have on K.P., I spent by collecting one-dollar bills. I ran a number of card and dice games, and my luck was real good. They must've paid the whole Army in one-dollar bills, and I was getting more than my share of them.

We hadn't been in camp very long before they decided to ship us across the big pond as replacements to outfits which had lost a lot of men. When we loaded on a train for Camp Merrit, New Jersey, I thought my K.P. days were over. Everything went along smoothly until we stopped somewhere in Ohio. I never saw so many pretty girls in one town in my life, and the one I helped up to my window was the pick of the lot. About the time I got into full swing telling her how many Jerries I was going to knock off, and that she could rest assured that the war would be over soon, I felt like one of the German's bombs had hit me. It was the Commanding Officer, who'd been coming through my coach, and ran into my feet, which were sticking across the aisle. That officer was plenty sore, for he almost fell. It was embarrassing, and officers can't take being embarrassed. He told me to sit at attention, and then he bawled me out, ending up by saying if he caught me with my head out of another window, he would clap me in irons the rest of the way across. It was quite a bawling out, but he hadn't more than left the coach before I had my head out again, bidding the girl good-bye.

After we arrived at Camp Merrit, we had lots of time to gamble, and I made several winnings. I also bought several decks of cards, and marked them to take across with me. That was a bright idea, for it turned out that cards were scarce in France. At Camp Merrit, they gave us all a short haircut, and headed us for the boat. The captain of the boat was now the law, and he didn't care how much we gambled. I started a blackjack game. The commanding officer came by where we were playing. He really wanted to stop us, but he couldn't. You could tell it really bothered him, almost as much as it delighted me. He really showed his colors on the boat through. All he did was stand on deck and watch nervously for submarines even though there were none reported in the vicinity.

While we were on that boat we were all wondering what would happen to us once we got to France. We would sit and talk about what we would do over there. Of course most of us had heard about France in the newspapers, but we really didn't know what to expect. The boys did talk about the good things they had heard. Mostly about the French women, but they talked about other things too. They said that the French liked wine, and except for eating snails, they like a good feed, too. One boy had heard that there were a lot of painters in France, and I always was one who enjoyed looking at pictures. We all wanted to see the Can-Can dance, and one guy told us there were a lot of castles in France. I never had seen a real castle, and I sort of looked forward to seeing one. I was really starting to look forward to my little trip across the big pond.

When we finally made it across to France, I was in for a big disappointment. As soon as we landed, they sent us out to a rest camp, but very little rest we got. I was on so many work details I called the place Camp Detail. Just before we landed, the Commanding Officer gave us a lecture and told us to stay out of the cafes and leave the Mademoiselles alone. He said that if any of us ended up in the brig, he'd just let us rot there. That didn't sound so bad to some of the boys, who figured that jail was better than being shot at. The Commanding Officer soon changed his mind about leaving us in the brig. The first company formation we had there was only about one third of the company present.   He asked the sergeant where the rest of the men were, and the top sergeant told him he might find some of them in the brig. The Commanding Officer turned red in the face, dismissed us, and stomped off. Two or three hours later, he came back, marching the rest of the outfit in.

There weren't many boys in the outfit who seemed to like the Commanding Officer. I guess the Army did the Commanding Officer quite a favor, just after we left Camp Detail they transferred him to another outfit. It might have been good for him, for some of the boys who came across with him might have mistaken him for a Jerry when we got to the front.

Finally, they loaded us into little boxcars, just like shipping cattle. Here I was, riding the rails again. We traveled for some time, then they unloaded us off the train, and loaded us onto trucks. Then we unloaded off the trucks, and we had to walk the rest of the way. The officers tried to deceive us, telling us the war was about over, and we wouldn't ever be in any danger zone. I had other ideas the night we went to the front, for we could hear the big guns. The officer in charge of our detail told us the guns we heard were some of our boys practicing. He also told us that when we got to our destination we'd get a hot feed. I don't believe there was a doughboy in the whole outfit who wouldn't have faced the whole German army for that hot feed.

We went on for some time, the guns becoming plainer. As we passed a dead mule that one of the shells had killed, I hollered to my buddy who was ahead of me, and asked him how he liked the climate. He answered back by saying "O.K., but one of our boys sure played hell with that target, didn't he?"

It wasn't long after that until we stopped. The officer in charge told us to find some holes and get in them. I asked about the feed. He told us we would get it the next day, then he ducked in a hole. We started out in the dark to find a hole. We had orders not to strike any matches or make a light of any kind. The first hole I came to was already taken. I tried several times before I found one that wasn't occupied. I soon found out why it wasn't occupied. When I tried to get into it I could only get my head in. I began to cuss the soldier that had dug that hole, when someone hollered and asked, "Is that you, K.P.?"

I answered, saying "Hell, yes!" Believe me that was one time I was proud to hear someone call me "K.P.," for those Jerries were sure sending over a few shells. It was a fellow named Smithy who had hollered. He was a big boy I had trained with in Texas. The hole he was in was large enough for two, so I pulled off my pack and crawled in with him. The first thing he asked me was did I have any smokes. I told him I had a sack of Bull Durham. We weren't supposed to strike any matches, but we rolled us some smokes, and held a shelter half over the front of the hole and lit our smokes. We talked for some time. I was dead tired and hungry, so I dozed off to sleep, letting Smithy talk on. After some time, he poked an elbow into my ribs, telling me to wake up. I asked him what he wanted, but before he could answer, a shell hit a few feet from our hole and exploded, causing some dirt to fall in on us. We were both a little shook. Smithy said, "Don't you wish you had taken out another ten thousand dollar policy?"

I shook the dirt off and told him to go to hell, and turned over and tried to go back to sleep. But Smithy wouldn't let me. We talked on for some time. Another shell hit just back of the second hole from us, knocking the two boys out of their hole. They began hollering "Gas!" We were supposed to put on our gas masks at that first alarm, but we couldn't smell any gas, so we decided we would rather risk a little gas than put those damn gas masks on. They were hell.

The next morning, we saw the hole where the shell had hit. It was right behind the hole those boys got blown out of. All I can say is that was a lucky pair of Yanks.

In the morning, Smithy and I were both starving. We had just decided to eat our iron rations, when a sergeant came along and told us to line up about ten feet apart and march on up to the kitchen and get our breakfast. The idea behind the ten feet apart was that if a shell hit it would only get a few of us. On our way to breakfast, a shell hit the second boy ahead of me, tearing his head off, leaving only his chin. Hungry as I was, I couldn't eat much breakfast after that.

After breakfast, Smithy and I were separated once again. I was put in Company L, in the 82nd division. That outfit had seen plenty of action.

The night we were relieved, I stayed in a hole with two other soldiers. One was an old timer in the outfit; the other was a rookie like myself. We had been told we were going to be relieved for some time. The old timer told me he had a hunch he would never get out alive and he didn't think we would be relieved at all. My being a gambler, I believed in hunches. I was lying between the old timer and the rookie, and if they got the old timer tonight, I figured they'd get me too. A shell flew over and exploded a ways behind us, and the other rookie began talking about his wife and children back in Tennessee. The shells began to fall all around us, for the Germans knew we were moving troops. The boy from Tennessee began to get on my nerves. I asked him what he did back in the States. He said he worked on an extra gang on a railroad. I asked him if he had a ten thousand-dollar insurance policy. He said, "Yes!" Then I told him to stop worrying about his wife and his kids, for they'd be better off if he didn't come back. I made him sore, but he stopped his chatter.

We had all stopped talking. I heard a shell coming. I knew it was a low one, and it sounded like it had my number. It hit just below us, and when it exploded, I thought I was cut in two about the waistline. Nobody said a word for some time, then I shook myself and found out I was all together. I asked if anyone was hurt. Nobody was.

When the outfit finally left that night, I got lost. I took a short cut, trying to find my outfit and got the scare of my life. Before I knew it, I guess I was lost. Of course, I didn't know it right off. I was walking along, thinking how lucky I was, when one of our big guns exploded within ten feet of me. Thinking it was a German shell, I guess I would have sold out pretty cheap. I thought that General named Sherman had been a pretty smart man, for war sure is HELL. I soon caught up with some troops on the road, and asked what company it was. Someone answered me saying "Company L." I fell in with them, thinking it was my outfit. In the morning, I found out it was another Company L. I also found an old friend I'd trained with in Texas. Instead of worrying about my own outfit, I thought I would let them worry about me. I stayed with this outfit for four days. We were camped in an old town the Germans had built before they were driven out of France. I was lining up for chow when I saw my sergeant. He looked at me as though he was seeing a ghost. He said he thought I had been killed. They had me marked with the missing. I told him I was quite alive, and would be more so when I got that mess kit full of chow into me. After we ate, he took me to my old outfit, which was a short distance away. The outfit had some supplies. We had underwear issued to us, but we didn't have anywhere to take a shower. By then, I had so many cooties crawling all over me; I could see them in my sleep.

The next day, we were marching back to a rest area when the captain gave us orders to fall and rest. It was November 11th 1918. The captain told us the war would be over at eleven o'clock. That was fifteen minutes away. None of us believed him, but sure enough, when it was eleven, the guns ceased firing. After we got to the rest area, they took us to be deloused. That is where I made a million cooties homeless.

IV

Show Me The Way To Go Home

My outfit passed in review for Woodrow Wilson, on Christmas Day, 1918. The French General, Foch, General "Black Jack" Pershing, and several more big shots were all there.

After that, we moved into a camp, and I went AWOL a number of times. The sergeant and I were good buddies, so he would always report me present. One day, several of the boys went AWOL, and I was the only one to get by, the rest making the guardhouse. The next day, it fell my luck to pull guard duty. Were those Yanks in the guardhouse pleased! I kept them in drinks.

We threw a big drunk one-day, and forty-five of us got court-martialed. They handed me the loss of two-thirds pay for two months and fifteen days hard labor. But I only did two days on K.P. For the "hard labor" I ended up with the flu and had to go to the hospital, where I stayed sixty-four days. I was lucky; I had a mild case of the flu, many of the boys who got sick with this flu went home in a pine box. I gambled most of the time I was there. When I left to go back to my outfit, I had almost a full gunnysack of French francs.

There were five of us left in the hospital together, all of us privates. The fellow in charge of our papers was a good sport, and he did a little paperwork for us. Did we see France! We stopped at every good town we came to. We all expected to get court-martialed but we got back to the 82nd and got by. A short time after we got back, we were loaded on a boat for the good old USA. Was I happy! We had some great games on the boat coming back. You could get a gamble on any game you could name, for any amount you could count. When we landed in New York, I had a real bankroll.

The 82nd Division got quite a reception when we landed, for we had one of the world's greatest heroes in our outfit. He was Alvin York, from Pall Mall, Tennessee. I was gold bricking the day he received his Medal of Honor. A friend of mine was visiting me and the sergeant let me off. We were standing back of the officers' lines and heard them read off what York had done to receive his medal. My friend said to me, "Say, K.P., if they had two more like old York, you and I would have never had to go to France."

After I got to Camp Merrit, New Jersey, I had a 24-hour pass almost every day I was there. I started out to see little old New York City. I had a big bank roll when I got to Camp Merrit, but when they shipped me out for Camp Taylor, Kentucky, I found I had left most of that bankroll behind in New York.

I stayed in Camp Taylor long enough to build up a new bankroll. On June 3, 1919 I received my discharge, then I headed West to the sweet little girl who was waiting for me. I could just hear her saying, "Daddy, I just knew you would win that old war!" But when I unloaded in the town where I had left her, I had an awful shock waiting for me. Instead of finding my sweet waitress with open arms waiting for me, I found out she had married a Greek and moved to St. Louis.

That's when my old friend, John Barleycorn, came to my rescue. I looked up one of the town bootleggers and began buying his business, one bottle at a time. I ran into another soldier who had hard luck. He hadn't lost any girl, but he had got drunk, and someone relieved him of his bankroll. I wanted someone to talk to, I took him with me and we got a room in a hotel. There I met a little girl who was only fifteen years old. Her name was Ethel. I was surprised to find a kid like her there. She told me a story that was hard to believe, but I could tell she was telling the truth. I asked her if she would like to go with me and quit her current way of life. She answered me by saying I was just kidding her. I told her about my other girlfriend, and why I was in that town. I also told her I was a gambler, and I could make enough dough for both of us. She said she would like it fine, if she could believe I meant it.

I talked the other young soldier into going on home and forgetting he'd ever been to the war, and then moved the girl in with me. I stayed with her for about a week, during which time I told her that it had been several years since I had seen my mother. She said I ought to go visit, and I told her that was my plan, and I would come back within a week and get her. When I left, she told me not to do her like my girlfriend had done me. When I left her, I was feeling that the Greek had done me a favor taking that waitress.

I caught a train for the old home town, Urbanette, Arkansas. I was feeling pretty good; thinking it wasn't a bad old world after all. When I reached my hometown, I unloaded off the train, and went to my mother's house. She was very surprised to see me, and we had a happy reunion, at first. Then a number of things happened that put a damper on my stay. Shortly after I left Urbanette the first time my mother remarried. Her new husbands' name was Alfred P. Haynes. Haynes hated me, he said I was a bad influence on his sons and made it very clear he did not want me around. Then, two days after I got home, out rode the sheriff. He didn't know me at first, but he knew I was there. After he recognized me, he stammered a little, then said, "Jones, I have a warrant for your arrest."

This made me sore, and I told that sheriff where he could put that warrant. People around here were quick to forget a war, but awful slow to forget a warrant. That pinch hurt me worse than any pinch I have ever had, and I have had a lot of them. It took all the joy out of my homecoming. I made my bond, and was turned loose. I went to see the sheriff to see it we could fix it so I could leave. I didn't want to put my bondsman on the spot. The sheriff said he guessed we could work something out. I handed him enough money to square things, and asked him if I would have to appear. He said I wouldn't. I then told him I was leaving the state.

I said good-bye to my mother, and caught the night train for Oklahoma. That pinch had caused me to lose whatever respect I still had for the law. When I arrived back in the town where I had left Ethel, she was one happy kid. I asked her if she was expecting me. She surprised me by saying, "I knew you would come back, regardless of what you have told me about yourself. I knew you were honest," Hearing that sweet kid say that helped me some to forget the sheriff back home.

We started in to enjoy life, and in a few days we left for the town where I had worked in a gambling house. At the rate we were spending money, I would have to look up something to do in a short time. When we arrived at the town, we took a taxi to a hotel I had stopped at before. I knew they didn't ask any questions at that hotel. Thinking Ethel and I would be safe, I found a woman I had known before, who was still in charge of the hotel. I introduced Ethel as my wife. We picked a room that suited us, and I paid a month's rent in advance. For a while there, we took life easy. After three weeks had passed, I counted the bankroll I had left, and I knew I had to do something. I wasn't holding enough to go buy a load of booze. I thought of a game up North I could make if I had good luck. It would put me on my feet again. I told Ethel I had to make a trip. I might be gone a week, and I gave her some money, telling her if I wasn't back within a week for her to go home until she heard from me. She wasn't happy about it, but she said, "Okay." I got my bag and left. I went to a second-hand store, bought a good rod and some rough clothes. Then I took the night train north.

After I reached the town I was headed for, I changed into my rough clothes, and then I headed for the game. It was in full swing. Knowing how to knock in order to gain admittance, I put a muffler on my face, and knocked on the door. I knew that the man who tended the door wore a rod, I covered him with mine as soon as the door opened, telling him to "go high"---and go high he did. I relieved him of his rod and made him walk in front of me to the room where the game was going on, telling him if he tried anything funny, I would give some undertaker a job. He must have believed me, for he did as I told him. When he opened the other door, I covered the men in the room, telling them to put their hands up, which they did. Then I made them line up with their backs to me. Keeping the doorman with me, I started to frisk them for rods. I found only one of the men carrying. I made all of them put their money on one of the tables, and then I made the gamekeeper open his safe. I gathered up all the money, keeping them covered with my rod. Then I walked back to the door, telling them not to come out for five minutes. I didn't wait to see if they did or not. When I got outside, I went to the spot where I had left my bag. I picked up the bag and walked off. I walked about five miles to another town, leaving the rough clothes at the spot where I changed. I went into a cafe, got something to eat, went out, and took a taxi to another town, where I caught a train back to where I had left Ethel.

When I went up to the hotel where she was, she seemed real pleased that I had got back so soon. Ethel was a smart girl. She asked me no questions, so I did not have to tell her any lies.

The trip more than paid me back the money I had given the sheriff back home.

A short time later, I made the acquaintance of a man who owned a drug store. He asked me if I could handle a supply of Jamaica Ginger, better known as "Jake." He told me the police were checking up on the drug store. They were only supposed to have so much Jake on hand at any one time. He was overstocked and afraid the officers of the law might take it from him. I knew that Jake was the Osage Indians' favorite drink. I told him that I thought I could handle it. When he made me a price on what he had in stock, I told him I would take all he had. I then looked up a friend I had in town, who went by the handle of Slats. He was a little down on his luck, and I asked him if he wanted to go to work for me. He said, "Yes." I asked him if he cared that he would be risking getting jailed. He wanted to know how big the risk was. I then explained to him that I wanted him to help me sell Jake. He laughed and said that was easy. We got a car and took a load to Pawhuska, a town near the Osage Indian reservation. We had no trouble finding a market. We sold out in no time, and promised the customers some more on the next trip. My business soon got so large I had to hire more help. Through my druggist friend I got lined up with the rest of the drug stores that handled Jake, helping them balance their inventory and keep it legal. I put my friend, Slats, on the road running it into Pawhuska. Then, knowing I might land in jail any time, I sent Ethel home to visit her folks. I told her I would send for her later. I then moved to Pawhuska, and really got down to business.

V

Runnin' Jake

One day I ran into an old schoolmate I hadn't seen for years. After we talked awhile, I asked him what he was doing. He was working for some oil company. I told him if he worked for me he could make a lot of money, more than he was making at the oil company. He decided to quit his job and go to work for me.

One night, Slats was bringing in a load when the train he was riding on wrecked. I had to meet him at a crossroads with a car. I waited all night at the crossroads. The telegraph operator told me it would be several hours before the train got there. I decided to go back to my room and get some sleep, then come back later. I had just got undressed and laid down when Slats knocked on the door. I let him in, and was surprised at how nervous he looked. He set a bag down, and then told me a bull was following him, after that he left. I didn't lock the door, thinking he would be back. A few minutes later, the door opened and in walked a plain-clothes dick. Not knowing him, I asked who the hell he was, and he pulled back his coat, showing me his badge. He asked where was the guy who'd just come into the room, and I played dumb, saying no one had come in, except him. He looked around and spotted the bag Slats had left, and said that was the bag the guy had been carrying. He started to get the bag, but I reached under my pillow and got my rod, telling him not to touch the bag unless he got a warrant first. Then I told him to get the hell out and leave me alone, as I wanted to get some sleep. He left, and I went to sleep.

The next morning I went to the cafe to get my breakfast, the Greek who ran the place came in. He had just got back from the police station, where he had taken Slats his breakfast. He spotted me, and came over to my table, saying, "Your brother is in jail." Then he told me that Slats had called up and ordered his breakfast. The Greek thought Slats and I were brothers, and that I was foreman on a job, and ran a big crew of men. That part about me being a foreman and running a big crew was sort of true. I was a bootlegger, and I had a crew working for me. I'd often take the boys to eat in the cafe, or order lunches to take out.

I asked the Greek what my brother had done. He said he didn't know, but that he had told the chief of police that I was a foreman on a big job. I wanted to laugh at how the Greek seemed to believe anything I told him. He asked me why I didn't go to the police station and make them turn Slats loose. I wanted to laugh again. I wasn't going to any police station unless some bull took me there.

I told the Greek I had to get out to the job, and I was late. I asked him to go down, spring Slats and tell him to come out to the job. I offered the Greek money, but he said I could pay him later if it cost anything. It turned out it cost twenty-seven dollars to get him out, but Slats covered it himself.

Still, Slats had lost the load of Jake. The bull had pinched it. The bag he'd left in my room belonged to some other passenger on the train, which is something I didn't know right off, and Slats didn't know either. If I'd known, I would have let the bull have the damn bag. I figured we'd got off lucky, only losing the load of Jake and paying a small fine. But it caused us to be more careful.

One day one of my friends introduced me to a young fellow of about fifteen. He wanted to run a load of Jake to his hometown of Atkins, Arkansas. My friend introduced him as "Chock". I sold him a small load of Jake and after he left, my friend told me his real name was Charley Floyd, that he had got the nickname "Chock" from all the "Chocktaw Beer" he drank. In about ten years young "Chock" would be public enemy number one and would have the new nickname of "Pretty Boy".

All this time, the country had been changing, and I hadn't been paying any attention. For one thing they decided to give women the right to vote, and as soon as they did that, all those Anti-Saloon League and Women's Christian Temperance Union women started raising hell because fellows liked to relax and drink now and then. So the next thing coming down the pike was "Prohibition", and what was being prohibited was anything to drink with alcohol in it.

Still everything ran smooth for us until one day my old schoolmate and I were out to where we had a load of stuff planted. We were on the Indian reservation, letting the boys drive out for their orders. We had just got through eating our lunch and sent the car back into town when we heard a car coming. Thinking it was our car, we didn't pay much attention to it until it stopped and a load of bulls got out. I got up, and we were surrounded.

The officer in charge started in to shake us down, asking us if we were making a lot of money. I answered him by saying, "This would be a hell of a spot to make money." He said, "I have a guy up town that knows you."

They hunted through the woods around us, but found only eighteen bottles. When they came back to where they had left us, they asked the officer they had left guarding us if he knew how to mix up a drink. It was some kind of joke, but I didn't find it funny. They loaded us in the car and headed for the police station. After asking a few questions, they took us to the county jail and booked us on a charge of possessing intoxicating liquor on an Indian reservation, which was a Federal charge. Then they locked us up in jail, which was the first jail my buddy had ever been in.

There were several boys in the jail on different charges. I knew they would kangaroo us, and when they did, we really got a laugh out of my buddy. We paid our fines, which amounted to five dollars each. Still, we weren't getting out, so I sent for a mouthpiece. After we talked to him, he said they had nothing on us, and he could spring us. After being arraigned they set the amount on our bonds. Having all our money tied up in Jake, we weren't holding enough for our bonds. My buddy wired a brother, who came and sprang him on bond. I was transferred to another town, to a Federal jail, where I got another mouthpiece and made bond. We beat the rap.

While I was in the Federal jail, I met a fellow who had been pinched for stealing a car. He belonged to the Drumright gang, which was one of the best-organized gangs at that time. This fellow wanted me to spring him when I got out. Thinking that my Jake plants would be lifted when I got out, I decided to help him. He said he would line me up with the gang. When I left the jail, I had three letters concealed on me, addressed to three members of the gang, and a message to another boy's father, who ran a cafe in the town I was going to.

I looked up the cafe, went in, sat down at the counter, ordered something to eat, and asked the girl who waited on me if the boy's father was there. She told me he was, and I had her send him to me, and I delivered the message. A man sitting at a nearby table overheard us talking. I told the father I had just left his son. The man, hearing me say that, thought I had just got out of the pen. He was waiting on the outside for me when I walked out. I thought at first he was a bull. He asked me if I had just got to town. I told him I had. He wanted to know if I was looking for a job. He told me where I could find him if I was interested in working, then left. I went back into the cafe and asked the boy's father if there had been a bull in there. He told me "No." Then I described the man who had waited outside for me. The cafe owner knew him. He told me the man's name was Ed, and wanted to know if he had made me a proposition. I told him the man wanted me to look him up. He said, "Ed is okay

I got a room and went to bed. The next morning, I left town to try to make the car thief's bond, which was five grand. I looked up the men I had letters for. I didn't know what was in the letters, but I soon got the impression those letters had something good about me in them. Without those letters, it would have been a one-sided conversation, but after reading them, those fellows couldn't treat me nice enough. Each one of them gave me expense money. When I left, they told me if I wanted to join them to come on back. I didn't go back, though. Those babies were too tough for me, at least at that time. Instead, I just turned the bond fixing over to them, and went back to the town where I had left Ed. I looked him up the next day, and asked what he had in mind. He told me he had a partner and they were making booze, but they needed a guy to sell for them. I told him I was the guy they were looking for, just give me a sample, and I would start right in. He left, and a while later he was back with the sample. In three days time, I had sold it all out.

One night I got a telephone call from a landlady to whom I had sold two cases of Ed's liquor. She asked me if I could come to her place. When I got there, I saw she was mad, and I asked what was wrong. She said that was the question she wanted to ask me. She had a man there at the point of death, and she figured that the whiskey she got from me caused it. I told her, all I knew was that I had bought the booze from another party then sold it to her. When I left her, I was pretty uneasy. The first thing I did was to look up Ed. I asked him what the stuff he had me peddling really was. I was mad, and I made sure he got scared. He owned up that it was denatured alcohol, not moonshine at all. The next day I went to the place where the sick man was, and found he was okay. I felt a little better then. I sure didn't need a possible murder rap.

I got to thinking about the drug stores I handled Jake for. I knew they had real alcohol, and I knew it wasn't poison. I looked them up after I had made some inquiries, and found out they all had some Jake, even though some of them wanted more for it than the others. I made them a price, and all of them told me they would sell it to me. I contracted to take all they had, and all they would get in the future. I looked up Ed, taking him as a partner. We went out to a junkyard, and talked to a colored boy who worked there. He said he could supply me with bottles. I made arrangements with him to also wash the bottles for me. I gave him some money and told him not to say anything about the deal. He looked at the bill I had handed him and said, "I don't talk, Boss---I don't talk." I knew I had a good man. When we returned to get the bottles he had them all ready for us.

In a short time I worked up the best business I ever had. I made more money than I could spend, but that didn't stop me from trying to spend it all. I got in with a fast mob, and I started drinking again. Ed was more scared of a pinch than any man I ever worked with, even my old school buddy. To listen to Ed, who looked more like a bull than a bootlegger, Uncle Sam now had more prohibition agents than he had soldiers in the A.E.F. Every man Ed saw was a prohi.

One day I received a telephone call from a party who wanted a case of liquor. When I looked up the address that had been given me, I found it was in the heart of "Little Africa," which was what the colored district was called. I was worried at first that it was a frame, but we had some liquor on hand, so I told Ed we'd take a chance. I knew that part of town was tough. I got a bag with a case in it. Ed and I got in the car to deliver it. We stopped the car around the corner from the place, and I looked around. "Little Africa" wasn't too fancy a place, but it wasn't much worse than the rest of the town. I knew there was no chance of getting Ed to make the delivery, so I got out, got the bag, and took it to the door. I knocked on the door. A colored woman opened it, and said, "What you want?"

I told her what I was there for, and she let me pass through, closing the door behind me. I had a hunch I might have to shoot my way out of the joint. I asked the woman if she had ordered the booze. She said she would get the boss. She opened another door, and a big buck came into the room. He asked me if I had a case in the bag. I told him I did. He wanted to sample it. There was a girl standing by one of the windows, and she kept looking out. After the man opened a bottle, poured out a glass and tasted it, I asked him how he liked it.

I noticed that he glanced toward the girl at the window, who seemed sort of nervous. He said it tasted all right. I asked him what he was waiting for. He said something about "the boss." I said, "I thought you were the boss.” Then I pulled my rod, told him to put the bottle back in the bag, and fasten it. I kept him and the girl covered as I reached for the bag. I backed to the door, and I felt a lot better when I stepped into the street again. Then I saw Ed. He had got nervous and got out of the car to come and see why I was staying so long. Then it dawned on me why the big buck stalled and hesitated and didn't go through with the stick-up. The girl must have seen Ed through the window, and thinking he was a bull, had kept the buck from making his play. Ed saw I still had the booze when I put the bag into the car.

I stuck out my hand and said, "Shake, Flatfoot. You saved the booze, and maybe my life, too." Then I told him what had happened. For the rest of the time I worked with him, Ed carried the name "Flatfoot." I was real glad he looked so much like a bull.

One night I was out with a bunch of the boys. We had a real wild night of it. I banked my money at one of the bars I hung out at, and when I ran short, we went back to the bar, as I wanted to draw some money. After I drew the money, I lined everybody up at the bar to have one on me. Some man crowded in beside me and hollered to his buddy who hadn't heard me telling the bartender to fill them up. He was telling his buddy to come alive, some fool was buying. After we drank, I got the bartender to set them up again. I told him that my friend was buying. I nodded toward the man next to me, who had said some fool was buying. "This fool is buying this time," I said. He looked at me and said he wasn't buying. I stuck my rod in his side, and said. I think you are." He took one long look at the rod, and got generous real fast. He bought the drinks, all right, but I put a lot of heat under me with that play. His buddy ran for the law, so we loaded into our cars and headed for a roadhouse.

From there I called up to see how hot I was. The bartender told me the bulls had my description, but didn't know who I was. Later that night, we went into a cafe to get something to eat. One of the waiters got tough over an order. I stuck my rod on him, and told him to bring my order. When he left us, he ran for the kitchen. The manager came over and wanted to know what was going on. I put the rod on him. Somebody sitting at a table back of us saw the rod, and let out a scream.   I marched the manager to the cash register, and instead of taking his money, I paid our bill and we left.

After that, I knew I was plenty hot. I stayed in my room for a few days.   One night, a friend of mine drove me to another little town nearby. I wanted to cool off or get the heat fixed up, but I couldn't get it fixed. They seemed to want to put me in jail, which I disagreed with. I slipped back into town one night, and looked up Ed. As I had some alcohol I was due to pick up, I asked him if he would go ahead and make the deliveries. I told him that I would take the rest of the alcohol out to our plant until I got cooled off. He said he would rather not. But he said he would take the alcohol off my hands if I wanted him to. I could see then that Ed was trying to take advantage of me, and I didn't like it, but I didn't let him know I was on to his game. I asked what he would pay for it. He said he'd pay what I was paying for it, and no more.

Then I knew for sure what kind of a man I had for a partner, trying to kick a man while he was down. I told him I would let him know the next day. Then I looked up a friend, and got him to help me. The next day, I went and gathered up some alcohol cans, the kind we had been handling. I rented a room in a good spot. I filled the cans with water, putting a plaster of Paris seal on them, wrapping them in green paper, fixing them just like the ones I got at the drug stores. Then I placed them in different drug stores where I had some due.

After that, I went and looked up Ed, and told him I would let him have what I had on hand, but he would have to stay in the car and let me go into the drug stores and get the cans, just like always. I had ten cans scattered in different stores. Ed said he could only handle six that night, but I finally got him to agree to take eight. I would get the other two the next day, as they were in a drug store on the edge of town. I had been paying one hundred and fifty dollars a can. Ed, knowing that, got a taxi we had used when we were partners. The driver asked me if we were going into business together again. 1 told him it was only for that night. I wanted to tell him what I was doing, but I knew better. He'd know soon enough anyway.

I had him drive me to the store where I had stuck four cans. Before we got to the store, I told Ed to give me six C-notes. I knew better than to ask him for all of it at once. He counted the money over twice before handing it to me. We stopped in front of the drug store. I was afraid he would get wise. I went into the store, took the druggist back out of sight of Ed in the car, and talked to him awhile. I offered to pay him for leaving the cans in his store. He wouldn't take anything. Then I walked on up front, stepped behind the counter and picked up two cans, loaded them into the car, went back and got the other two.

At the next drug store, we only had two cans. Ed counted out three hundred dollars and handed it to me. I told him he might as well give me the other three hundred, for the drug store where the other two cans were was in the same block. Ed said he wanted to wait until they were loaded. After that, we drove on to the other drug store. Ed counted out three hundred dollars more and handed it to me. I went into the drug store and stalled around long enough to count the money. Then I offered to pay the druggist for leaving the cans in the store, but he wouldn't take any pay either. I told him I might leave town, and for him not to hold the alcohol for me if I wasn't back in two weeks. He said he hated to see me leave, but if I thought I was hot, it was the best thing to do. I got the two cans of water, took them out to the car, and loaded them in. I then asked Ed if he needed me to help plant them. He said he could make it okay without my help. He said, "I'll be seeing you," as he drove off. I thought he wouldn't be seeing me if I saw him first.

I looked up the boy who had helped me fix the cans. It was the same colored boy from the junkyard who helped with the bottles. I gave him a double sawbuck, wishing him luck. I then got a friend to drive me out of town. I had sold Ed twelve hundred dollars worth of good city water, and I was feeling pretty damn good about it. I guess some people would think I was pretty much of a rascal in that transaction, but they didn't know Ed.

When I arrived at the town where I was staying, I packed my clothes and sent Ethel a wire telling her to meet me in a town up North. Then I boarded a train. When I got off the train, I went to a hotel and engaged a room, telling them my wife would be there in a day or two. The next day, Ethel arrived. We started in on our second honeymoon, which lasted about a month. Then I got restless. I told Ethel I wanted to ramble around some, and I thought it was best for us to split the bedroll. She could go her way and I could go mine. It took some reasoning, but I finally got her to see it the way I did, so we parted the best of friends.

I wanted to get back on the road and bum around some more. I didn't know where I wanted to go, I just wanted to go. I went down to the railroad yards. I hadn't yet made up my mind where I would go. I walked over to a creek. Nearby there were some bums cooking a meal in the jungles. I sat down and talked to them. They offered to share their chuck with me, but I told them I had just eaten in town. They were heading for the Kansas harvest fields. That helped me to decide where to go. I thought I would go up into Kansas and gamble some. We loaded on a night freight train. I knew then why I wanted to split with Ethel, and it had nothing to do with Ethel. I just wanted to feel free and ride freight trains again.

We headed for one of the main wheat belts and traveled for some time. We unloaded to feed and met some other bums, who told us there was a bad railroad bull at the next division point ahead of us. He was in the habit of catching bums and beating them up. Of course, none of us wanted that to happen to us. We were on the lookout for Mr. Bull as we pulled into his town. We soon spotted him---he was coming at a run to catch our train as we pulled into the yards. All of us bums unloaded and got clear of the yards. He was one mad bull. He began to bluster and cuss, shouting after us, telling us what he was going to do to us if we didn't get out of his town. Since we were younger and had better wind than he did, we were far enough away we could laugh at him. While he yelled threats, we headed up to town, looking for a cafe.

On the way up to the town, we met some farmers who stopped us and asked if we were looking for work. I thought here was a good chance to put the bull on the spot. I did the talking for the bunch. I told the farmers all of us wanted jobs, but not in this man's town. They wanted to know why. I told them we had orders to leave town that night or we'd be put in jail or shot. They wanted to know who gave us those orders. When I told them it was the railroad bull, one of them spoke up and said, "So that's why we can't hire any help, and our wheat is going to ruin."

When they left us that was about the maddest bunch of farmers I ever saw. They told us they were going to run the bull out of town instead of him running us bums out, and if we wanted to stay and work, we could get jobs. That did me so much good, I thought I would go to work. But then I happened to think of the times I had worked in the header barge, and I changed my mind. I got something to eat and headed for the railroad yards, thinking I might get there in time to see some fun. But to my disappointment, I didn't see anything of the farmers, or of that railroad bull.

VI

Got Me A Black Derby

In Idaho

They captured me in Idaho,
A State I had done before.
They took me to the Boise jail
And then closed the prison door.

They locked me up in prison
Away from the things I love.
Stone walls all around me,
And damn those bars above.

They threw me in a dungeon,
A dark and filthy cell.
Then they handed right to me
A real dirty bunch of hell.

Eighteen months they kept me,
My hair and my whiskers grew.
So I'll guess that, my boys,
They will do the same to you.

Those fifteen long years I gave them.
You'd swear was a fiery death.
They kept me there; I lost my health,
And I'm still paying them yet.

Here's my tip dear stranger,
Don't ever mingle with crime.
Though you may think you're smart,
You'll end up doing time.

Oliver F. Jones

I took the next train west. I found that the World War had wised the boys up, and gambling wasn't what it used to be. I thought of my sister, Ina Ruth Smith, whom I hadn't seen for some time. At that time she was living in Idaho, and I decided I should go visit her. I made it okay, until I eventually unloaded in Colorado, to get something to eat. A bull grabbed me and told me I had to go to work, the local farmers needed hands. I told him I wasn't looking for a job, and he smiled and said that meant I was going to jail. When a farmer came along, he told the bull to turn me loose. He wanted me to work for him. The bull left me with him, and the farmer seemed to think because he was paying going wages, it was all right to load me in his car, take me out, and put me to work.

I told the farmer that I was under the impression that Mr. Lincoln had freed the slaves. I also told him I was overseas during the World War, and I thought that since we won the war, it was still a free country. For a moment it looked like I was going to have to fight him, but then he backed down, and I caught another train.

It was in July of 1920 when I got off a freight in Twin Falls, Idaho, where my sister, Ina, now lived. After a visit with her, I went out to look the town over. I had known the place before, but I also knew a town could change. I wanted to make some money because I was getting low on funds. There was quite a demand for liquor. It was an even bigger demand than before Prohibition. I was already pretty well lined up, and I decided this was my best chance to make some easy money. I looked up an old friend who used to be in the racket. He lined me up with two brothers. They were running liquor in, and wanted someone to handle it for them. They made me a good proposition, and I started in a wholesale business selling to other bootleggers.

One evening a couple of the bootleggers I was selling to, Cleo "Slim" Bush and Bob Linville, decided to try some of their merchandise. They really tied one on. Shortly after midnight, Linville, who was driving their Maxwell, crashed into a farmer's rig. The car overturned and both occupants were thrown out. Bush was just scrapped up, but Linville was pretty messed up. Bush was afraid that when the cops showed up they would confiscate their booze, so he staggered to his feet and stashed the keg they had with them near a fence. He then walked up to the farmhouse and called me, and the police. When the bulls arrived Slim was standing guard over the wreck and he tried to keep them away from the fence. A couple of minutes later, I showed up with another bootlegger named Porter Harrison and we picked up Bush and drove him back to town. I had the boys drop me off at the St. Regis pool hall and told them to go home. Harrison dropped Bush off at his house, but on his way home was picked up by the bulls for being drunk. The next morning I read in the paper that Linville had had to have surgery, he survived, but the bulls decided to crack down on all the bootlegging that was going on.

I was in the St. Regis pool hall about three weeks later, when Harrison came to me and wanted to trade a Paige roadster for six gallons of bootlegged whiskey. As I needed a car, I told him I would see him later. I went out to the Hagler place to see how much I had stashed. It turned out to be six gallons, so when I got back to town I found Harrison and told him I would trade for six gallons of hooch, but that he would have to give me a bill of sale stating that I had paid cash for the car. I took him back out to the Hagler place and showed him the booze. He said he would take one gallon then and come back for the rest later on. He gave me the bill of sale and the keys to the car and I drove him back to town.

The next morning I was downtown with a friend, Hubert Snow, when we passed a clothing store. In the window

I spotted a hat and told Hubert I wanted to go in and see it. The hat was a black derby made by Stetson and really took my fancy. I bought it and wore it out of the store. Later that evening Snow and I got into a poker game and I was still wearing my derby. There was a new man at the game and as the evening progressed he was getting drunk. The drunker he got, the less he remembered. He couldn't remember any of our names. During one hand he had raised the pot and turned to me and said "O.K. Derby, are you going to stay in?" Snow really thought that was funny and for the rest of the night all the guys called me "Derby". And for some reason the name stuck. I wore that derby for many years and for the rest of my life I was known as Derby Jones. The nickname "Derby" is sure a hell of a lot better than "K. P. Jones!"

Everything went okay for about a week after that. I was making lots of money again, but then I started to drink once again. On the evening of October 11, 1920, Hubert Snow and I was drinking pretty heavily, and happened into a man who bought a bunch of booze from me, then forgot to pay for it. As it had been several weeks, I thought it was a good time to collect. I asked him about it, and he began to give me a song and dance. I didn't like the way he acted, so I told him I would give him until five o'clock to raise the dough for me. Snow and I began looking for him at five, and finally found him at the depot. He was fixing to leave on the five-thirty train.

I made him get into my car, and we took him back uptown. He said he would pay me. We looked up several of his friends, but none of them seemed to want to help him. We went into a joint to get a drink, and he tried to give me the slip. I had started taking the money out of his hide, when some bulls ran in and pinched us.

I had a rod on me, and I didn't want the bulls to find it. I had it inside my belt. I drew in my stomach, letting it fall down my pants leg. The trouble was, one of the bulls heard it hit the floor. I kicked that rod away from me, and when they found it, they didn't know where it had come from. I woke up the next morning in jail with a headache. I had no idea what the charges were. The sheriff came in with my breakfast, which I wouldn't eat. He came back later, took me out and put me into the bullpen, where there were several more boys. I ran into to Snow in the bullpen and he was really mad. They had arrested him for carrying a rod, because they thought the rod I had dropped was his. I overheard one of the other prisoners say that his mouthpiece would be down to spring him in a short while. The judge had given him a fifty-dollar fine and thirty days in jail. I told him to send his mouthpiece to me. About twenty minutes after that fellow left the jail, his mouthpiece, A. J. Myers, came and called for me.

Myers asked me what I was charged with, and I told him I didn't know, which was why I'd sent for him. Then he asked if I had any money. I told him I had, and he said he would go and find out what the charge was, and come back and let me know. A few minutes later, he came back, took me outside, and told me I was charged with being drunk. He said he could spring me for ten dollars in fines, and ' his fee would be fifty dollars. I told him to get busy, for I wanted to get out of that jail. They took me before the judge, and he read off the charge. The judge asked me, "Guilty or not guilty?" I copped a plea. Then he asked if I was ever in trouble before. I told him I had been, and he asked how many times. I lied to that judge and told him a couple of times. I couldn't have told the truth because I'd been in trouble so many times I didn't know how many it was. The judge fined me ten dollars, and I walked out with my mouthpiece. Just as we crossed the street, Sheriff Adelbert. N. Sprague hollered at us. We stopped, and he called us back.

When we went back into the courthouse, the sheriff said he had a warrant for my arrest. Myers wanted to see it. Sprague said the D. A. was making it out. When the District Attorney finished, Sprague handed it to me. I read it, and handed it to my mouthpiece, telling him there wasn't anything to it. I was charged with possession of ten gallons of liquor. They put me back in jail. Was I mad! I had a lot of booze planted around that town, and it must not have been planted too good. That was the reason I wanted out so badly.

They arraigned me, and the next day I had my hearing. Did I get a surprise! Both Snow and Porter Harrison, the man I had traded with for the car, were testifying against me. Snow was saying that he had helped me sell the moonshine and Harrison took the stand and swore I traded him the booze for the car. He also testified that I had cheated him out of five gallons of booze. He said that when he went back out to the Hagler place to get the rest of his booze all but one small jug was gone. I knew he had gone back for the booze, and got all of it because he had been selling it all over town. Even though I had a bill of sale stating that I had paid cash for the car the judge did not seem to impressed. The next day in the papers' account of the arraignment they stated that "The officers procured a sample of the stuff, which is said to have a savage kick and to be the real western 'moonshine hooch'." Now I know how they got Harrison to testify against me.

I sent my mouthpiece to see some of my friends, telling them what Snow and Harrison had done. I knew my friends would take care of them. Then my sister heard I was in jail and came to see me. She tried to buy me out, but Sheriff Sprague called her out and had a talk with her. When she came back, she told me what he had told her. The sheriff didn't want me; he wanted to force me to turn on the fellows who were running the booze. I told my sister to tell the sheriff to go to hell on her way out. If there is one thing I am not, it's a rat.

My friends took care of Harrison, and my mouthpiece forced them to put me on trial. The D. A. dismissed the case, due to lack of evidence. It seems that Snow had left the state and Harrison had left ahead of a sheriff's warrant for defrauding an innkeeper. So, after 75 days in jail I walked. When I hit the bricks, it was December 13. It was cold and snowing, and I still had my summer clothes on. When I made the rounds of my plants, I found I had lost all of my booze. I had also lost my rod when I was pinched. I had no money and no means to get any and I needed new clothes.

I went to see my sister and gave her the lowdown. I borrowed a double sawbuck from her, and went down and looked the poker games over. They were tough, but I had to do something. I finally took a seat in one of the games. That was one time I played conservative poker. When I cashed in my chips, I had the game broken for over two C-notes. The first thing I did was go to a clothing store. When I came out, the world was warmer and looked a little brighter. The next thing I bought was a good rod. I knew I was lucky to beat that game, and I was going to play it safe, for I felt like the law had given me a raw deal on the last pinch. However, there was one positive thing about the law; there was an election while Sprague had me locked up, and an election he had lost.

One day, as a gambler friend and I were walking down Main Street, we saw a fellow stick a shiv into another man, then turn and run across the street. We walked on up to the man who was hurt. Some other men had come up. The assailant had stuck that knife into the guys left eye. He took hold of the knife with both hands, trying to pull it out, but he couldn't do it. They took him to the hospital, where he died later that night. The bulls pinched the fellow who did the job. He was a Mexican, and not too well liked around those parts.

The next morning, I was sitting in a poker game when my friend came in and hollered, "Come on, Derby, let's go see them hang the Mex!" When we came out on the street, we saw a large mob coming up from the jail. My friend said he guessed they had already hanged him. But then the mob turned up Main Street, and we fell in behind and followed them to see what was going on. We soon found out. One of the men had a rope. They stopped at one of the newspaper offices and wanted to publish a notice for all of the Mexicans to leave town, or they were going to run them out. While they were arguing about what to do, the chief of police came and pinched the man who carried the rope, and the rest of the mob scattered. Several years later, I would run into the man who had carried that rope, in the state penitentiary. When I saw him again it would be with a different rope, he would be hanging from the end of a rope in the penitentiary rose garden.

I went back to the poker game. I sat down and began to play. Some of the boys asked me what had happened. I told them about the sheriff making the pinch. One of the boys asked why they pinched him, and I told him I didn't think he had the knot tied right. When they began to laugh, I looked behind me, and there stood the new sheriff, E. R. Sherman. I thought I was pinched, but he only laughed and went out.

There were a lot of stick-ups being pulled. Almost every night someone was robbed. The boys were talking about what they would do if somebody should put a gun on them. One fellow named H. B. "Mac" McCollum had been shot up a time or two, and he was plenty tough. He said he wouldn't put his hands up for any hijacker. I told him I would, and if asked to politely, I'd even go up on my tiptoes. A few nights later, on January 22, 1921, Mac paid with his life when he would not put his hands up. It seems that Mac, J. L. Wenger and G. W. Jensen had gotten up a poker game at the St. Regis. Wenger had invited Ed L. Slagle, a sheep camp tender, to play. The three men were already in the room setting up for the game when Slagle came in, pulled a gun and ordered the men to put up their hands. When Mac refused Slagle shot him in the chest. Jensen slid under the bed and Wenger attacked Slagle to try and get the gun away from Slagle. Slagle hit Wenger over the head several times. It was then Jensen crawled out from under the bed and started helping Wenger push Slagle out of the room. All the noise had alerted the bulls. When Slagle ran out of the room and down the hallway, he ran straight into the arms of Frank Austin, one of the Twin Falls bulls.

I was in a barbershop when it happened. Some other gamblers and I went to the morgue and saw old Mac. He was lying on a marble slab, looking just as dead as he was. As we walked out, there were some comments. One man said old Mac had thought more of his bankroll than he did of his life. I said something about how a man could always get another bankroll, but when he was dead, he was dead for a long time, and wouldn't have an easy time getting another life. Later on, I was to do time with the sheepherder who had bumped off old Mac.

After this killing, the law got hostile and they made it plenty tough on the gamblers. There wasn't much to do, but a fellow had to live. They didn't seem to be catching the hijackers, and since I still had my rod, I thought I might try this line of work. If I could have known what that thought would cost me, I might have passed it up. But I wasn't much for passing up what seemed like opportunities back then.

I got some rough clothes and my rod. I knew there was a game out at the edge of town that I thought would pay off. I found a spot and changed clothes, then went to look over the game. It hadn't started, so I left. When I started back to town, I met three gamblers. I was in a good spot, and I thought, "Why not?" I covered them with my rod, and made them turn around. I first shook them for rods, and found none. Then I took their dough. I started them back towards town, ducked down an alley, taking a short cut, and beat them back to town. I had changed clothes and was standing at a bar having a drink, when in came the three gamblers I had just robbed. They all seemed to be excited. The bartender asked them what it was all about, and they told about being robbed. Each one gave a different description of the robber, but they all seemed to think he was a big guy, a lot larger than me. They told how much they had lost. Two of them told the truth, but the other one lied. I wanted to tell him he lied, but that would not have been very good poker. I bought them a drink and left them talking about the robbery. I laid low for a few days before I pulled another job. Then I pulled a few more jobs of simple robbery, and left town.

VII

Doin' Time

I moved to Hansen, a small town about six miles from Twin Falls, where I met O. R. "Slim" Kendrick. He and three others, Harold Smith, Ernest "Curley" Davis, and William Bronson were a gang of burglars who seemed to consider burglary the highest of all callings. We pulled several jobs, but I had trouble with Smith, so I decided to quit them. I just did not trust Smith; he was always whining and acted like he would turn on us in a heartbeat. One night they were going out on a job, and there was a safe they wanted to open. They drove to where I was staying and asked me to go along. I told them they didn't need me. They said they wanted me to open the safe. I asked if Smith was going. They said he was, so I told them I wouldn't go. Then they said they would leave him out, so I decided I would go. We pulled the job, which seemed easy enough, and we got away.

Slim ran into a guy who offered to buy auto tires, if we could get hold of any. It sounded like easy pickings so we started robbing auto part warehouses. The guys asked me to let Smith go with us, they had all been raised together and they thought Smith was really an O.K. guy. I said O.K. but that turned out to be one of the worst decisions I ever made. On the evening of June 14th, we robbed the Hazelton Auto Company. We got six tires and a number of parts. As we came out Smith yelled, "Hey there is someone watching us". The noise he made caused a man who was walking across the street to look up and get a good look at all of us. We jumped into our car and sped off.

I decided things were going to get hot around there real quick and that I would leave Idaho for Oklahoma. My mother had moved to Cyril, Oklahoma and I thought it would be a good time to visit her. Slim had a jewelry store cased, and he wanted me to help him pull it. He said that it would give me traveling money. The store was in Jerome. I told him I would. I knew a fence in the East who I could place the stuff with. We left for Jerome where the Coates Jewelry Store was. Slim had a brother living near Jerome on a ranch, and went out to visit him. I stayed in town, and got tired waiting for him. I was going to give him one more day, then leave for the East.

The next morning, June 20th, I was reading the Twin Falls paper while I ate breakfast. There on the front page was an article stating that Slim and Smith had been pinched, Slim and Smith had been in Hansen when they were arrested and taken to Twin Falls. When the constable, Martin Krum, was opening the door to the Twin Falls jail, Slim made a break. He ran around the north side of the building and escaped into the shadows of the trees. Krum fired at him but missed. The fool Krum had not even bothered to place handcuffs on Slim. I decided to go to Twin Falls to see if I could find Slim and get him to go to Oklahoma with me.

The morning of June 27th I was eating breakfast in a cafe in Twin Falls when a bull came in, walked up to me and said "Derby Jones, you are under arrest." After they pinched me, I saw Curley and Bronson. I found out that Smith was squawking his head off. I told those two boys that if they didn't stand pat and make Smith out a liar, we would all get a trip up the river. They promised to stand pat. But when their folks came to the jail and talked to them, they both confessed.

When they transferred us back to Jerome County where we were wanted, those two boys never told me that they had talked, but I knew they had. The sheriff kept me in the office after locking them up. He asked me if I had anything to say. I told him I was guilty as hell. He laughed, and said I might as well cop a plea, for the rest of them had, and tried to lay everything on me. Then he locked me up in jail with them all, except for Slim; they hadn't caught him yet. I lost no time in telling those burglars what a weak bunch of sisters they had turned out to be.

The next morning, the D. A. had us brought out. He talked as though he would get us suspended sentences, if we all plead guilty. The sheriff's son was the jailer. He also had been in the service during the war, and he seemed to take a liking to me. He told me I was going to get the worst of it, the other boys all belonging to the state, and my being an out of state guy. I told him I was expecting it, but I wasn't expecting what was handed to me.

The newspapers really gave us the works. They wrote us up as one of the biggest organized burglar gangs ever captured in the state, and of course, being an out of state guy, I was the leader. They laid every job that had been pulled on us.

On July 13, two days before we were to go before the judge, they caught Slim. He was at his family's farm near Buhl. When the bulls went out to the farm his mother and sister were there. They told the bulls that Slim was not there and they hadn't seen him. The bulls kept pushing when his sister broke away from them and headed for the house. That gave the bulls all the excuse they needed to search the house. Slim was in the cellar, going out the cellar door when one of the bulls spotted him. He got out of the cellar and started to run when they ordered him to halt. There was no cover on the farm so the only thing he could do was stop. They brought him to the Jerome jail the night before our trial.

On July 15, 1921 three of us went before judge Baily Lee. I had a mouthpiece to put up a talk for me, but it was a cut-and-dried proposition. The judge called Curleys name, gave him a talk, and then gave him a fifteen-year sentence---which he promptly suspended. He did the same for Bronson. Smith had turned states evidence, so he had already gotten off. I had a hunch he would run out of suspended sentences before he got to me, and sure enough he did. He finally called my name, and I stood up. He asked me if I was guilty or not guilty. I told him I was guilty, and about that time the D. A., Keith Ferguson, jumped up and began to stammer.

He told the judge he would like to say a few words before I had a sentence passed on me. Then he started in. If what the D. A. said was true, I was the meanest man in the state of Idaho. After he got through, the judge turned to me and said, "Jones, I will now sentence you from one to fifteen years in the Idaho State Penitentiary."

I waited for him to follow up with "Sentence suspended," like he had for the others, but it didn't come. I remembered what my dad had told me. He only missed it by four years, for I was twenty-five, not twenty-one. Curley and Bronson came over to me and extended their sympathy, but I brushed them off and told them to give their sympathy to their friend, the D. A. The sheriff led me to the jail and locked me up. When Slim finally came to trial he was also given a suspended sentence, even after he lammed. All of us were guilty, but again the law had made me its goat.

Before they took me to prison, I was held for several days in the county jail. While I was there, Lydia Southard, Idaho's "Woman Bluebeard," was being tried for killing one of her husbands with poison. They gave her ten to life in state prison on a guilty verdict for second-degree murder, even though the statutes say death by poisoning is first degree murder with a death penalty. The all-male jury just could not bring themselves to condemn a woman to hang.

I also made the acquaintance of A. D. Pollock, who had robbed his own bank. Ironically it was a bank I had cased and planned to rob. I told him about it, and he said he wished I had gone ahead and done it myself, for maybe then we'd both be on the outside. They had about a dozen charges against him including forgery and embezzlement. He had been found guilty and was appealing to the State Supreme Court. I tried to get him to withdraw his appeal and go on up the river with me, telling him he was going there anyway, so why waste the money on an appeal. Neither one of us had ever been in a pen. There was a boy in jail with us, who had been in before, and he really showed us a good time, telling us what we could do, and that we could learn any kind of trade.

The banker was going to take up electricity. He asked me what trade I was going to take up. I told him anything that put me close to the chuck, for most jails I had been in, getting a good feed was the biggest battle. The boy who had been in the pen told us that the warden was a swell guy, and there were two gates at the prison, a front gate and a back gate. He said that if a fellow was wanted in some other state, when his time was in, if there were some bulls to take him back, the warden would turn him out the back gate, so those bulls would not see him leave. I thought that was pretty strong, but I didn't say anything, not knowing much.

The day came when I had to leave my new friends. On July 27th a deputy sheriff was going to drive me over to the prison and not wait for the traveling guard. The deputy told me I was getting special treatment. I told him I'd had enough of that from the judge. When he laughed, I laughed right along with him. It didn't seem all that funny at the time, but what else could I do?

Jerome, Idaho - Early 1920's - From the Jerome Historical
Society Collection

VIII

A New Fish In The Fish Cell

It was about a hundred thirty-mile drive from jail to prison, and when they put me in the car, they put an Oregon Boot on me. This "boot" was probably the most torturous device ever invented. The boot was a type of shackle. It weighed about twenty-eight pounds. It was made of a heavy iron band that was locked around my ankle and rested upon another iron ring, which was supported by braces attached to the heel of a leather boot. When you tried to move with the heavy weight on only one foot it was almost impossible to walk, and it would rub your ankle raw. This was my first encounter with the boot but would not be my last. Many a time my ankle would be shredded and bleeding when they finally removed the boot. When we stopped for something to eat on the way, the deputy expected me to walk into the cafe with the boot on. I protested that I'd rather go hungry, and the deputy took the boot off, but watched me very carefully, to make sure I didn't lam out on him. As soon as I ate, the Oregon Boot went back on.

Late that afternoon, we arrived at the prison. As the car pulled up, I gave the walls the once over, and once was enough. Those gray stone walls didn't look easy, and I couldn't help but wonder what kind of hell they contained inside. The deputy didn't let me out of the boot until we were inside, and I figured he did that to impress the state officials that I was a bad character, and he was one tough bull having got me all the way there by himself. The officer he turned me over to was Deputy Warden D. W. Ackley, who told me to sit down. The deputy who had brought me gave him some papers, said, "Here he is," then left. After Ackley had looked over the papers, he told me to follow him to another room, where I changed into a suit of rough prison clothes of wide black and white stripes. Ackley told me that if I was a good little prisoner that at the end of my first three months I would be given new clothes made of narrow black and white stripes. Both outfits were called "zebra gear". He went on to tell me that if I stayed a good little prisoner at the end of six months I would get yet another set of clothes, these would be a gray suit made of a cloth called "cadet gray."

Then the deputy warden took me into the prison itself and locked me into the "fish cell." A "fish" is what they call a new prisoner, and I guess it's a good name, because anyone who ended up in prison sure is a poor fish. While I was in the "fish cell," Warden William Cuddy came to see me and told me that if I obeyed his rules my stay in his "hotel" would go quickly, but if I didn't mind my step he would make my life a living hell.

They brought me a little chuck the next morning, and after I ate breakfast, they took me out, took mug shots, asked all sorts of questions, looked me over for scars and tattoos, and fingerprinted me. They found I was 5 foot 8 7/8 inches and weighed 130 pounds. The also found my four tattoos, a woman's head and an American flag on my left arm, a nude woman and a dancing girl on my right arm. Then they handed me a number, for which I had to more or less trade in my name. That number was 3015, "Derby 3015 Jones." I later learned that that meant I was the 3015th convict to be incarcerated in the Idaho State Penn since the first 11 inmates had entered the grounds on March 12, 1872.

A screw took me back inside the walls, and showed me the "deadline," telling me not to cross it unless I wanted to be shot. The "deadline" or "no mans land" as the cons called it, was a twelve to sixteen foot dirt perimeter located between the

75

wall and the yard. They kept it raked and free of debris so anyone walking on it would leave nice clear footprints. Then they assigned me to another cell and turned me into the yard.

In each cell there were a number of printed rules on the wall, which you had to live up to, or you'd be in the hole on bread and water. Since I was here, I decided to get to know what was what. I walked over to a group of cons, and on the way to them, I recognized a boy I had met in Pocatello some months before. He recognized me, and introduced me to a few of the right guys. He also pointed out a number of the rats. I asked him about Slagle, the sheepherder who had bumped off old Mac. He took me over to where he was. After we talked a while, we went over behind a building where some of the boys were smoking grujo that they had managed to smuggle into the prison. Some of those boys were so high they didn't even know they were locked up. They offered me a smoke, which was tempting, but I passed it up. I had made up my mind to keep my nose clean in here. They had told me I could get a parole at the end of eleven months if my record was good, and I didn't want to stay any longer than that.

The truth is, I didn't even want to stay that long, but I didn't have any choice in the matter anymore. I was soon to find out that there were a number of disappointments ahead for me.

When I was booked in, I told them I was a cook and waiter, thinking it would place me where the chuck was, which it did. At the time, Idaho had an easy stir. There wasn't any work going on, it seems the unions were protesting the use of convict labor, probably because so many union members were being sent to prison. The prison had been built by convict labor. They had quarried heavy sandstone block from the ridge above the prison. Now only the shoe shop, which had been opened early in 1921 and the upkeep of the prison, kept the boys busy.

A few days after I was booked in, the captain sent a runner to me and asked if I wanted to work, which I did. There was an opening in the dining room, waiting on tables, and I got it. After I was introduced to the headwaiter, I was put to work. I soon found out that the food was better than jail food. I also found out the ex-con in the county jail had given the banker and me a lot of baloney. There wasn't a chance to learn a trade of any kind except the criminal kind, and we had to pick that up from conversations with each other. There also wasn't any back gate, because I looked for one, thinking they might forget to lock it. No such luck.

The Idaho stir had a rather interesting past. It was pretty much built by the cons themselves. One con, George Hamilton, designed the dinning room I was working in while doing a seven-year stint for robbery. He did such a good job they let him out early. The day he was released he took an overdose of morphine and killed himself. According to the papers he was "despondent over his unconquerable appetite for liquor".

I had been in the stir about three months when the Jerome County D. A., Keith Ferguson, came to see me. The trial for one of the boys who had been in the Jerome county jail with me was coming up. The D. A. was having problems getting anyone to testify against Roy Claxton, and since we had been seen talking together in the bullpen he wanted to know what Roy had told me. I told him I wouldn't rat on anyone, that he was just wasting his time. He told me that if I would testify against Roy in his upcoming trial he would see to it that I got a parole on my first board. I told him I wasn't a rat and would not testify. He said to me, "We'll see about that," and walked out. A couple of days later Warden Cuddy called me into his office and handed me a subpoena. He said that he knew I didn't want to testify, but I didn't have any choice. I told Cuddy about the deal Ferguson had tried to make me and what I had told him. Cuddy told me that since Ferguson had subpoenaed me he would see to it that Ferguson kept his end of the bargain and write a letter to the board recommending my pardon. I told Cuddy I would not squeal on a buddy, even with a subpoena or a chance of getting out of the stir early.

The trial was set for the twelfth of October, but the D. A. kept getting it postponed. Finally on December 21st the case was dismissed due to lack of evidence. Cuddy was true to his word and had Ferguson write a letter to the board recommending my parole. Cuddy even had Ferguson go to the judge that sent me up and got him to write a letter of recommendation. What Cuddy and I didn't know until later was Ferguson wrote his letter but went to the attorney general, Roy Black, and told him that I was a "persistent violator" and he was really "opposed to any clemency being granted." That letter from the attorney general is what kept me from getting my parole in 1922.

On November 8th, 1921, Lydia Trueblood-Dooley-McHaffie-Lewis-Meyer-Southard, Idaho's "Lady Bluebird," arrived in the women's section of the prison, where they kept her away from the rest of us. Lydia was the first known female serial killer in the United States; she had been convicted of killing her fifth husband by boiling fly paper to collect the arsenic, then baking it in apple pies. Circumstantial evidence suggested she might have killed her previous husbands, a brother-in-law and her baby daughter as well. Definitely not a woman I would be interested in marrying and not just because she was a killer. I always had a liking for a pretty woman and from the pictures I saw and the talk I heard she was a pretty woman, but I liked brunettes and she was a redhead. It's like they say, "one man's meat is another man's poison".

A short time after she arrived, my friend, Pollock, the banker, also arrived at the prison. I was anxious for my friend to get out of the fish cell. I had been there two months already at this time, but it felt like two years. The day after he arrived, my banker friend saw me. I was on duty, and he noticed my apron, and congratulated me on getting a job where the chuck was. We joked a little about the trades that ex-con told us we'd be learning. I told Pollock I had my name in for aviation. There was an airplane flying near the prison, I had told him it was one of the prison planes and that the landing field was just on the other side of the hill outside the walls. Then I had to get on with my work.

The next time I was with Pollock, he had been wised up. We had a laugh about the back gate. My friend had a job milking cows under guard outside the walls, but just about every day he got the chance to stop by and talk with me.

There were men in that prison for just about every crime on the statutes. There were a lot of good fellows there, and some of the worst, whose crimes would make your blood boil. Some of them were very famous. For example, there was Harry Orchard, who had been given life for bombing the Idaho governors' house and killing Governor Frank Steunberg, and was accused of killing thirty-something other people. He had been tried with Big Bill Haywood, George Pettibone, and Charles Moyer. Clarence Darrow defended those three, and got them off. But Harry Orchard didn't have Clarence Darrow, and he took the fall. He was in there with the rest of us, and he was in there to stay. He became the penitentiary's longest serving tenant and was even baptized into the Seventh Day Adventist Church in the communal plunge bath in 1926. I heard later that in 1932 he was allowed to live in a cottage behind the prison where he raised chickens and turkeys until he died.

There were two men I met that I became close friends with. Clarence Rousch had arrived at the stir about four months before me. He was serving his second one to fourteen sentence for grand larceny. When they arrested him he pulled a rod on the bull that was trying to take him and shot the bull in the mouth. Walter Smith had been serving a one to fourteen year sentence for forgery but had been paroled about a month before I arrived. About three months after I arrived they arrested him in California for violation of his parole; this was following his disappearance from Boise following a grocery store holdup. They were considered two of the toughest men in the stir, but I got along just fine with them.

There were seven of us working in the dinning room. As boys would go out, you'd move up a place. After I was there for some time, I got to be headwaiter. I had some say in picking my help, and I got some good boys. I had been there long enough to know who the rats were and that the rats were worse than the screws to get you in bad.

Two boys were brought in one night for robbing a bank. They both seemed to be okay. One of them was a barber. I got the head barber to get him into the barbershop, and I got the other into the dining room, and ended up celling with him. Every Sunday, we had services in the dining room. It was the headwaiter's job to arrange the songbooks and tables for the services. Not caring about that kind of job, I let Duke, the bank robber, take care of it. In the meantime, I would go to number three cell house, where we would post some of the boys on the lookout for screws, then we would gamble, my kind of worship service. If the screws caught us, it would mean the hole on bread and water.

One day, another con came to where I was shooting craps, and said, "Say, Derby, one of your waiters just got saved." I asked him which one, and he said it was Duke. I said, "Well, that's another bank robber gone wrong." That night, after we went to our cells, I noticed Duke didn't have much to say. He got up on his bunk and lay down and began to read. When I got up for something, I noticed he was reading the Bible instead of a magazine. In prison, when a con finds Jesus, all the others think he is trying to get a parole or a pardon. The officials are smart enough to think the same thing. These cons are called "Bible backs." I have seen several preachers fall in prison for one crime or another, and they are treated worse than the others.

That night, when they blinked the lights for us to get ready to retire, Duke got down from his bunk, knelt, and began to pray. I asked him what the hell he thought he was pulling, he couldn't kid me. Duke looked at me, and sort of smiled. The next night was the same. I told Duke I didn't know if he was on the up and up, or trying to get a pardon, but if he did any praying in that cell, he could do it on his bunk. Jesus could hear him there as easy as on the floor. The next day, I told Duke to hunt another cellmate. He could stay on the job in the dining room, but I wasn't celling with any Bible backer. Duke found himself a new cell, and when they later took me outside to cook in the guards' quarters, he moved up to headwaiter. We stayed good friends.

I worked at that job until I almost had my first year in. I had tried one board, and been turned down. The warden told me he thought he could get my time set to one year. But then I was denied again. At the time I did not know that the prosecuting attorney, Keith Ferguson, in his report to the parole board, had said I was a "menace to society", that I was one of the lead members of a gang of "robbers and thieves". He had also stated that "other members who were young men just out of the Army and of good families had been led into the commission of the crime by the prisoner", me. I began to change my mind about going straight after I got out. There really didn't seem much point in it. I began to think that going straight wouldn't be much different from being in prison. Every day, I had to get to work at five in the morning, and work until seven at night. I was getting tired of that sort of life, and the straight life outside looked like it would be more of the same. Living, or should I say surviving, in the stir was not very glamorous or exciting. The cell house was cold and drafty. There were three tiers of forty-two steel two man cells about six feet long by eight foot wide. The beds were metal racks that hung off the walls with straw mattresses and one cotton blanket. There were no toilets, only "honey" buckets in the corner that had to be emptied every day. There was a ventilation shaft in each cell for air, but during the winter, the wind would whistle down those shafts and it seemed there was no way to keep warm.

One morning, I lay in my cell, and told the warden's cook, who I was celling with, that I was sick, and for him to tell them I was too sick to work. After some time, I got up and went into the con's kitchen and got something to eat. Late that afternoon, the deputy warden came and got me. I thought I was going in the hole. He said Warden Cuddy wanted to see me. When we got to the office, the warden told me to sit down. Then he asked how I was feeling. I told him I was almost okay now, but didn't feel so hot this morning. He told me he was glad I was better, because he had got a call from the Old Soldier's Home for two boys, and he was planning on sending me and a young fellow named Phil down there. They worked eight cons at the Old Soldier's Home, paying them thirty dollars a month, the state getting fifteen, and the con fifteen. The warden also told me that he thought I would make the next board, which was only three months off. He then told me to go to the commissary and draw my clothes and wait at the guard's kitchen. I left the office feeling like a new man.

Some time later, the car came to the kitchen where Phil and I were waiting. We had changed into our own clothes. We didn't look like convicts anymore, and I didn't feel like one. The warden made the drive with us. He was a square guy, for a warden. When we arrived at the Old Soldier's Home, they assigned us to our sleeping quarters. There I met the other cons, most of whom I knew. We were almost the same as free men. We could go anywhere we wanted to go, just so we were on the job at work time. After we had breakfast the next morning, the commander of the Home sent for Phil and me to report to his office. He shook hands with us, told us to sit down. Then he turned to Phil and asked him what kind of work he had done before he was sent to prison.

Phil told him he was a farmer. "Fine, I need a man on the farm." Then he asked me. I told him I was a cook, and he said he needed a cook. He then told me to report to the kitchen, telling Phil to go to the barn, where they would tell him what to do. I got a surprise when I went into the kitchen and asked for the head cook. One of the women there spoke up and said she was the head cook. I told her I was sent there to work. She smiled and she said, "It's about time we were getting a man on the job." Then I found out all the help were women. I thought what a change it was. I hadn't had a woman to talk to for over a year. She told me what to do, and I liked the job fine.

All of the cons at the Old Soldier's Home gambled. I soon had a bankroll. Then I began to go into town and sit in the games there. One evening, I was sitting in a cafe downtown. I had just put my order in, when I saw a real good-looking woman come into the cafe. She was a tall, slender, brunette with the prettiest smile I had ever seen. I had been drinking, but I wasn't drunk and I wanted some company. I called the headwaiter over and asked him if he knew the woman. He said, "No." I handed him a good-size tip, and asked him if he could arrange for us to eat together. He went over and talked to the woman, who had already seated herself at one of the tables. I saw her smile and look in my direction. The headwaiter came over and told me the woman would be pleased to eat dinner with me. I went over with him and met her, and we had dinner together. I should have left that lovely lady alone, because before long I would serve her up one heaping dish of trouble.

Her name was Dora Douglass, but I called her Doris. I found out she didn't drink much, but she didn't object to a fellow having a few drinks. After we had finished our meal, we went to a show that she wanted to see. She was a young widow, and had two small boys. Her first husband had worked on the railroad. He had died of the flu during the World War and she had a small pension coming in. I didn't tell her much about myself, thinking that if she knew the truth she wouldn't talk to me. I made an engagement with her for the next evening. I made up my mind I was going to win her. Then I would tell her the truth about myself. And that is what I started to do.

A few weeks passed, and I had almost forgotten I was still a con, when one evening we were out for a drive, and out of a clear sky she asked me what I did for a living. I told her I was a gambler. She said that is what she had me figured for. I asked her if she thought gambling was wrong. She said she didn't see anything bad about it. She told me her husband had been an engineer on the railroad and he liked to sit in on a game now and then. I started to tell her I was a convict, and that I was doing time, but I changed my mind. I could just see her telling me that she didn't want to see me anymore.

A few evenings later, we went to a show, and the plot was built around a boy who had lived part of my own life. In the end, he had been sent to prison, the others going free. On our way to her apartment, I asked her how she liked the show. She said she didn't think the boy who had been sent to prison got a square deal handed him.

Then I told her I knew a boy who had been cold-decked something like that. I went on telling her a part of my life. I told of this boy meeting a woman, and being afraid she would turn her back on him if she found out about his being in prison. She said if the woman had done that, then she wasn't worth the boy's love. Then I told her I was that boy, and she wanted to know where I had been in prison. When I told her I was doing time right then, she could hardly believe me. Doris was a good sport. She told me she could feel I had a secret, but she had thought it was another woman.

Doris had talked about getting a job. When I told her about being at the Old Soldier's Home, and that they were needing girls to work there, she said she would go out the next day and put in an application. She did, and the matron promised her the next opening. Three days later, she went to work.

The head cook introduced us. I thought of the time that I had bribed the headwaiter to do the same thing. We had a laugh at being strangers.

While I was doing time at the Old Soldier's Home, I made a good friend who was doing time, too. We were going to double up after we got our releases, but he got out ahead of me, and got shot up and sent back to prison.

Soon the board had a lot of complaints made to them, wanting them to hire free labor at places like the Old Soldier's Home. They ordered us cons sent back to stir. I had been in almost two years. I had been at the Old Soldier's Home for over seven months, and now I went back to the pen. Doris stayed on her job. After I was sent back, she would come up and see me on visiting days. They put me back in the guard's kitchen, where I worked until I got my parole.

I was paroled on April 12, 1923; I had been in the stir twenty months and sixteen days. It was good to get out, and I was fairly happy, except when I reflected back on those burglars who had all got their sentences suspended. The thought of that was almost as bitter a feeling as the parole was sweet. I tried to think what I had learned in prison, but about all I learned was how to do time in prison. The only bright spot about prison was working in the Old Soldiers Home, because if I hadn't been sent there I would never have met Doris.

Old Idaho Penitentiary - Idaho Historical Society Collection

North Wing of the 1899 cell house

Administration Building at the Old Idaho at the Old Idaho
Penitentiary
Idaho Historical Society Collection

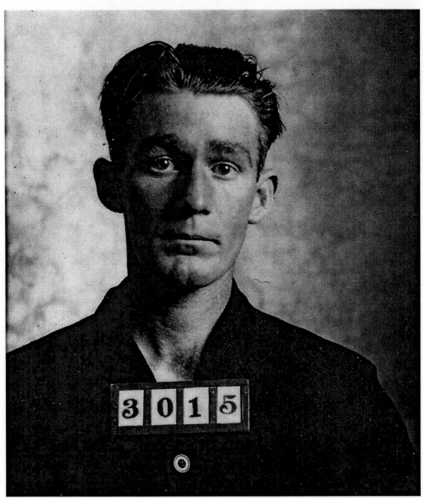

Mug Shot Oliver "Derby" F. Jones 1921 - Idaho Historical
Society Collection

IX

I'll Make Him Pay

As terms of my parole I had to report back to Jerome County, and could not leave the county without permission, I also had to have a job. A friend of mine got me one as a cook in a lumber camp. We were going to gamble, of course, for they had some big games in the camp. He knew I was a crooked gambler who could win without even being crooked, but that didn't seem to bother him a bit. My new job was outside of Jerome County where I'd been sent to prison, but the Jerome county sheriff, E. B. White, had told me I was okay as long as I stayed in the state. There was a whole long list of rules and restrictions I was supposed to live by as condition of my parole. Some of them were kind of easy to live by. But others were impossible for a man to live by if he really wanted to call it living. And if he wanted to supplement his wages with some winnings, he was already in violation of parole just for thinking about it. I was not allowed to drink, gamble, and I had to "avoid all evil associates and improper places of amusements." Of course, I was moving in with just such "evil" company, when I went to that lumber camp. I also had to agree that in case I violated the conditions of my parole I would pay "all expenses incurred by the State of Idaho in causing my arrest and return to the Idaho State Penitentiary." They really had me coming and going.

I rented a house in Boise. Doris quit her job in the Old Soldiers Home and she, her sister, Olive, and her two boys, moved into the house I had rented. Once I knew she was settled and safe, my friend and I drove out to the lumber camp. Once we started working I ran into a problem. Working as a cook meant I had to work too late to get in on the games. My friend and I finally talked a foreman into giving me another job. It was easy. He knew I had just got out of stir, and I told him I needed to be out in the open again.

We made several good winnings, my friend and I. I also took several chances on my life. If any of those lumberjacks had found out I was a crooked gambler, I wouldn't have got out of that camp alive, and chances are, no one would have had to go to jail for killing me. Remember I was a "menace to society." I got along good with those boys, but there isn't anyone tougher than lumberjacks, and the work could be dangerous enough. They could always arrange an accident if they didn't just kill you outright. I had to get a bankroll and one for my friend too, since we were kind of working together. That meant I had to win. But I had to be careful, and time my winnings, manage the cards to pace things just right where I looked lucky, but not too lucky. And to do that, I had to call on all my skills as a cheat. I must have done pretty good, because I got along good with the lumberjacks, and they never were suspicious of me. Instead, they must have figured I was just kind of lucky at cards.

Still, I almost didn't get away from that lumber camp alive. One afternoon, my friend and I were headed into Boise with some of our winnings, and we had a car wreck in which I almost cashed in my chips. I went headfirst through the windshield, landing several feet from the car. I don't think there was a spot on me that wasn't cut, scratched, or bruised. We left the car where we wrecked it, and flagged down a guy in a Hupmobile. He gave us a ride into town to get patched up. I thought for a minute maybe we ought to steal the man's car, that Hupmobile was sharp! But what we needed was some patching up, and it was pretty square of him to give us a ride. We offered to pay him, but he wouldn't take it, not even after he realized we were bleeding on the seats of his car. It's a good thing we were hurt so bad, for I would have felt terrible if we had robbed him and stolen his car. We might have done just that, if we'd been in better shape.

On June 21, 1923, while my wounds were healing, five cons escaped from the stir. I knew all five, J.J. Wright, Hugh Henry Wilson, Frank E. Walters, and my two good friends, Clarence Rousch and Walter Smith. They had sawed through the iron bars on their cell, and crawled into the corridor of cell house No. 1. Once they were out of their cell they called out to the screw that was on guard. When he came in they overpowered him and bound and gagged him. They waited until the screw that was coming on duty showed up, hit him on his head and knocked him unconscious. They took the keys from the screw, unlocked the door and ran out into the yard. When they reached the yard they took some planks from the roof of the shirt factory that was being built, placed them against the wall and went over it. Their escape really caused an uproar. Warden Cuddy was on sick leave at the time of the escape, and he was so upset he had a relapse that put him into the hospital. The governor, C.C. Moore, fired the two guards that the boys had overpowered and named seven additional guards to the prison. He also fired Dan Ackley, the Deputy Warden, and replaced him with the traveling guard, George Roberts. The governor also decided that the prison needed a new dungeon and ordered the construction to start immediately.

This was not the first escape attempt by these same five men. Shortly before I was paroled they were in the dungeon when they sawed their way out of their cells. They were ready to leave when a guard happened to walk into the dungeon and found them out of their cells. The guards took them to cell house one until repairs could be made on the cells in the dungeon. I really wished them luck, and hoped they would get away clean.

After my friend and I had rested and mended up a few days, I filled out and signed five blank parole forms, and sent then to Doris to mail, one each month to the prison. Then my friend and I bought another car, a second-hand Ford, and left town. We headed north.

My friend knew of a bank he had cased, and said it was a set up. We were going to take it. To do that, I had to leave the state. That didn't matter to me. I had already violated my parole. The officials didn't know about it, and I thought what they didn't know couldn't hurt me. At least they weren't looking for me, and that was an advantage.

We stopped in a town in Oregon, where we picked up two more ex-convicts. One was from Idaho, the other one from Montana. They both had some heat on them. They had pulled a job and got in trouble, and had to do some shooting. No one was hurt, but they had to leave their car. They thought we were good sports for giving them a hand. We were good sports; just maybe we weren't to smart.

The car we were driving wasn't hot. We had bought it, and we had our bill of sale. We didn't want to use it on the job, and so we decided to get another car. We soon spotted a new Buick, parked in a good spot under a tree without too many windows looking our way. We drove around the block and parked our car beside the Buick. One of the boys was good with locks, and he said he could make it. He got out and got into the other car. In a few seconds, he said, "Okay." One of the other boys climbed in beside him. We let them drive on and followed behind them. After a while, we found a garage where we could leave our car, and loaded in the stolen car, still headed north. The next afternoon, a carload of bulls tried to stop us. Thinking we were pinched, we didn't stop. There were several shots fired, but no one was hit, and we soon left them behind. When we got to where we thought we were safe, we stopped and gave the car the once over. The back end of that car looked like it had been in No Man's Land. I don't know how we escaped without one of us stopping a bullet. It was clear we had to ditch that car because those bullet holes would have made the law ask too many questions.

We drove on until dark, when we came to a good town. We wrecked the car on one of the side streets, and left it, thinking that when the bulls found it, they'd be looking in the hospitals for the thieves. We got another car, and went on our way. We had good luck, until we hit a town in Washington. There had been a bank robbery pulled, and they had most of the roads blocked. Thinking they were looking for us, we drove around the roadblocks, having a few bullets fired at us, but no damage done. After a long series of chases, we finally made a good getaway.

Thinking we had too much heat on us, we passed up the bank job, and split up in Spokane. I went back to the town where we had left our car, then drove it back to get my pal. From there, we went on back into Idaho, where we made some easy money gambling. Then we had another car wreck and split up, abandoning our car where we had wrecked it. I caught a train for Boise. I had been gone for several weeks, and I didn't know if I was wanted or not, but I didn't intend to be pinched if I could help it. I ended up changing my direction before I got to Boise, and caught another freight train. Before too long, I was somewhere in Oregon, traveling with another bum. We were rattling along when we spotted a railroad bull going over the train. He was a bold one; we could tell by the way he was moving over that speeding train. I thought about how I couldn't stand a pinch. If I had been pinched outside of the state, it would have been the same as committing a felony. When I saw that bull, I decided that I would pinch him if it looked like he was going to try to pinch me. I told the bum what I was thinking and he said, "I'm with you." When the bull jumped down in the car we were in, I put my hand on my rod, and he did the smart thing. He made no effort to arrest us, or to unload us either. The other bum told me this was one of the toughest bulls on the Oregon Short Line, and the bull nodded, and allowed that it was true. He wasn't too tough with us, though. Before he left our car, he just told us to be careful and keep out of sight.

I unloaded at the next stop and hired a taxi to drive me to another town, where I stayed a few days, for I felt sure they were looking for me. Then I caught the night passenger train for Nampa, from where I took the electric line for Boise. It was night when I went out to the house where Doris was waiting for me. She had sent in two parole blanks for me. When I asked if anyone had made inquiries about me, she said "No." After resting up a few days, I felt safe. I went downtown and looked around some. Doris asked me why I didn't go to work, and I told her I might. Instead, I got lined up with a guy who was in the whiskey business. If I had taken Doris' advice, I might have saved myself a lot of grief. But I didn't think I could make expenses working a real job.

I handled several loads of booze before hard luck overtook me. I had been in bed, sick, for about three weeks, when one morning about two o'clock the doorbell began to ring. Thinking it was some friend; I turned on the porch light, and stepped to the head of the stairs, telling whoever it was to come in. When the door opened, I saw I had made a mistake, for a bunch of bulls came barging in. The sheriff, Lee Allumbaugh, said he wanted to shake my place. I asked him if he had a warrant. He sure did. He came up the stairs and handed it to me, and I read it.

When I thought Doris had had time to get to her sister's room, I told them to go ahead. I felt safe with the booze, for I had it planted where those bulls would never look, all of it except one bottle in the clothes closet in my room. I had been drinking out of that bottle. I started into my room, the sheriff going with me. I was in my pajamas. I told him I wanted to put on some clothes, then he noticed the room where Doris and her sister were in bed. He wanted to know who roomed there. Then he started to go in. I told him there were some ladies in there, and if he wanted to talk to them, I would have them get dressed and come out.

The bulls were still shaking the place downstairs. The sheriff started into the girls' room. I stepped in front of him, telling him again to stay there, that I would call the ladies out. When the other bulls came upstairs, they told him they hadn't found anything. I felt pretty good hearing that. They looked my room over, passing my bottle by. I didn't think the sheriff would pinch me. Then he accused Doris of being in bed with me. He was going to pinch both of us. I didn't want Doris to go to jail, so I told him if he wanted to pinch me to go ahead and put any charge he wanted on me, but he had no right to pinch her. One of the bulls was a Federal Agent. He tried to get the sheriff not to pinch me, telling him he didn't have anything on me. But the sheriff took me along and threw me in jail. He charged me with lewd cohabitation on a John Doe warrant. I knew he wouldn't have had a Chinaman's chance of sticking me, if I hadn't been on parole. The next morning I talked to a mouthpiece, and he told me not to be uneasy. They couldn't stick me.

Doris sent another mouthpiece down to the jail to see me. He told me the same thing. There was an ex-convict in jail with whom I had done time. He was said to be phony when he was in stir. After the sheriff found out I had talked to two mouthpieces, he came to my cell, and said, "I thought you were going to plead guilty." I told him I was not pleading guilty because I wasn't guilty of anything, and he might as well turn me loose, because he didn't have anything on me. He got mad,

95

and told me I would "find out just what he had on me." The ex-con must have tipped him off, for the sheriff came back in a short while and unlocked my cell, told me to get my hat and coat; he was going to take me back to prison. I asked him what he meant, and all he said was, "I know you."

We loaded into the car, and headed toward the prison. The sheriff began to talk to me. I told him I had been in prison, but I was out on parole and that Warden Cuddy was a good friend of mine. He would have to show the warden that I had violated my parole before he would receive me at the prison. My bluff worked, for he turned the car around, and we headed back to the jail. Sheriff Allumbaugh talked like he was going to turn me loose. When we got back to the jail, he told me he didn't think I had anything to do with the whiskey, but then he mentioned Doris. I didn't like what he said about her. I fell right into his hands; I blew up and gave him a good cussing. He told me to shut up, or he would punch me in the nose. I told him he didn't have guts enough. He unlocked the bullpen, and as I went through the door, he gave me a shove that would have caused me to fall if I hadn't been expecting it.

Sheriff Allumbaugh had only been sheriff since March of 1923. He had been appointed to finish the term of Sheriff James Agnew who had been convicted of six counts of conspiracy to violate the national prohibition laws. Agnew was sentenced to ten months in the Caldwell County jail and received a fine of $10,000. Speculation over who would take his place had been running wild. In order to be considered for the post, the applicant had to acquire twenty signatures on a petition that supported him for that position. Chief Deputy Sheriff Robinson's petition had the signatures of twenty county jail prisoners. It was a complete surprise when Lee Allumbaugh was appointed. This guy was a building contractor by trade, and the only law experience he had had, was as a deputy in Iowa, some twenty years before. I felt like he was making me his own personal "I'll show them I can do this job" fall guy. What made me even angrier was that he was using Doris to get to me.

I wasn't currently in a position to do much about it though. Allumbaugh called up the prison board; fed them a line of bull, and the board ordered me back to prison. On September 24, 1923, the traveling guard came to the jail and got me. While he was putting handcuffs on me, the sheriff came in. I asked him how many lies he told the prison board to get them to come for me. He smiled and said I would find out, sometime before I got out again. When we got to the prison, I found out that warden Cuddy was sick and not able to be on duty. He had never completely regained his health after Rousch and Smith had escaped. George Roberts, the Deputy Warden was in charge; he didn't like me, and was pleased to get the chance to lock me up again. I told him that Sheriff Allumbaugh had framed me. He didn't believe me, so I didn't say any more. He dressed me in, giving me my same old number. That meant a year, at least, for I was booked as a parole violator.

As soon as Doris heard about them taking me back to prison, she sent my mouthpiece up to see me. He said he would get me out in a few days. I told him to get busy. I wanted to believe him, but I was looking out of a steel door again and didn't feel very optimistic.

I found quite a change when I was turned into the yard. I had only been out a little over five months, but they sure had turned that playhouse into a workhouse. The state had finished the shirt factory. We were now making the clothes we wore, plus the state had signed a contract with some shirt company in Chicago. Believe me, every convict in that stir was working, even the cripples. They assigned me to the shirt factory, and put me on a sewing machine. This was something

I had never been near before, but they put me on a task, and they meant for me to do that task, or else. The "else" was the hole on bread and water. When they built the shirt factory they had also built a new, larger hole, just as the governor had ordered. This one actually had six cells, and was not a hole in the ground. They did, however still use the deep dark holes that were built under the cell houses.

The job I got was sewing labels on shirts. It was easy work for me to get the task done. But there were lots of boys who couldn't get their job done. We had a gun guard in the factory who sat up in a cage where he could see all the cons. When a con wanted a drink of water or wanted to use the toilet, he had to hold his hand up so the gun guard could see it, and then the screw might give permission to leave the machine if he thought the con needed it. If he happened not to like the con, he wouldn't give permission. There were two floor screws who carried clubs. They kept the floor hot, going from one machine to another, seeing that the boys kept busy.

My mouthpiece came to see me and promised to spring me in another week. Doris came up the next visiting day. She didn't like the mouthpiece we had. She said she didn't think he was trying to get me out. She wanted to get another one, so I told her to go back and tell him we were through with him, and to get another one, for I was wanting out of that sweatshop. She got a real mouthpiece, Pete E. Caveney.

During this time, Warden Cuddy had regained his health and was back on the job. It was December and when the next visiting day came, Doris and her sister, Olive, came up. Warden Cuddy overheard our conversation. He spoke up and said, "Jones, you are booked as a parole violator. You will have to stay at least a year with a good record before you are entitled to another parole." I told him I didn't think I had violated my parole. He looked in the book and said I was booked as a parole violator, but there was no charge against me. Then Doris and her sister told how Sheriff Allumbaugh had pinched me, and about me being in bed sick for three weeks. Also, they told about the different doctors I had. Then the warden spoke up. "If I had been here at that time, I would not have received you back. No sheriff has the right to arrest a man and order him back to prison just because he is an ex-con." The warden said I didn't need a mouthpiece. He would get my parole back for me.

Then I told him I had almost a year in since I went out on parole, and I was on the next pardon board. He said that as we had paid the mouthpiece, we should keep him, as a mouthpiece is always a help when it comes to pardons, Doris thought the warden might be kidding us, but he wasn't. He meant just what he said. He wrote to District Attorney Elam and asked him why I had been sent back. He had talked to Roberts who told him that Allumbaugh had said I was caught in a place where whiskey was for sale and with some women of bad repute. Elam wrote him back saying that I had actually been picked up at my residence and that I had been sleeping with a woman of questionable character. He also said that the sheriff had reliable information that I had been selling liquor, but that at the time of the raid no liquor was found.

Before Cuddy could do anything with the information he had received he had another relapse and was put back in the hospital. While he was there it was discovered that he had diabetes. He had to resign due to his health. He was really a good warden. As long as he stayed at the prison, he was as tough on the screws as he was on the cons. And he had no use for a rat.

The new warden appointed to replace him was John W. Snook. Snook was not new to the job; he had been warden from 1909 through 1914. Some of the cons who had been in the stir under him said he was a fair man, a good replacement for Cuddy.

In prison, I met two Chinks, Dong Sing and Lo Ming, who had been given life for a tong killing. They had been locked up in a county jail for over five years before being sent to the stir. Their interpreter at court, Charley Emow would take a question from the lawyer, sing it in several keys for five minutes, then when either Dong Sing or Lo Ming would answer, Emow would make up answers in English. They had carried their case to the highest courts, but they had lost, and had to come on up to the stir. They were trying every board, and burning up a lot of money trying to get out. Dong Sing was over sixty years old and didn't have much time left on this earth. Lo Ming was in his early thirties and was looking at a long life behind bars. I told them I could connect them with a mouthpiece who could spring them.

On April 12, 1924, I finally received my pardon. They opened those iron gates, and let me out. I felt like a new man. I made up my mind that somehow, some day, I was going to make sheriff Allumbaugh pay for framing me. When I made the board, Dong Sing and Lo Ming gave me a message to deliver for them. I delivered it the day after I got out. I made a lot of friends by doing that, for it got those two Chinks pardons. I believe every Chinaman in Boise's Chinatown knew me.

Doris had been working at the Silver Grill in Boise while I was in prison. She was waiting for me and she sure looked great. She wanted me to go to work, so I took a job cooking in one of the hotels. Doris stayed on her job. I thought I would work until the bulls got used to seeing me on the job, then I would even things up with Sheriff Allumbaugh.

I believe that the hotel I went to work at had the hottest kitchen in Boise. I know it took all the nerve I had to stick on that job. I had been hitting the booze again, which really made me sweat on the job. I would have been sweating anyway as hot as that kitchen was.

Doris and I were throwing some good parties. She had a girl friend who had smoked hop. Doris got the idea she wanted to try the pipe. I had smoked some, and I knew if there was any hop in Boise it would be in Chinatown, and I could get it through some of my Chink friends. One night we took in Chinatown, we went first to the Mandarin Inn on Eighth and Grove for dinner. It was an elegant place run by Louie Lai. Louie only let non-Chinese in his restaurant on special occasions and only if they were invited. This was a special occasion; Chinatown was celebrating the release of Dong Sing and Lo Ming. We saw everything there was to see, and some things besides. Doris and I smoked a little hop. The next day she told me she was glad she had tried the stuff, but it really wasn't to her liking. I was really glad to hear that, that stuff can become quite a habit.

About this time, I was beginning to need more money than we were making. I didn't intend to let Doris know I was making some on the side. When I would see easy dough, I would go get it.

One day, while I was on shift at the hotel, a friend of mine came into the kitchen, and told me he had a friend who wanted to meet me. I told him to bring him in. He said he wanted me to come out to the car if I could leave the kitchen. I went out and met the man. He looked like a gangster. My friend introduced us; his friends' name was Chet Langer. Chet said he had a proposition he would like to talk over with me. I told him I would be off work in a short while, and he could meet me at the depot. When I got through work, I walked over to the depot. Chet was there waiting for me.

Chet told me a friend of his had recommended me to him. He went on to tell me he was out of Los Angeles, where he belonged to a gang, and he had some heat under him. He had been staying with his brother in Los Angeles. Now he was up in Idaho cooling off, staying with his parents and he was running short of money. I asked him what he had in mind. He told me he knew some Chinks who had a chunk of money, and it would be easy to get. He thought it was a safe job, and he wanted me to crack the safe for him, so I asked how much the safe had in it. He said he didn't know if they had a safe or not, but he thought we could stick them up and make them dig up their money. Chet kept changing his story, which made me think he did not have as much experience on the wrong side of the law as he said he did.

I asked him if he had ever robbed a Chink. He said he hadn't, then I shook my head and told him not to try to make a Chinaman dig up his money, for they didn't like to give it up. I said I had robbed some once, and I knew. Then I told him that almost every Chink in Boise was a friend of mine, and I wasn't interested in robbing any of them. I told him if he had a bank job that would pay off, I might try it. Then I told him I hadn't been out long, and if I tried anything, I wanted it to be worth taking the chance. I told him I would see him again, then I left.

I knew that Chet was desperate for money, and I needed a partner, for I was getting tired of burning grease. I had a show job there in Boise I was casing. It was the biggest show in town, and they gathered the money from two other shows and banked it in the vault at the big show. A harness bull would ride the car with the collector when he gathered in the money. I thought it would pay off about six or eight grand on a Sunday night. I thought if Chet proved to be okay, I might cut him in on this job.

I mentioned Chet to Doris that night, but I didn't mention our conversation. She asked if he had a girl friend. I told her he did, so she said we might throw a party and invite them sometime. Doris was beginning to get very fond of parties.

I was walking along a street one day when I saw a large car parking just ahead of me. Two men got out. I thought there was something familiar about them. They went into a cafe, and as I passed the cafe, I glanced in. I recognized them. They were two brothers that I had done time with.

I went into the cafe, walked over to their table, and sat down. They were really glad to see me, wanting to know when I had been sprung. Then they asked me what I was doing. I told them I was cooking, and they didn't believe me. They told me they needed another man to work with them, and wanted me to join them. I asked what they were doing. They had a good racket, but there was some work attached to it. They were robbing fur and wool trains. They had a fence in Salt Lake City, who handled their stuff for them. I told them if I did any more stealing, it would be in Idaho, and in that county, and no place else. Then I told them about the sheriff who had framed me. They said they didn't much blame me, but they still tried to get me to go to Utah with them.

When they finished their meal, I got in the car with them. They wanted to look Boise over. Their car was loaded. They had rifles, sawed-off shotguns, six shooters, and enough soup to blow Boise off the map. I laughed when I looked inside that car, and asked them if they needed any more artillery. They said they did. They had spotted a machine gun they were going to get on their way back. One of the brothers, Joe, said, "If those monkeys ever take me, it will be in a wooden box."

And that is just what happened. A few months later, he stopped a volley of slugs from posses' gun, not having a Chinaman's chance for his life. I read about it in one of the newspapers, and not knowing what was ahead of me, I thought myself lucky in not joining up with them.

Dora (Doris) Douglas with sons Luther (Babe)
and Gilbert - 1924

Doris and Babe – 1924

X

The Bobbed-Hair Bandit

One day, along about the time that my train robber friend was killed, another friend and I were at my apartment relaxing and discussing an article we'd just read about Lucille Wilson, alias Lucille LaVallette, a gun moll in New York that the press called "the Bobbed-Hair Bandit," when in came Doris and a girlfriend. Her friend had just had her hair bobbed, and when my friend and I saw her, we started to laugh. Of course, this upset Doris and her friend, so we showed them the article we'd just read, and both of them started laughing, too. The friend looked kind of cute with her new hairstyle, and I told Doris she could get her hair bobbed if she wanted to, and I would make a bobbed-hair bandit out of her, too. Knowing I was kidding, Doris and her friend went off to the beauty parlor, and Doris got her hair bobbed. We didn't know it at the time but it would be the first step to making my joke a reality.

That evening, my friend, Chet, came into a gambling joint where I was sitting in on a game, and he gave me a wink. I played a few more hands, cashed in, and followed him out. We got in the car, drove out to a good spot, and stopped. Chet wanted to know if I had anything planned, as he felt he had to do something right away. I couldn't be sure whether he needed money desperately, or was just getting antsy to do something. But either way I had made up my mind to try him out before going on a big job with him. I told him I had a few things in mind, but he'd have to be patient. Then I arranged a party for that night, and he brought his girlfriend over to our place.

We made it an all night party, and we ended up in Chinatown. Chet was already very drunk when we went to a Chinese noodle parlor, where we had a run-in with a gang at another table. The Chink owner being a friend of mine saved us from a pinch. We went back to my place, where Chet and his girlfriend went to sleep. I went to work the next morning. I was feeling pretty tough, so I got a bottle on the way to work. The boss came into the kitchen just as I burnt up an oven full of pies. I told him to get another cook to relieve me. The boss thought I was feeling sick, so he told me to go ahead, and I'd feel better after a while. I told him I quit. He finally got a cook to take my place, and that was my last workday in a free world for a long time to come.

That night, I told Doris what I had done, and told her to call up and get someone to take her place at work. We were going to take a rest. After she had done that, I asked her what she thought of our new friends. She said she liked them okay, but she didn't trust Chet. She explained that Chet couldn't look anyone in the eye, and she had a hunch that he would be the cause of my going back to the big house. I laughed at her, and told her to pour out another drink. I figured she was just nervous about what had happened in Chinatown the night before. But then I started thinking, and I could see that she had a point. I had noticed the same thing about Chet. That was one reason I wanted to try him out on a job I could handle myself, just to see how he acted. He was supposed to have robbed several banks, but I had my doubts.

Doris must have known what I was thinking, because after she called the cafe and told them she would be out of town for a few days and that they would need to get someone to replace her. Then she turned to me and said, "Derb, you are planning a job with Chet, aren't you?" Then she said, "I would rather go with you myself than have you double up with that guy, I don't trust him!" If I had played her hunch, I might have saved myself a lot of hell.

107

I heard what she was saying, but I did not like the thought of putting her at risk, and I dismissed it from my mind. Doris was the light in my life, the only really good thing I had going in my very rough life. I really loved her and did not want to see her ending up on the run, or worse, in jail.

A few nights later, Chet and I went out on a job. It paid a little over three C-notes. Chet did his part well, and never showed fear. I liked him, and felt better about him then. Doris kept saying that she didn't trust Chet, and that she would rather pull the jobs with me than watch me pull them with him. I should have trusted her instincts. One night we were out drinking, and I was feeling no pain, when she again told me how she felt about my working with Chet. She said she would rather go out on the next job with me. I finally gave in. I told Doris that if she wanted, she could go along on our next trip. All she said was "It's about time." Chet said it was okay with him, so we took her along. I wanted her to trust Chet. We made several small jobs without a rank. They were robberies and burglaries, and Doris got a thrill out of it. When we got back, we began to plan our next job. I told them about the show job I had planned, and about a bank I had cased out. They both wanted in.

We were going to pull the Boise show job first, hit the theater, then take a bank I had been casing. The bank was in Eagle, a small town northwest of Boise. We decided we needed to get another car so we decided to snatch a taxi. I called the Central Livery Company for a taxi and told them to send it to 21st and Jefferson, which was the address of a vacant house we had found. I told them I needed the pick-up at about ten p.m. When the taxi came, I went to the sidewalk and covered the driver with my rod. Doris and Chet then got into the cab and Chet covered the driver while I got in. We were all three masked, and Doris was wearing one of my suits, so she would look like a man. I told the driver we didn't intend to harm him.

All we wanted was for him to drive us where we wanted to go. He was a good driver, but he was a little nervous. We had him drive us to the show house, and park across the street. Just as we parked, the towns new motorcycle cop came by and slowed down. We waited a few minutes and the pay car collecting the show money came. The harness bull got out of the pay car, then the motorcycle cop came up and stopped. I told the driver to drive on. When we started moving, the cop pulled in behind us. I told the driver to ditch that bull. We did, but it took several blocks. We decided to pass the show job up, and get the bank the next morning.

We stopped at a cafe. Chet got out, went in, and ordered us some sandwiches. We picked him up later, then we left town to find a place to stay the night. As we left Boise, a black cat crossed the street in front of us. I laughed, and said that if we got caught, it would be that cat's fault. Chet and Doris laughed too, but the driver only gave a nervous smile. I don't think he was too happy being a part of our job. We had him drive down State Street, out through Eagle, Star, and up to the Darling Station area. We finally found a deserted ranch house where we would put up for the night. I told the driver to get out of the car, keep his eyes ahead and no moves. I kept him covered while Chet and Doris went into the house to make sure it was empty. When they found that it was empty, they came back out and got the driver and me. We parked the taxi driver in a closet. At first, we tied him up, but then I told him I would turn him loose if he promised not to try to get away. He promised. We were going to need him the next day, and I knew he couldn't rest if he was tied up. We guarded him, but we fed him, and treated him well. We didn't let him see us with our masks off. After eating breakfast the morning, August 11, 1924, we took off for the town of Eagle. We timed ourselves, getting there just when the Bank of Eagle opened, at nine A.M.

When we drove up to the bank, it was full of people. I told the driver to drive on out of town. In about twenty minutes, I told him to drive back; thinking the people in the bank had plenty time to clear out. The bank was empty of customers now. I told Doris to keep her rod on the driver, and to shoot him if he tried to get away. When Chet and I got out of the car, Doris kept the driver covered. Just as when I'd cased the place before, there was only the bank manager and a clerk on duty. We scuttled under the low plate glass window in front of the bank and then burst through the front door. Even though we were masked, we got to the bank cage before the manager noticed us. I covered the manager at his desk. Chet went to the cage window and covered the clerk. I told the manager to go stand by the clerk. I told them both to get their hands in the air. The clerk was a gal about eighteen, and she either had some real spunk or was scared to death. She said she wouldn't put her hands up for anyone. I said okay, as long as she didn't try anything. About that time the manager, keeping one hand in the air, put his arm around the clerk. She then put one of her hands in the air.

I found out later the girls' name was Margaret Fikkan, daughter of the bank manager E. H. Fikkan. Meanwhile Chet went inside the bank vault. When he got to where he could cover through, I joined him by the vault. I covered the bank manager and his daughter with my rod while Chet was getting the money. The banker kept looking outside, so I told him "You're looking around too much," and told him to face the wall. Then I told Chet to make it snappy. While Chet was clearing out the money, the banker tried to run inside the vault. For a second, I thought I would have to shoot him, which I didn't want to do, because that would have alarmed the town. That banker was smart enough, I guess. When I told him to stop, he stopped. After Chet cleared out the money, I ordered the banker and his daughter into the vault, and locked them inside, telling him he shouldn't have rushed to get inside before because I was going to let him in the vault anyway. As we started towards the door we could hear the clerk screaming and making all kinds of racket.

We burst out the bank door, breaking the doorframe, and ripping two of the hinges from their fastenings. As we were getting in the taxi, I saw a woman across the street, pounding on the back door of a poolroom, hollering as loud as she could that the bank was being robbed. As Chet got into the car, he spilt a bag of coins, bent down and started picking them up. I realized that the alarm had been sounded, and that the bulls were probably on their way. I told Chet to leave the money, that we needed to get the hell out of here. I told the taxi driver to "Drive like hell." At the same time I made Doris get down on the floor of the car, thinking we would get a volley of bullets shot at us. But we were lucky; we got away without a shot being fired. The driver took me seriously about driving like hell; we almost wrecked going around a corner on two wheels. As we neared the spot where Doris and I were going to leave the car, I told Chet to either tie up the driver, or knock him out before leaving the taxi. I found out later that he didn't do either.

When we got to the crossroads, Doris and I left the car, taking the money with us. When the taxi took off, we took off on foot. Chet went on to where his car, a Hudson Super Six, was stashed, let the driver go and then headed to his parents ranch just outside of Eagle. Doris and I headed to the Dave Sommers ranch, which was about a mile south of Star. Doris was paying the Sommers fifteen dollars a month to look after her two boys. When we got to the ranch house, we went in, finding the rancher's daughter Nettie, who was only fourteen, and Elmie, one of the ranchers sons, who was a little younger, than Doris' oldest boy, Gilbert. Nettie was in the kitchen, washing dishes. I set the bag down and glanced at the clock. It was nine twenty-seven. I stepped into the kitchen and spoke to

Nettie. I took my watch out, saying, "We got here early. It is only a quarter to nine." Nettie answered, saying we sure were early, because she didn't even have the breakfast dishes washed yet. I knew she would swear a lie, thinking it was the truth. We stayed at the ranch until later that night.

Dave Sommers was helping a neighbor thresh, and did not come home until that evening. His wife had gone to Caldwell to hear Matty Crawford, the evangelist, speak. She had taken Doris' youngest son, Luther, who we called Babe, with her. We had some trunks in one of the rooms upstairs. Doris made some remark about getting some things out of the trunks, and I took the bag and went upstairs with her. While we were upstairs we counted the money. We had snatched $2772 from the bank. We separated out the gold and silver coin from the paper money and the pennies. We put about twenty-four dollars in pennies in a bag marked $500. I wanted to get rid of the gold and silver, thinking I would ditch them some place on the ranch, and come back for them later. I put them in a sack and left it in one of the trunks, thinking I could find a safe place to hide them later, not wanting the kids to see me. But when I looked for a place, I found I would have to walk some distance. Not wanting to leave the ranch house, as it was our alibi, I left the bag where it was, thinking I would have a chance to hide it later.

When Dave came home that evening, I was intending to get his son, Lester, to drive us to Caldwell to get Babe. While we were eating supper, the rancher asked us if we had heard about the bank being robbed. I told him I had not heard, and asked him when it was robbed. He said a little after it was opened in the morning. His daughter spoke up and said "No, they could not have heard about it Daddy, they were here before it was robbed. I didn't have my dishes washed when they came in." I asked if anyone had been hurt. He said, "No," and that the bandits had got away without a trace. I glanced at

Doris. She had turned a little pale, but then she spoke up, and said it was getting to be a common thing. In almost every paper you picked up, there was a robbery pulled somewhere.

After supper, we hired Lester to take us to Caldwell, where we picked up Babe. Then we had him take us to the Inter Urban depot so we could catch a streetcar for Boise. When I got out of the car I laid a five-dollar bill on the seat and told Lester "here's a little something for your trouble." Lester said, "Ah, its no trouble, I wouldn't charge you anything for the ride." I said "you keep it, the next time you see Doris and me we will be driving a Cadillac."

When we got to Boise, we stopped in a cafe for something to eat. There were quite a number of people in the cafe. They were all talking about the bank robbery. I had the waitress bring us a copy of Boise's evening newspaper, the *Boise Evening Capital News*. The headlines read "Masked Automobile Bandits Hold Up The Bank Of Eagle And, After Locking Cashier Fikkan And His Daughter In The Vault At Point Of Gun, Make Away With $2600 In Cash." After reading the article, I told Doris everything looked good, except the banker thought one member of the gang was a woman. The paper said they were also holding Hank Endsley, the taxi driver. It said that he was telling everything that he knew, which wasn't much. It really bothered me that three of the witnesses thought the person in the taxi was a woman, but I didn't say any more about it to Doris. The article also said that the money Chet dropped totaled $476. It was also through the newspaper that I realized how close we came to murder. The bank vault was airtight and the bank manager and his daughter only had about twenty minutes of air. Mr. Fikkan had, fortunately, hidden a screwdriver, a pair of pliers, and a hammer in the vault just in case some one got locked in. He had used the tools to undo the lock and get his daughter and himself out.

113

Doris thought it might be best to take Babe and spend the night with her sister. I could get a room at some hotel. As it was after midnight, I thought we were safe, and said that wasn't necessary.

When the taxi stopped at the Kurri Flats on South 10th street, where our apartment was, I had the driver wait, leaving Doris and Babe in the car. Everything seemed to be okay, so I went back out and got them. After we had been inside for a few minutes, Doris noticed a note on the dresser. It read, "Will be back in a short while; wait until I come." I told her I didn't like the looks of the note, for it was printed. We thought it might be that Chet got uneasy, and came to town, thinking he would find us. And not finding us, he had left the note. I had her take Babe and sleep in another room. I slept in the front room. I had just dropped off to sleep, when the door burst open and a bunch of bulls swarmed in, holding their rods and flashlights on me, telling me not to move. I asked them what the hell they wanted. One of them said they wanted to talk to me. I told them to turn on the lights, and take their flashlights out of my face. They did, and I recognized my old friend, Sheriff Allumbaugh. When he saw the door leading to Doris' room, he started in. I told him to stop, and asked if that was all he did, raid people, and go into rooms where the women folk were. Then he recognized me. He turned around and said, "When did you get out?" I told him it was none of his business. I had a pardon, and he would have to tell his lies to a jury of twelve before he could send me back.

He then started into Doris' room again. I told him I would have her dress and come out, and he stopped. I called to her, telling her there were some men wanting to talk to us. She came into my room. She was pale, but seeing all of those tough looking bulls with their rods turned on me was enough to make any woman pale. The sheriff wanted to know what we knew about the bank robbery. I told him nothing, only what I read in the papers. He wanted us to go to the station with him. There wasn't anything else to do, but go. They would have taken us anyway. I got up, got Babe, and we all loaded into the car and headed for the station, stopping along the way to pick up District Attorney Elam. When we arrived at the county jail it was one a.m., August 12th.

As soon as we got to the jail office, the sheriff booked me on lewd cohabitation charges. They kept Babe and me in one room, taking Doris into another one. They would talk to me awhile, then go and talk to her. I knew we had them guessing. The D. A. asked if we knew a man called "Chet." I told him I might, but couldn't recall anyone by that name. He then told me they had pinched Chet in my apartment, and had him in jail, and he had owned up to being one of the robbers. I told Elam I was an ex-con, but had gotten a pardon. He then asked me about Doris and me living together. I told him we were planning on getting married. I told him to ask her, and if she was willing, we would get married that night. He went and asked her, she told him "Okay." He came back and said, "I don't believe you had anything to do with the bank robbery, but you two had better get married." Then I asked him if he would let Doris take her baby and go spend the rest of the night with her sister. I didn't mind spending the night in jail, but I didn't want the little boy to grow up and find out his mother had spent a night in jail. I patted little Babe as I said it.

Elam told me that could be arranged, and after we got married he would turn me loose. About then Sheriff Allumbaugh said he thought he could get enough evidence against me to change the lewd cohabitation charges to robbery, so I was just going to stay put. I asked Elam if he could keep this out of the newspapers for the time being. He said he could try, and picked up the phone. But when he got the editor of the *Idaho Statesman*, it was too late; they had already started printing the morning addition. I could just see the headline telling about the big bank robbery, and how O. F. (Derby) Jones, Idaho ex-convict, was leader of the gang. And sure enough, that was just what I saw the next morning on the front page of the *Idaho Statesman*. Reading about the outlaw Derby Jones in that paper, I couldn't understand why anyone would ever want to be that famous. There on the front page was Chet, Doris, and myself. The caption under the picture read, "Oliver Jones an Idaho ex-convict, who covered the banker, Dora Douglas, bobbed hair and all, the woman bandit, and Chet Langer who looted the vault". My joke about Doris being Idaho's Bobbed Hair Bandit was no longer a joke. The paper also told how the bulls had found that bag marked $500 in Doris' trunk and that they were real excited thinking they had found $500 of the bank money, only to find it contained $29.50 in pennies. I would have loved to see their faces when they opened that bag. I also did not know that, at that time, they had Chet in the city jail and that he was squealing his head off.

They sent Doris and her baby out to her sister's. I knew she would send a mouthpiece to the jail to see me. The first thing the next morning, she sent Pete Caveney, the mouthpiece who had gotten me a pardon. Pete didn't think any more highly of Sheriff Allumbaugh than I did. He said they had nothing on me, and he would spring me on a writ. But when he found out they still had me booked on a charge of lewd cohabitation that stopped him cold. He also told me that the bank job was all over the front page of the Idaho Daily Statesman, he had even brought me a copy.[1]

---

[1] "Sheriffs Scour County For Three Bandits Who Loot Eagle Bank" The Idaho Statesman August 12, 1924 (Newspaper Reprints page 295)

The Idaho Daily Statesman, August 12, 1924, Front page

A load of bulls and Elam went out to check our alibi. When they got out to the Sommers ranch, Nettie told them we got there before nine o'clock and stayed until that night. They asked if we went anywhere while we were there and she told them only upstairs. Two of the bulls went upstairs and looked through the trunks, finding the bag of pennies which I had intended to throw away and the paper money. Thinking they had all the money, they rushed back to the jail. At about three p.m., they drove out and pinched Doris again, bringing her back to jail. They booked her on robbery charges, and changed my charges to robbery. My mouthpiece came to the jail, and told me what had taken place. He also told me that Chet had talked. I told Pete to get hold of Chet, and shut him up. Pete did just that. He said the bulls had not found all the money, that $776 was still missing. He said if everyone stood pat, we could beat them, but it had begun to look bad to me.

At about the same time they were booking Doris, they brought Chet over from the city jail and put him in the county jail. They brought in Mr. Fikkan, the bank manager, who identified us. He said he was positive it was me who held the rod on him. He said, "This is the man who covered my daughter and me with the gun. I can tell from his actions and his movements, and he has a way of crouching, just as he did when he placed the revolver close to my body." He was equally as positive that Chet was, "The bird who looted the vault and carried out the money." They took us out and mugged us. Then they arraigned us, setting our bond at twenty thousand dollars, which was close to a record at that time.

The bank was insured by the Burns Detective Agency out of Salt Lake City. Some of their bulls came and went to work on Doris. A.M. Pritchard was their head bull and one tough cookie. Everyday for weeks they would question Doris, but she hung tough.

I made the acquaintance of a man who fed me. He and his wife had been convicted of making moonshine, and they were both trustees. His wife would feed the women, and I would get her to slip Doris a letter, and Doris would use her to get one to me. In that way, we could correspond, as they wouldn't let us talk to our mouthpiece together. They had done everything to get her to squawk. They even had a bunch of businessmen go to the jail and talk to her. They threatened to take her boys away from her, and put them in a home. She wrote me a note asking me if they could do that. I wrote back telling her no, and if they tried it, I would break jail, and get everyone who had a hand in it. When she got my note, she was far from talking.

Early the next morning when the trusty came to feed me, he also brought me a copy of the Statesman. He thought I might like to see my picture in the paper.[2]

---

[2] "Charges Of Robbery Filed Against Four In Eagle Bank Case" The Idaho Statesman August 13, 1924 (Newspaper Reprints page 300)

The Idaho Daily Statesman, August 13, 1924, Front page

The next day, the bulls started in on Doris again. Again they failed to get any information out of her. They were getting pretty angry, since they had already had the newspapers publish that "they were going to get a full confession out of the woman." It was turning into a lie. Day after day they would start in on her, and day after day they would fail.

After a couple more days, the bulls came into the tank, and cuffed me. I thought I was going to have a hearing. I asked one of the bulls, and he said they were taking me to the pen for safekeeping. I asked permission to call my mouthpiece, and when I got him on the phone, I told him what they were doing. One of the bulls got tough. I began to argue with him, knowing that Pete would be at the jail in a few minutes. They were dragging me out, when I heard a car drive up, and Pete came charging in and wanted to know what was going on. The sheriff wasn't there, and the deputy in charge told Pete he had orders to take me to prison. Pete told him he had no right to do that, and if they did, he would bring me back on a writ. He told the deputy to put me back in jail until he had talked to District Attorney Elam. And being a more reasonable bull than the sheriff, that's what the bull did. When Pete came back with Elam, the D. A. ordered them to put me back in the tank, and leave me there.

About three weeks later we were still in the county jail with no court date set. The bulls were still looking for the missing $776 and didn't want me going to trial until they found it. They were worried I might beat this rap. One night when they brought the boys over from the bullpen to sleep in the tank, the sheriff came in, telling me to get my things and come along. Thinking I was going to the prison, I said, "This is pretty damn good. Pete will just bring me back." It turned out I had misread the situation. Instead of taking me to the pen, the sheriff handcuffed me and took me to an empty cell, where he beat the hell out of me. I had to take the beating, because I knew he was trying to get a rise out of me, hoping I'd do something that would let him take me to stir until my trial. I took that beating. The only thing I did was to ask sheriff Allumbaugh if he'd blown his top, which he had. He seemed to know that he had, too, because as soon as I said it, he stopped beating me, and locked me in another cell, with a railroad brakeman, Nick Watkins, who was accused of killing another brakeman, Dave Jennings.

It was then that I made my mind up that if I could, I was going to beat that jail. It was an election year; I wanted to see what a jailbreak would do to Lee Allumbaugh's chances of getting elected sheriff for a full term.

The Summers Ranch in Star

Lester Summers with mother and sisters and the car he drove
"Derby" and Doris in

XI

Jail Break

A few nights after the sheriff beat me up; they took Watkins out of the tank, and brought Chet in. I asked Chet if he wanted to break jail. He said yes so I told him we would. Some of my teeth were still loose; my lip was still fat. I ached everywhere and was covered with bruises, but I was still determined to break that jail, in fact, I was even more determined than before. If I had been given a choice between being released and breaking jail, I would have chosen a jailbreak. I was going to make Allumbaugh pay.

I figured that to break jail, I would have to have help from someone on the outside. After I got to know the fellows in jail with me, I thought I had found the outside man I was going to need. He was an ex-con named Bob, who was facing a Federal prohibition charge. Not only was he facing a trip to McNeil Island, he was also broke. After listening to him tell me his situation, I told him I would have my mouthpiece put him back on the bricks, if he would slip me a saw once he got outside. He said he would do better than that---he would slip me a rod. I saw my mouthpiece, and leading him to think I was going to use Bob to gather evidence for my trial; I paid him a C-Note to get Bob out. Not only did I pay my mouthpiece to spring him, I also gave Bob some expense money, and he said he would come back, stick up the jail and break us out. If there was any way, I was also hoping to break Doris out too, but I knew that wouldn't be easy. I felt real bad that Doris was in jail. This was definitely no place for a lady, much less the lady I cared so deeply about.

The night after Bob left, Chet and I got ready to leave. But Bob didn't come that night, or the next, or the night after that. I began to get the hunch that Bob had blown town, which he had. With that chance gone, I told Chet we were going to have to do it ourselves. We began to look around real carefully, looking for a way to break out. I knew that there were weaknesses in every system, and I also knew that weaknesses could become opportunities.

Whenever we got a shower, they would take us over to the bullpen. I had noticed that they never locked the bathroom door, so I asked for a shower. When they took me to the bullpen for my shower, they left the bathroom door unlocked. When the bull went out, I waited a minute, and then sneaked out to the room where they kept the dishes. There I picked out a good case knife, and planted it in my sock. When I finished my bath I also hid a safety razor with the case knife. They took me back to the tank, and didn't bother to shake me down.

After the bull locked the tank and left, I showed the knife to Chet. I told him we were going to leave that jail with the help of this knife. He didn't see how, so I showed him. I pulled out a small block of wood that I had smuggled in from the bullpen a couple of days earlier. First I whittled a crude looking gun out of the wood. Then I had Chet hold the knife, and I went to work on it with the safety razor. When I got through, I had a good hacksaw, at least good enough to saw what we had to saw. There were two locks on our cell. I could pick one of them, but we had to saw the other one. Outside our cell was a corridor with a door we'd have to get through. I told Chet we'd have to get our cell fixed first, then we would figure out a way to beat the corridor door.

I started on our cell lock, and even with that good case knife saw, it was slow work. I had to stop often, working only at night so no one would hear me. But I finally got through to where we could snap it, but the bulls wouldn't notice the cut. During the next few days I started picking up all the tin foil cigar wrappers I could find. I used the foil to wrap my gun in so it would not look so much like a chunk of wood. I figured we would break out at night when there was very little light, and the gun would look convincing enough. All I was thinking was about the immediate future. I was thinking that the screws would unlock the corridor some night, and we would stick them up.

Federal court was in session at the time, and the jail was full because, thanks to prohibition, the Federal bulls were pinching all kinds of people. Because the jail was so full, some of the boys slept on the floor. There were two "hypos" in the jail, and one of them slept on a cot in the corridor. There being no toilet in the corridor, they would take him out to the bull's toilet. The hypo would always go when there were a bunch of bulls there, never giving us the chance we needed. For a hypo, he was damned regular. But one night, he asked the jailer for some salts. The jailer told him to wait until morning. I spoke up, and told him to take some C.C. pills. He didn't know what they were, and neither did the jailer, so I laughed, and explained that C.C. pills could regulate a man's calls of nature, and that was what won the World War for us. It was a load of hokum, but I was thinking that the jailer wouldn't know that, and would just get the pills from the dispensary without checking up on what they really do, which is to give a man a bad case of the runs. Sure enough, that's what the jailer did, and as I told the jailer I wanted some too, he brought more than enough. I slipped my pills to the hypo, and only pretended to take them. When the hypo lay down, I gave Chet a big wink, then told him we were leaving that night. We kept our cloths on and lay down.

About two o'clock, the hypo, Charles Smith, began calling the jailer. When I touched Chet, he was already awake, and when the jailer unlocked the corridor door and let Charley out, we got up. I picked the spring lock, and Chet snapped the lock I'd sawed through. We went out, closing our cell almost completely behind us. I had Chet get under Charley's cot, where he could grab the bottom of the corridor door. I got behind the pot-bellied stove. When the jailer unlocked the corridor door to bring Charley back in, I jumped up with my fake gun, telling him to put up his hands. The jailer was so scared he jumped back out of my way. But I was on him, grabbing him. I fanned him for his rod, but he had left it in the office. I shoved him inside. He saw Chet, swung on him, and scratched his face. Chet hit him with a stove lifter. At the same time, I shoved his head hard against the door, both blows breaking his nose. I demanded the keys, but he said he didn't have them. We shoved him into our cell, locking the spring lock. Then I told the jailer that I was going into the office and get a rod, and if he didn't give us the key when I got back, I was going to knock him off. When I came back with a rod I found in the desk, he had a mattress over the cell door, and one hand was through the bars, dangling the keys. He told us he just wanted us to leave and I do believe he meant it. I picked the spring lock again, moved the mattress aside, and tied the jailers' arms with an old shirt. I told Chet, "Hit him a crack on the head and knock him out, so he'll keep quite." Chet looked at me kind of funny but finally did what he was told, and we shut the door and locked the spring lock again.

There was another boy in the tank who was going to the big house. He had told us he wanted to break jail with us, but when he saw the blood on the jailer, he got cold feet. We left, locking the corridor door behind us. In the office, we busted into a gun case, and picked out some rods and about a hundred rounds of ammunition. One of the pieces we took had the initials L. A. engraved on it. It was Sheriff Allumbaughs' personal rod. Then I went to the women's ward, and unlocked the door with the keys I had taken. There were several women in there with Doris, and at first they were scared to see us. I asked Doris is she was coming with us, but she said she believed she could beat the rap, and didn't want to go. They still had not officially charged her yet. They were just holding her on suspicion. I told her to lay all the blame on me, and to tell the D. A. I had forced her to do what she had done. She said she wasn't about to do anything that low. Once again, I told her to lay it all on me, and then I bid her farewell, first telling the other girls I would give them a conditional pardon, they were free on the condition that they didn't get caught. I left their door unlocked; taking the key with me, but none of them came out. Back in the office, we jerked the telephone wire out of the wall, and then we left.

We didn't try to get a car. I had a friend who lived on a ranch a few miles from the jail, and that's where we headed. We skirted next to the highway for a while, hiding whenever a car came along, and a good thing we did, for all of those cars were full of bulls, and all those bulls were bristling with guns. Finally we found a haystack, and hid there the rest of the night and all the next day, feeling like we were starving to death the whole time. We hung tough, and then after it was dark, we headed for the ranch where my friend, Jerry Firestone, stayed.

It was about ten when we got there. I went to the back door, leaving Chet by the garage. I had almost reached the door, when Jerry's dog, whom I had forgotten all about, lunged to the end of his chain trying to get me. I still had my rod in hand, and not thinking too clearly, I almost shot that dog. When I knocked on the door, it opened, and I was staring into the muzzle of a double-barrel shotgun, with Jerry's wife on the other end of it. Jerry was running off some moonshine, and thinking I was the law, she was going to hold me at gun point until Jerry got everything in the clear. But when she recognized me she called to Jerry, saying, "It's Derby!"

I brought Chet around, and before long, Jerry's wife was cooking us up a feed. When I told them we had broken jail, they didn't seem too shocked, but they were a little surprised because they hadn't been to town for a couple days, and weren't up on the news. Jerry asked if we had killed anyone getting out, and I told him that the jailer might have a sore nose for a day or two, but nothing more serious than that. He looked relieved to hear that. He said he guessed we were plenty hot, and he offered to let us stay there for a while until we cooled off. Jerry said he would go into town the next day and get the low down on the manhunt. We wouldn't have to worry about anyone sneaking up on us, he said, thanks to his dog outside, and when I heard that, I was plenty glad I hadn't shot that dog.

Jerry went to the mailbox and got the paper. There was plenty in it, everything but the truth. In jails and in the pen, I often met men who were proud of the way the newspapers played them up, and I never could understand why. Almost every time I knew firsthand about something, then read about it afterwards in the newspapers, the papers were either wrong or lying. And besides, newspaper always managed to turn up the heat, and make a man look worse than he really was. There Chet and I were on the front page of the *Idaho Statesman* again, along with a picture of the sawed off lock. They said nothing about that wooden gun I had so lovingly carved or anything about me suggesting to the jailer that he give Smith those C.C. pills. We were hot, all right. A couple days later, the papers would even come up with a story about a tall thin man who had been seen hanging around Eagle for a few days before the robbery. They would tell the readers that this guy must have been our scout. We had no idea who they were talking about.[3]

---

[3] "Bandits Still Free After Jail Break" The Idaho Statesman October 17, 1924 (Newspaper Reprints page 303)

The Idaho Daily Statesman, October 17, 1924, Front page

We were so hot I had to tell Jerry that if we got pinched at his place, he was to tell them we had taken them hostage and forced them to feed us and give us a place to stay. Jerry laughed at that, and nodded his head toward the kitchen door. "There won't be any unannounced visitors out here," he said, and once again I was real glad I hadn't shot that dog.

Jerry really knew how to make moonshine, and he gave us a bottle apiece, of the booze he had been running off. When we showed up. He got us blankets and led us to a good spot to stay the night. He stayed and talked for a while, saying he'd go into town the next day, and come back with the news. He also told us if anything happened he would notify us in plenty of time to make a getaway and that he would bring us breakfast in the morning, when he left, Chet and I went to sleep. Chet said he thought Jerry was a regular guy, and he was.

Jerry went into town. While he was gone I sat down and wrote two letters, both telling exactly how Chet and I had escaped from jail. I sent one to the *Idaho Statesman*, and one to my good friend Sheriff Allumbaugh. I wanted to really rub his nose in it. When Jerry got back from town he told us just how hot we really were. We were in all the newspapers, even outside the state. There was a reward of five hundred dollars for any information leading to our apprehension. A wanted poster had been issued and we were known to be armed and very dangerous. There were guards and roadblocks and patrols on all the highways out of the valley, and Jerry said it would be suicide for us to try to travel. We were out of jail, but we weren't out of trouble.

We were still in the valley, and the valley was bottled up. The only thing to do now was to lay low for a while.

That was all right for a day or two, but we soon got restless. I had a little talk with Chet. This was one of those situations where you have to try to change the bad for good, and to make opportunities out of problems. Jerry was doing us a good turn, and we ought to pay him a little for his troubles. I told Chet I thought that was the right thing to do, and when Chet pointed out that we didn't have any money to pay Jerry with, I kind of smiled, and nodded, and allowed that it was true. But just because we didn't have any money at the moment, didn't mean we couldn't get some money. And if we were lucky, and raised enough of a fuss without getting caught or getting killed, we just might be able to wage us a nice little campaign against my old friend, Sheriff Allumbaugh. That snake was running for office again, and the election was only about a month away. The more trouble we could cause him, the more people were likely to vote against him when the election came.

Chet didn't share my personal grievance against the sheriff, but he liked the plans I laid out, for he was getting restless too. First thing, we needed a car. We couldn't go pulling jobs in Jerry's car. Jerry knew a guy with a good car that was laid up in a garage because it had a bill against it. We decided to take it. It was to the guy's advantage to have it stolen, and if we did well, and got it back to him safely, we'd pay off the fellow's note for him. Jerry introduced us to the fellow. His name was Slim, and he volunteered to help us case jobs, which was welcome help, because we couldn't do too much unnecessary travel.

There was an ex-screw I'd done time under, who had retired and opened a store. We really showed him a good time, getting his store three times in the first week we were out. Then Slim lined up a garage he said would pay around a grand. It was a Friday night stick-up, and we went and got it. The owner, S. V. Royston, and his wife lived in an apartment above the garage. While we had the owner in one of the rooms and were looking for the safe, I heard a noise in the bedroom. I left Chet with the owner, and stepped into the other room just in time, for the owner's wife had got to the stairs and was fixing to make a run for the bulls. I made her go back to bed, telling her if she would be good, we wouldn't harm her husband. When we got the money, we fell short by half of what Slim said was there, but that didn't make us give it back. We told the owner and his wife to stay put and not leave the room for five minutes, and they did better than that. I later found out they didn't report the robbery until the next morning.

By that time, we had Jerry's basement looking like a wholesale grocer's warehouse from all the things we stole from that ex-screw's store. We decided we had better find another place, for we had been chased by a load of bulls one night, and we were afraid that they might get wise to Jerry. We found a cabin in the foothills near Orchard, got a supply of groceries, and lay low for a while. We even gave Slim back his car, with the note on it paid. We had really gone to earth, and that was probably the smart thing to do. But then we got restless again. The newspapers were reporting us in Oregon. There was a gang up there doing robberies, and the newspapers laid every job they pulled on us. There was a bank job pulled up north, and in the getaway they had to kill a bull. The sheriff went to Doris, and told her it was Chet and I who had pulled the job and killed the bull, and they would be sure to hang me when they caught me. It seemed like time to pull another job, just to remind everyone we were still in the area.

Chet and I stole a car and went to a nearby town to get a job Slim had lined up for us. It was a large grocery store, with a safe inside. There was also several hundred dollars worth of silk inside, and Slim had a fence who would handle the silk for us. Slim said there wasn't anyone in the store at night. We waited until about midnight, and then we tried to get inside. The front of the store was heavy plate glass. The side doors looked like jail doors, with all the bars on them. We tried the front doors with a jimmy, but we couldn't spring the lock, so we went back to one of the side doors. Chet said he thought he heard someone inside, but I passed it off as nerves. I told him we could take the night lock. I took my rod, and hit one corner of the glass, making a hole so I could reach through the bars to get the night lock.

We just about had that door open, when someone---or something--inside began shooting through the door. Chet fell, and I ducked back to one side, thinking Chet was hit. I was wrong. Chet wasn't hit. He began to crawl, then he raised up and ran for the alley. I ran after him. He stopped, out of breath, in the alley, and I asked if he was hit. "No," he laughed. "But if those bullets had turned a little sideways, we'd both be goners." It was a close shave. Chet still thought it was someone inside shooting, but I thought it was probably a gun trap. Either way, we weren't going back. We made it to our car, and left in a hurry.

The next night, we stopped in Boise. We were going to the jail to see Doris and find out why she hadn't had a trial yet. I remembered one of my Chink friends talking about how if you wanted a tiger whisker, you had to go to the tiger's cave to get it, and I was pleased at the thought of plucking a whisker off Sheriff Allumbaugh in his own cave. We drove around the jail in our stolen car, noting all the cars parked there. Then we parked and got out, and strolled toward the sheriff's office, intending to stick them up, then go in and get Doris out. But glancing through the window before we committed ourselves, we saw almost every bull on the force crowded into that office, and we decided that discretion was the better part of valor, so we went back to the car. On the way out of town, we decided to stick up a large grocery store, pretty much to let everyone know we were still around.

It was October 28th; we had been free for ten days. It was about 8:15 in the evening when we entered the Fairgrounds Grocery. The owner, Walter Hamm, was going over his books. I asked him for some smokes, and when he turned to get them I pulled my rod on him. When he turned back around he was looking straight down the barrel of my revolver, and did he start shaking. He said to me, "Now you be careful with that gun. I'm here to serve you gentlemen, and I don't want anything to happen." I told him to give us all his cash and nothing would happen. In the meantime Chet was loading up on groceries. Hamm really seemed like a nice guy, just scared, and he kept calling us gentlemen. We had the car stashed about a quarter mile away, so we were on foot. As we left, I grabbed Hamm and made him go with us. I knew he would call the bulls as soon as we let him go, so I wanted to send them on a wild goose chase. We walked over to the railroad tracks. Chet and I climbed the fence leaving Hamm on the other side. I told him, "You're the best sport we have ever robbed, and sometime we are going to return your money and pay you for the groceries." We then headed towards the fairgrounds until we were out of Hamms sight. We doubled back to the car and left. Our little rouse worked. A couple of days later, the paper told how Sheriff Allumbaugh followed our trail from the fairgrounds to Perkins, which was in the opposite direction from where we actually went.

A few minutes after we let Hamm loose, we had a run-in with a car full of bulls, and had to abandon our car, a beautiful Hudson roadster with red wheels, and make a run for it on foot. When we thought we were safe, another carload of bulls was right on us. We looked for a place to hide, but there wasn't any. We lay flat on the ground, partially hidden by sagebrush. The moon was full and shining bright. I told Chet I was going to take a bull out with me. He said he was, too. The car full of bulls was driving real slow, shining a light around. We could plainly see every bull inside. I told Chet to cover the bulls in the back seat, and I would take the front seat and if they saw us to take his Sunday shot. The car was driving real slow, we could almost see the color of the bulls eyes.

Those bulls had plenty of artillery, and they were really looking for us. When they found us, they were sure to shoot first, and so we figured that as soon as they spotted us, we would open up. It's funny how your mind works when you think you are about to die, I wasn't scared, but I was tense and suddenly this little ditty pops into my head,

> *Here I lay, old Derby Jones,*
> *I guess the worms will soon eat my bones.*
> *There are only two places from here, to go.*
> *Going above I have nothing to show;*
> *How far down I go, is hard to tell,*
> *But I guess I will stop, when I get to hell.*

Lucky for those bulls, and lucky for us, they drove right past without spotting us, and in a short while they were gone. As the car drove on, Chet said, "What do you know about that? I know one of them bulls looked straight at me, I still got the dents on my finger, I was holding the trigger that tight."

The next day, we decided we had a better chance of getting out of the area if we went back and got the car we'd left. After we got the car, we drove on into Boise, and left the car at the station so we could get to it easily. Then we caught a streetcar to Huntington. We sat quietly, not talking to anyone. When we got off in Huntington, we started off across country on foot. We walked on to our cabin without being spotted again. The next morning in the paper, there we were again. We were the suspects in the grocery store robbery, and the brake man on the street car, J. Q. Hoagland, had called the bulls and told them he had seen us get on the line going to Huntington. It is amazing how, when you become famous, everyone knows you. The fireman on the streetcar, a Jess Slade, told the bulls that he knew me, and that we had stopped to chat. I am glad he knew me, because I sure didn't know any Jess Slade. They did, unfortunately, give the bulls a description of our car. It was very plain to Chet and me that we would have to get another car before too long. That night we went out, and got one. We had to drive through town after getting it. We saw several bulls, but none of them recognized us.

By now, people knew we were still in the area, and the press was really eating up my old friend, Sheriff Allumbaugh, over the jobs we were pulling. Slim came by one day, and told us he had heard that the deputies were aiming to kill us, even if we surrendered peacefully. We were embarrassing the sheriff that much, and I was glad. We pulled a couple of jobs during the next three days before the election, then Chet and I waited for the returns. Thursday night, November 6th, two nights after the elections, we went into town to get a newspaper and read the election results. There had been a republican landslide, but Sheriff Allumbaugh was not one of the Republicans to be re-elected. The vote was Emmitt Pfost, 6628 to Lee Allumbaugh's 5654. Chet said it was a sure sign that the voters were behind us, I told him he was crazy. Who did he think we were robbing, if not the voters of this country? Besides, 5654 of them were in favor of Allumbaugh! Sure I was glad to see my old friend the sheriff loose, but I wasn't thinking we should go taking all the credit on ourselves. We had left the final choice up to the voters of this county, and they had done the smart thing for all of us.

About a week later, the night of November 12th, we were out by the Hillcrest wye. We saw a streetcar coming on the belt line, and we decided to rob it. When the train stopped and the conductor got off to open the switch I put a rod in his side and told him to get back on board. When we stepped into the streetcar I covered the conductor, W. H. Smith, while Chet shook him down. He had a real nice gold watch, which I took. Neither of us must have been thinking very clearly, because neither one of us paid any attention to the motorman, R. R. Bullock. However, Bullock paid some attention to us. He struck at Chet with an iron bar and almost got him. When I turned, Bullock hit me along the side of the head, almost knocking me out cold. I fell off the streetcar, and I shot as I fell. When my head cleared, the streetcar was gone. Chet was close by, and he helped me up. The only thing I got for that headache was about sixteen dollars and that damned gold watch, which would eventually help bring me down.

As we stood up I asked Chet what the hell he was carrying that rod for, if he didn't intend to use it, no matter what happened. I was glad that he hadn't shot the bull who had looked right at him the night we had robbed the grocery store. But now my head was throbbing all the way down to my knees, and I sure wished he had shot that damn motorman before he could hit me with that bar.

I told Chet we would lay off this county for awhile. We would take it quiet for a few days and then maybe we ought to be moving on to someplace were we weren't quite so hot.

The evening of November 17th, while we were still lying low, Chet went out to the spring for some water. I was cooking dinner, when I heard someone talking. I stepped to the door and opened it a little. I saw two boys coming toward the cabin. I waited until they hollered, then I opened the door, and they asked directions to a town nearby. They said they were tourists, and had lost their way. One of them said something about being hungry, so I offered to feed them, but they said they were in a hurry, and couldn't stay. When they were gone, I had the feeling there was something phony about them. When Chet came back with the water, we talked it over, and decided to pull out the next day.

The next morning, after we had breakfast, we packed up what things we meant to take with us. We were cleaning our rods, when someone knocked on the door. I had just loaded my rod, but Chet's was still unloaded. I told him to answer the door, and I would keep him covered. As he opened the door, I saw a prisoner I knew to be a rat, holding a shotgun. I told him to drop that gun, and he did, raising his hands in the air. I pulled him in, and shook him down. I knew this rat, he was Jack Dykeman. He had been doing six months, with a five hundred-dollar fine, for stealing a car. He was widely known as a rat back at the jail, but here he was, at our door with a shotgun.

I walked him around back of the cabin, and asked him where the posse was. He said there was no posse, then he gave us a story about how he was a trustee, driving for one of the deputies, when he ran off from the jail. I knew he was lying, and I told him we were going to take him with us. To see if I could get some information out of him, I also told him that if I found out he was lying, I was going to give him the contents of that shotgun I had taken off him. This scared him into changing his story. He told us he was with Deputy H. W. Brown, and the posse already had us surrounded. They had forced him to come to the door because they were afraid to do it themselves. I asked him where he had left the deputy, and he said about a mile from the cabin. I knew he was lying again, but we left, taking him with us. I told Dykeman, that if I saw the deputy on the way, I was going to bump him off. That scared him into telling the truth, where Deputy Brown was. We were cut off from the car, and so we had to foot it. As we passed a draw, we saw the deputy standing some distance away, I then told the rat that if he hadn't told us the truth, we would have left him in that draw for the coyotes.

We traveled for several miles, working our way through the sagebrush to a ranch house, where my friend, T. R. Wilson, lived. I figured we could get a car there. But when we got to the ranch house, we found it vacant. The Wilsons had moved in to Boise. We tied the rat to the bed upstairs, and left the house. I printed a note and tacked it up on a tool house door of a section gang, telling the finder to notify the sheriff of Boise he could find his pet rat at the ranch house. A few minutes later, Chet and I almost stuck up a passing car, but we noticed in time that it was loaded with bulls. We split up that night, thinking we would have a better chance of getting away that way.

I went back to Boise late that night. The next morning I got a newspaper, and did I have a good laugh. Front page were two articles about our little encounter with Dykeman. The headline read " 'Let's Kill Him.'[4] Jones pleads when trusty is taken; Langer is afraid." Dykeman wasn't just a rat; he was a lying little rat. He had told the reporters that we were desperate for food; that we had been eating rabbits, and that we even "grabbed at and downed two onions." He told them that Chet had begged me not to kill him when we first hauled him in. I was glad that Chet had left the state so he wouldn't see the headlines calling him yellow. He made us both seem to be shaking in our shoes when he talked to reporters. "Jones and Langer had assumed less of a 'hard boiled' attitude in the recent exploits to turn suspicion away from themselves knowing they were regarded generally as desperate characters. They had striven to make their later hold ups committed mostly for the bare necessities of life, so it would appear the work of much less dangerous persons." He must have really enjoyed yapping to those reporters.

---

[4] "Let's Kill Him Jones Pleads When Trusty Taken, Langer Is Afraid" The Idaho Statesman November 20, 1924 (Newspaper Reprints page 308)

The second article was about Sheriff Allumbaugh, how he said it was the state appointed deputies' fault that Chet and I got away and those same deputies saying it was Allumbaughs' fault. That article really made my day.

One really bad thing in the article though, was they had arrested Jerry Firestone, for helping Chet and me, but it also said they didn't have enough evidence so they had to let him go.

While I was in Boise I wanted to find out why Doris hadn't had a trial yet. The reason turned out to be that the murder trial of Nick Watkins, the brakeman was in progress. D. A. Elam was going after the death penalty for Watkins and having trouble finding twelve good men who believed in the death penalty. The defense was saying that there was an "unwritten law" higher than the laws of the state or any statue of the law and that under certain circumstances a man is justified in taking another's life. If that failed they were going to plead insanity.

I got a car, and went to one of the hospitals, and got a nurse who was a friend of Doris and mine. We drove around for some time. She said she would go to the jail the next day, and see Doris. We were hungry, but I couldn't go to any of the cafes, as I was too well known. I drove into an alley near a kitchen I had worked in, got out, and left the motor running. I told the nurse to wait in the car, as I was going to get some sandwiches.

I walked to the kitchen door and knocked. The cook who was on duty was an old friend of mine. He came to the door and asked me what I wanted. I told him a sack of chuck. He told me I was going to get killed, and I told him I wasn't, not if I could help it. He grabbed a large sack, and began filling it. I was standing just outside the door, where I could see into the kitchen and the alley. I saw a big harness bull I knew well, coming down the alley, headed for the kitchen door. I took hold of my rod, and pulled my hat down low, then I thought of the nurse in the car. I was going to cover the bull with my rod if he acted like he recognized me, but fortunately, he didn't. Without a glance my way, he went into the kitchen, then on into the dining room. When the cook came to the door with my bag of sandwiches, he told me there was a bull in there, and I told him I knew, for he almost stepped on my foot on his way into the kitchen. I asked my friend how much I owed him. "Not a thing," he said. "You just get out of town before you are killed." I laughed, and thanked him, and told him I would be seeing him again.

When I got back to the car, the nurse said she had seen the bull, too. She asked what I would have done if he had stopped, and I told her I would have loaded him into the car, then dropped him off out of town. She laughed, and said she might have got her name in the paper.

We drove out of town, ate our food, then I took her back to the hospital. I drove to the depot, as there was a passenger train due. I parked on a side street, then caught the blinds of that passenger train, and rode it to Nampa, where I caught a freight train, thinking I would go east into Wyoming.

There were two other bums in my car. I gave them a smoke, and they gave me some news. They had just come down from Oregon. They told me the bulls were shaking all the trains down along the line for those two bank robbers who had broken jail in Boise. I knew then that bumming was as dangerous for me as traveling in a hot car, but I stayed on the train until we made the next division point at Mountain Home. There I gave the bums some money, telling them to go up to town and get some chuck, and we would jungle up. I never expected to see those bums again, but after I waited for some time, I saw them coming down the track with their arms loaded. After we cooked up, I told them I had changed my mind about going east. I knew a rancher about a mile out of Glenn's Ferry, and I decided to go there and see if I could get a job.

It was the end of November, we had been having a heat wave, on the day I tied up Dykeman, November 22, Boise had a record high of 66 degrees. But now a winter storm had blown in. I headed cross-country, and traveled until dark. The land in southern Idaho is flat and open. The Sawtooth Mountains were to the north, the Owyhee Mountains to the southwest and the Snake River to the south, with nothing to break the wind of that winter storm as it blew down from those snow-capped mountains. It was so cold I was numb. I knew I couldn't build a fire in that wind, so I decided I would stop at the next house I came to, stick them up, and make them let me thaw out. About an hour later, I saw a house. When I reached for my rod, I discovered that my hand was so numb I couldn't use it. I managed to get my hand inside my shirt and held it under my arm.

After a short while, it began to sting and I began to work my fingers. Before long, I could hold my rod. Then I walked to the door and knocked, hollering at the same time. Nobody answered, so I decided no one was home. I went to one of the windows, kicked it in, and went inside. I made myself at home. First I built a fire, and after I thawed out, I went in search of something to eat. I couldn't stay awake; I had lost lots of sleep. I didn't know what minute a car would drive up, and I would have to hit that cold wind again, but I was thinking that some hot coffee would help warm me up and keep me awake. I soon had a meal on the fire cooking. As soon as I ate, I fell sound asleep.

It was about nine o'clock the next morning when I finally awoke. The sun was shining. I walked to a window and looked out. There was a house across the highway. I watched it long enough to know people were home. I took the time to fix some breakfast, not knowing when I would have the chance to eat again. When I finished my meal I took a sawbuck and laid it on the kitchen table for the food and damages I'd done to the window. I couldn't go out the way I had come in for fear they would see me, so I went out the kitchen door, keeping the house between me and the other house. I made the barn just as a car drove up and stopped in front of the house I had just come out of. When I heard a car door slam, I took out across a field, and was soon out of sight.

XII

The Bells Are Ringing For Me and My Gal

I walked and froze, following the railroad, until I came to Twin Falls. I intended to look up a friend and lay low for a while, catching up on some much needed sleep. It was dark when I got to Twin Falls. I stopped at the police station on my way uptown, and looked into the office. I did not recognize any of the bulls in the office, as I hadn't been in Twin Falls for some time. Before too long, I found my friend. He had got married, so I didn't want to stay with him. He told me one of his brothers, Roy Standlee, had an apartment that would be a good spot for me. The Standlee brothers were actually distant cousins of mine; we had played together in Urbanette. Roy seemed pleased to see me, and I told him that if he would put me up for a short while, I would give him more money than he could make bootlegging. I didn't know it at the time, but this statement would come back to haunt me.

After a few days, I got reckless. I told Roy that if he would lease another house in a good part of town, I would take one of the banks in Twin Falls, and split it with him. He liked the idea. I told him he didn't have to help pull the job, and he really liked that too. After we had found a house that suited me, I hocked the gold watch I had taken from the train conductor and I gave him some money for rent and supplies, but didn't move in. I must have looked suspicious to the pawnbroker, because he called the bulls and showed them the watch. That is what alerted the bulls that I was in the area.

Roy and I were in the apartment a few days later. We had been sharing the cooking and it was his turn to cook breakfast. It was December 8th and getting real cold. Roy stepped down to the corner to get some cream for breakfast. I told him there was a bottle of milk we could use, but he went out anyway. Since I trusted him, I never gave it a second thought.

Pretty soon, he came back in. I was lying in bed, smoking. He stepped back into the hall, then he came in and set the cream down on the table. Suddenly all hell broke loose. The door flew open, and a squad of bulls poured into the room. I looked into the muzzles of more guns than I'd ever had pointed my way. The rod I had taken from the sheriffs' office, the night we escaped, with Allumbaughs initials on it, was under my pillow, right under my head. But it would have been suicide to try to get it. I glanced at Roy. They didn't have him covered. One of the bulls grabbed one of my hands, putting a cuff on it. Then he grabbed the other one, cuffing them together. The Twin Falls Chief of Police, P.O. Herriman, said, "We've got you now, Jones." I laughed and said; "I guess that's right." Then he said, "You are Jones, aren't you?" I could smell liquor on his breath; I said "Yeah, I'm Jones." Herriman asked me where Chet was, all I said back to him was "The chief still hasn't caught him yet?" and laughed. The bulls started shaking down the bed. When they found my rod, they began shaking down the room. All this time they hadn't pointed a gun in Roy's direction. Then one of the bulls put a rod on him, and told him to put up his hands. The bull, who handcuffed me said, "Well I guess you are going to jail now." I told him all indications pointed that way, but I would like to get dressed first. I thought it might be a bit cold to be going out in just my underwear. The bull unlocked one cuff and let me put my clothes on. When we got there, I told the chief that Roy hadn't done anything and they ought to turn him loose. The chief of police smiled. "I will say one thing, Jones," he said. "You are a good sport. " I found out later that this was the bull Roy had turned me in to for the reward.

They wired Boise, and told them they had me in jail. The sheriff wired back that he was coming to get me. A newspaper reporter from the *Twin Falls Daily* came to the jail to see me. He was a nice guy, and he seemed to be in sympathy with me. He said it seemed like the press had been giving me the worst of it. If I had anything I wanted the public to know, just tell him, and he would get the job done.[5] I told him about the sheriff beating me and bullying Doris. I said that the reason I broke jail was to embarrass the sheriff and cause him to lose the election, that I was happy to hear the elections results and grateful to the voters of Ada County. I never did tell him how I broke jail. I told the reporter about how close we had been to Sheriff Allumbaugh and his bulls on at least two occasions and that on one of those occasions I had been hiding behind the sagebrush like an ostrich and they hadn't seen me.

Finally, that afternoon, Sheriff Allumbaugh showed up. He had not been re-elected, but he was not out of office until the end of January. He had two more bulls with him, and they put a lead chain on me.

There were a number of people in the police station, including the reporter when we were ready to leave. I told the sheriff as they gave his gun back to him, "I ripped your initials off the gun and put my own initials on instead, I didn't think you would be using it again." Then I said "You don't need that chain on me, I'm not going to try and get away, you fellows are too willing to shoot me, that's why I held my breath when you passed so close while I hid behind the sage brush." I said this for the benefit of everyone standing there, and as a "life insurance" for me. I knew the Boise law wanted to kill me, and I could just see the headline, "O. F. (Derby) Jones, Idaho ex-

---

[5] Police Arrest Bandit Suspect In Twin Falls" The Twin Falls Daily News December 9, 1924 (Newspaper Reprints page 315)

convict and leader of the bank robbers, was killed while trying to escape officers on the way from Twin Falls to Boise. "

The two bulls the sheriff had brought with him were the two who had been present the night he beat me up. They loaded me into a car, and headed out on highway 30. As soon as we hit the rough country, I was expecting to get it any time. The deputy I was chained to asked me why I wouldn't be friends with the sheriff. He said the sheriff didn't have it in for me, which was sure news to me. We passed through a small town. I made a comment about my head aching, asking if they would stop and get something to eat, I'd pay for all of us. The sheriff spoke up, calling me "Derby," and told me we would stop at the next town, and the feed would be on him.

The news was out that I had been captured. As we stopped in front of the cafe in the next town, the street was crowded with people. The sheriff got out and led me into the cafe like I was some kind of animal. He picked a spot in the back part of the cafe. We were sitting in an open booth. The sheriff asked me how I made the saw I cut out of jail with. I asked if he was taking me to the pen to await trial, and when he said he wasn't I told him how I made the saw out of the case knife. The sheriff told me he hoped I wouldn't have to go to prison again, even though I knew it was almost impossible that I wouldn't. The sheriff also promised I could see Doris when we got to Boise. I couldn't understand why he was so good-natured for a change.

I think every person that lived in the town where we ate lunch came into that cafe to see the infamous Oliver "Derby" Jones. I felt like I was on display. But we had an even bigger surprise waiting us when we arrived at the jail in Boise. Roy had told the newspaper reporters about my fake gun, and about the letters I had sent to the *Idaho Statesman* and Sheriff Allumbaugh. Every newspaper reporter in Boise was waiting at the jail. I had promised the sheriff I would not let them interview me, so I didn't. In return, he promised to give me a break while I was in his jail.

Doris' sister, Olive, was waiting at the jail. She had heard about our trouble, and had come down from Alaska where she had been spending her honeymoon. I had a chance to talk to her, but the sheriff said I would have to wait until the next day to see Doris. When I saw her, I finally found out why the sheriff was being so good. Doris told me that Allumbaugh thought the reason I didn't leave the county was that I was trying to get a chance to kill him. . His suspicion was very close to the truth. I also found out that on December 3rd, Doris had been formally charged with bank robbery.

I kept my promise to Sheriff Allumbaugh and did not speak to any newspaper reporters, but the morning of the 10th Allumbaugh came into my cell, waving a newspaper under my nose, wanting to know who had let the reporters in to talk to me. I read the front-page article that had him so upset, and told him I had not talked to the reporters. That they must have talked to the reporter in Twin Falls, because a lot of what was printed was what I had told him. That seemed to calm him down some, but he was still pretty mad.[6]

I told Doris I didn't have any chance of beating my rap. I was going to lam again, if I had the chance. On December 13th I pleaded not guilty to the charge of bank robbery. The escape charges were dropped since at that time escape from the county jail was only a misdemeanor. The date of the trial was tentatively set for the first Monday of January 1925.

---

[6] "Jones Held Under Double Guard In Ada County Jail" The Idaho Statesman December 10, 1924
(newspaper Reprints page 319)

My mouthpiece told me he thought we had a chance to get a change of venue, taking my trial in some other county. Then on December 16th the newspapers came in with the news Chet had given himself up in Bakersfield, California, and that the sheriff had gone to Bakersfield to bring him back. I couldn't understand that play. Then I thought about the way Chet had squawked when he was pinched. I figured he was going to try to turn state's evidence.

I was real worried about Doris. I did not want her doing time in the state pen. I talked her into copping a plea and turning states evidence. I told her not to worry about me, that I still had some more tricks up my sleeve.

Doris told me that the taxi driver, Hank Hendsley, had also been charged with the robbery. Poor sucker, no one would believe that we had kidnapped him and forced him to drive us to the bank. I got a hold of my mouthpiece and told him to get a message to Hendsley. I said to tell him that I was truly sorry for the way things had turned out. I told him to cop a plea, say he was guilty of accessory after the fact, that since he had never been in any trouble before they would probably not make him do any time, but to wait until after Doris turned states evidence.

Doris did what I asked her, and turned states evidence. They cut her bond from twenty thousand to one thousand. I had my mouthpiece get hold of some friends of mine, A. J. Tucker and Allie Pollard, and had them make her bond. Doris finally was free. The next day Hendsley plead guilty to accessory after the fact and they put him on immediate probation. Doris was to appear against me at my trial, which I never intended to stand. If I got a chance to lam I would. My mouthpiece found out that Roy turned me in for the reward, and that he was turning states evidence against me, too. When

Chet got back, my mouthpiece learned he was not going to turn. He had just got tired of running.

I wasn't too worried; for Sheriff Allumbaugh had made it known to me that he was willing to help me break jail again when the new sheriff took office. When we talked it over, I could see Allumbaugh wanted money, so I made him an offer. If he would leave a car, with the tank full of gas, where I could find it and leave town, I would pull a jewelry store on the way out of town, and split with him. I had two other conditions, and he agreed to both of them. There would be two good rods and bullets in the car, and I could take Chet with me. Even though I believed Chet was going to turn state's evidence, I couldn't much blame him, and he was my partner. The sheriff agreed to all of this, except he didn't want me telling Chet that he was in on it, and he insisted we wait until the new sheriff was in office. He would fix it in advance. And as long as I didn't squawk on his part in it, he made it clear he wouldn't really mind too much if I stuck around and pulled a few jobs around Boise before leaving, just to put the heat under the new sheriff, Emmitt Pfost. Allumbaugh was pretty upset about losing the election. He figured if my little escapades had caused him to loose the election, maybe I could damage Pfosts' reputation too.

A few mornings later the sheriff came to the tank and told me he was leaving town that day to go after a prisoner. He said that "everything" was O. K. Doris knew I was going to try and lam again, and she didn't trust the sheriff any more than I did. She had my mouthpiece come to jail to talk to me. But when he tried to get me out of the cell to talk to him, the deputy on duty told him the sheriff was out of town, and had taken the keys with him. Doris was waiting in the mouthpiece's office when he went back and told her he couldn't get me out to talk to him. She knew the sheriff had double-crossed me.

151

Doris turned out to be the one with a trick or two up her sleeve. On January 5th, 1925, she got a marriage license and sent Judge Lawrence Johnston and my mouthpiece, Ivan Hiller to the jail. Then she and her girlfriend, Frances Fitzpatrick, slipped into the jail through the garage. It was quite a surprise to me when Doris came to my cell door and said in a low voice, "Hey, in there, do you want to get married?" I thought I was dreaming. "Hell yes! Anything your little heart desires." I said. "This is a hell of a place to get married, but hell yes I want to!"

When the judge and mouthpiece came in from the office, I could see Doris wasn't kidding. She reached for my hand through the bars, and the judge tied the knot for us. He had just finished the job when the deputy came barging in, hollering at Doris, telling her to get away from my cell. She thumbed her nose at him, and he drew a sap and started toward her. I hollered at him, and Hiller started toward him. He stopped, and said Doris didn't have any right to be talking to me. Hiller said he didn't know of any law that forbids a man's wife from talking to him. The deputy said she wasn't my wife, but the judge spoke up and said, "Oh yes, she is. I just got through making them man and wife." That stopped the deputy, but he still made Doris leave.

Soon I had every reporter in town down to see me. I told them I was the happiest man in jail. When one of them cracked about where we were going to spend our honeymoon, I told him we had plenty of time to decide, but for now it was postponed indefinitely. The press gave us the works. Our wedding made front page of the *Idaho Statesman* and the *Boise Evening Capital News*, while all those high society weddings were confined to page four. They told all about the Idaho bobbed-hair bandit slipping into jail armed with a marriage license, and marrying the man of her dreams. The *Boise*

Evening Capital News had the headline "Justice Defeated!"[7] and the *Idaho Statesman* would, in a later report say that our marriage was our next contribution to the gaiety of Boise.[8]

A few days later, the D. A., Laurel E. Elam, had a meeting with about a dozen of Boise's best attorneys, trying to find some law to annul our marriage. They couldn't. It was against the law for Doris to testify against me unless we both consented to it. The State's case was going up in smoke. Boy, I had thought I was the one with something up my sleeve. The sheriff asked me why I got married. I asked him why he double crossed me. Of course he denied it.

The law really started harassing me. They put me on a show-up everyday for over a week. Any one who had been robbed while I was on the lam came to the jail and gave me the once over. From then on, they had a special guard over me at night. All he had to do was see I didn't break out at night. He would flash a light in my face at all hours of the night. I never had any intentions of standing trial. With all the charges they had against me I didn't have a snowball's chance in hell of beating them all. I was more determined than ever to lam.

Doris couldn't come near the jail, but a girlfriend of hers slipped me a rod. She wouldn't get me bullets, though. My trial was drawing near, and I was getting desperate. I chewed up some paper, shaping it like bullets, leading it with pencil, and filled the chambers of the rod. They looked like real bullets. It was as good a bluff as my wooden gun. But let me tell you something, don't ever try to break out of a locked jail if

---

[7] "Justice Defeated When Alleged Bank Robber and Star ..." The Evening Capitol News January 6, 1925 (Newspaper Reprints page 323)

[8] "Dora Douglas Marries Alleged Bank Bandit" The Idaho Statesman Jaunary 6, 1925 (Newpaper Reprints page 321)

you don't have a loaded rod, you might just fail. Here is what happened when I tried it.

The brakeman, Watkins, and I were in the tank, when his wife came to visit. They took him out to see her, leaving me alone in the tank. I pulled my rod on Sheriff Allumbaugh, and told him to unlock my cell. He ran out, slamming the corridor door shut. I was still in jail when Allumbaugh came back with help. They covered me, and the sheriff said he was going to shake down the whole jail. I told him I had a bottle of nitro, and if he came in the cell, I was going to blow us all to hell, for I wasn't going back to the big house. He didn't come in, but I did end up turning over that worthless rod.

XIII

A Prisoner's Song

A few days later, the new sheriff, Emmit Pfost, came into office. The first thing he did was can the special guard who kept waking me up all night with his flashlight. He was an old friend of Mr. Wyley, Doris' father, and I think he appreciated my "campaigning efforts" on his behalf. Though he was always present, he let Doris and I visit, and he saw that I was not mistreated.

On January 15th our attempt to get a change of venue was turned down. My trial was scheduled for January 19th. On Saturday, January 17th at 2:30 in the afternoon, Chet plead guilty to the charges filed against him and received a six to sixteen-year sentence. I knew I didn't have a snowball's chance in hell. I called for my mouthpiece, Ivan Hiller and as the court house clock struck five p.m. I entered a plea of guilty. Sentence was to be pronounced January 19th.

The reporters had a heyday. Both Boise newspapers front-page headline news for Saturday was all about Oliver Jones changing his plea to guilty.[9]

When my sentencing hearing came I had three lawyers, Ivan Hiller, Pete Cavency, and S. L. Tipton, and because I was a veteran of the World War, the legion sent another lawyer, Thomas J. Jones, to make a plea for me. I had changed my plea, but even that did not help. D. A. Elam was still pretty pissed

---

[9] "Bandits Write Final Chapter in Bank Drama" The Idaho Statesman January 18, 1925 (Newspaper Reprints page 325) and

"Eagle Bank Robbers Confess on Eve of Trial" The Evening Capital News January 18, 1925 (Newspaper Reprints page 327)

off over Doris and I making fools out of him and his lawyer buddies when we got married. He had his say telling judge Clinton H Hartson, what a menace to society I was and that I did not deserve leniency.

The judge said that I had been given a chance at a decent life when I got out of the stir the first time, but I had failed to take advantage of it. He handed me not less than ten years and not more than twenty years in the Idaho State Penitentiary. So I was on my way back to the big house.

I was so proud of Doris the day of my sentencing. An article in the *Idaho Statesman* on December 22nd told how Lucille Wilson, Colorado's Bobbed Hair Bandit, had broken down in tears when she and her husband were sentenced to ten to fifteen years. Doris was there for my sentencing. She stood in the rear of the courtroom, near the entrance and showed no sign of emotion when the judge handed me my sentence. When court was dismissed I walked to the back of the court room, put my arm around her and we walked together out of the court room, and down the street, arm in arm to the county jail with a deputy scurrying behind us.

I was to make the front page of the Idaho Statesman one last time. The morning following my sentencing one finial article "Jones Goes To State Prison" was printed on the front page.[10]

Warden Snook, who was at the prison my first time around, came to visit me in jail before I went up. He had just been appointed warden at the Federal pen in Atlanta, and he promised to put in a word for me with the new warden, J. W. Wheeler. When the traveling guard came to take me to prison, he told me the new warden was a fine guy, and I was feeling

---

[10] "Jones Goes to State Prison" The Idaho Statesman January 20, 1925 (Newspaper Reprints page 328)

somewhat better about things. But when I got to the prison, I could see a lot of changes had been made. It suddenly became clear that if the guard thought Wheeler was a fine guy, he was looking at it from the other end of the gun. This warden might not be such a fine guy to the prisoners. I didn't like Wheeler as soon as I met him and I knew I would be facing a lot of hell. They mugged me and I traded my name for a new number, now I was Derby "3457" Jones, then they turned me out into the yard.

Doris came up the first visiting day, bringing me some things, but the warden wouldn't let us visit. He did let me have some of the things she had brought. I asked for an interview with Wheeler, and when we met, I asked him if I had violated any of the rules. He said no, I hadn't. I asked him why I wasn't allowed to visit with my wife the same as the others. He then promised I could see Doris on the next visiting day. When it came around, Doris and I did visit, but we had a special gun guard on us the whole time, listening to every word we said. The prison was becoming overcrowded and the only place for visitations was in the wardens' office. You couldn't even whisper without the screw hearing you. I had no chance to tell her I was going to try and lam, but she knew that if I got the chance I would. She told me the bulls were really harassing her about the missing money. I told her that I knew where the money was, that the bulls that had searched the Summers ranch had found it and kept it. I knew what I was saying wasn't true, but Doris and the gun guard didn't. I hoped that as this story got out the bulls would leave Doris alone.

I was assigned to the shirt factory, and before long, I was doubling my new job, which was to sew seams on seventy-five dozen shirts. That sounds like a lot of work, and it was. Chet was on a collar setting job, which was a little easier. Nothing in the shirt factory was easy, though we were turning out two hundred and seventy five dozen shirts a day. Our workday started at 8:15 a.m. and ended at 5:15 p.m. five days a week, on Saturdays we worked four hours. A lot of the boys couldn't do their tasks, and if they couldn't do it, they went to the hole on "cake and wine," which is what the cons called bread and water. Some of the boys would run the sewing machine needles over their fingers, hoping to get out of work, but all they got was either the hole, or a splash of iodine on their fingers. I tried hard to make my task plus some, hoping for better treatment, but as the months wore on we found that if you did well in the shirt factory, when it came time for you to go before the board, you were not given parole. After all this was a money-making business.

Shortly after I arrived I ran into an old friend, Walter Smith. He and Clarence Rousch were among the five who escaped right after I was pardoned in 1924. I asked him what had happened to Clarence and him and he told me he had made it to St. Paul, Minnesota before they captured him. He said that they never did find Clarence through.

One day, towards the end of 1925, I was in the cellblock where the boys loafed on Saturday afternoon and Sundays. I saw a fellow coming toward me, and I thought I knew him. He stuck out his hand, and I shook it. It was John Jurko, the man I had seen carrying the rope in the lynch mob at Twin Falls, who the chief of police had pinched when they were trying to hang the Mexican. At first, I thought he was a "fish" just coming in, but he had been there since September 25, 1924. He was on the condemned row for murdering his business partner, W. B. Vanermark. Vandermark had been running his mouth all over town that Jurkos wife was a woman of loose morals. Jurko heard about it and he and his wife went to the pool hall where Vandermark was gambling. Jurko walked up to Vandermark and yelled "You have been talking about my wife and I want you to prove what you said." Vandermark denied saying anything and Jurko drew a rod and began firing. He hit Vandermark five times. Vandermark was dead before he hit the floor. Jurko had appealed his case on reasons of insanity, and they had turned him into the yard while waiting the verdict on his appeal. The State Supreme Court turned him down, and he went back to condemned row. On July 9, 1926, I saw them hang him in the prison rose garden.

I got to know a colored boy, Mike Donnelly, who was doing life for killing William Crisp, a storeowner in Hope, Idaho, during a robbery. They had hanged his partner Noah Arnold on November 14, 1924, for the same killing. He was one of the most feared prisoners in the prison. He had been doing a life jolt in Washington State at Walla Walla, and had lammed twice before ending up here. On his first escape attempt he had been shot in the arm, but that didn't stop him from trying again. One day, shortly before I would be pardoned, he sawed off the door of his cell, knocked a screw over the head, and got shot before he could make the wall. It was about his fifth, but not last escape attempt. Mike would eventually get pardoned in 1944, after spending over half of his life behind bars.

On August 3, 1926, there was an attempted jailbreak and riot. Mike, Walter, and about fourteen others who were in the dungeon, cut the locks on their cell doors, lifted the 200 pound doors off their hinges, and were ready to rush the guards and go over the wall. The guard didn't show up when they expected him to, and they couldn't get through the cell house door without a key. When they realized that the jig was up they tore the place apart. When the morning guard was doing his rounds he heard unusual noises coming from the "bughouse". He ordered the tower screws to train their rifles on the door and then he and Deputy Warden Ackley opened the cell house door. The boys started jeering and bragging about the destruction they had caused. I didn't have anything to do with it, but I was still among the twenty or so who were pinched for it and I went to the hole for four months. The hole was a concrete building that had six cells that measured about eight feet wide by seven feet deep by nine feet high. After the cell doors were repaired, they put six of us in one cell. The building was not heated so it was always cold. The only toilet available was a hole in the floor and we were only allowed out once a week for a shower, so it always stank. The only light in the cell came through a small ventilation hole in the ceiling. There was a door of solid steel with a small hole about two feet wide by five inches tall at the bottom. There was another small steel door that closed over that hole. The guards would open the small door and pass our food to us. That was the only time that door was opened. There were two small ventilators at the top of the door, with caps on them to keep out the light

After this little escape attempt Warden Wheeler started construction on a new solitary confinement cell house. It would have ten rooms, and was to be made out of concrete and steel. That cell house would come to be known as "Siberia."

During the time I was in the dungeon, Doris came to see me but they wouldn't let us visit. Doris left word for me that the bulls in Boise were still making it tough on her so she was moving to Portland, Oregon. That she wouldn't get to visit as often, but she would come every chance she got. Those damn bulls were still looking for the missing money; my little ruse hadn't worked. If they only knew that I was the only one who knew where that money was hidden, and I would never talk, no matter what. I made up my mind while I was sitting in that cold damp hole that I was going to beat that prison, and as soon as I did, I was going to get those bulls that were badgering Doris, and get Roy for turning me in. Yep, I was going to beat that prison, or get killed trying.

There were a lot of boys who did just that. One boy, who had made several trips to the hole, got up from his sewing machine, one day, and just walked away, right in front of the gun guard. He went out into the yard, where they grabbed him, and threw him in the hole until he was so weak they had to put him into the hospital, where he tried to kill himself by swallowing a bottle of iodine. The doctor saved him, but a few days later, he made a rope out of his blankets, and hung himself. He was in the cell next to mine, and I could hear him kicking and struggling for breath. He died, and his prison days were over. I saw boys commit suicide by cutting their throats or wrist, eating ground glass, jumping off landings onto their heads, and in almost every other way imaginable. There were boys who got murdered while they were in the stir, by other convicts, or by the guards. It didn't matter what sort of sentence they had; it was a death sentence in their case. I made up my mind that no matter what, I would come out of that place alive, I wouldn't give them the satisfaction to see they had broken me.

That prison was a lot tougher than it was before, and the problem wasn't just the screws. There were plenty of rats everywhere, and they were well protected by the screws. I think everyone knows that nothing is more hated in prison than a rat, and I think even the screws that used them and protected them probably hated most of the rats. If two cons had a disagreement the screws would bring out the boxing gloves and allow the two to go one round with each other. Of course one round lasted until one of the two called "uncle". A lot of rats got beat up that way. Another way we got a rat was if the screws got called away to do something else and we were left on our own we would throw a coat over the rats head and everyone would beat and kick him until either the screw came back or he was unconscious.

We were not allowed to gamble with dice or cards, and if we got caught at it, it was "cake and wine" in the hole. However, we could bet on ball games and prize fights. We had two prison baseball teams, the Hillmen that was made up of trusties, and the Yardmen that was made up from the rest of the convicts. When these two teams played each other it could get real rough. You'd sometimes think your were at a very large billiard game, the way the balls would ricochet off those stone prison walls. We had a fight card almost every holiday. I became friends with one fighter who made a lot of money for us after he got out. He took up boxing as a livelihood and did quite well.

When Doris would come down from Portland, we couldn't talk freely, and I couldn't write freely, either. I had a Chink friend they had working in the laundry underneath the dinning hall. He told me they had him iron all of my letters before sending them out, to make sure I wasn't using invisible ink. Just before one visit I wrote Doris a kite. I rolled it real tight and wrapped it with thread. When the screws came to get me for our visit I coughed and as I did I slipped the note into my mouth. Was Doris surprised when we kissed and I passed the kite into her mouth! From then on we began to pass notes that way. The main trouble with this was that sometimes both of us would have notes. When we passed them, we had to be careful not to let either one of us have two notes in our mouth at the same time because then we couldn't talk without the screws getting suspicious. If the screws grabbed one of us, we'd have to swallow the notes, and two notes had to be at least twice as hard to digest as one note. The screws must have thought we were really in love because we had some really long kisses.

(Untitled)

I was born into this world a gambler;
Quite young I left my home.
All over this world I have rambled.
Wherever I cared to roam.

I have taken my love where I found it;
I have always played on the square;
I've smiled when I had to pay my bit,
I was never considered unfair.

I've met, I've loved and I have parted
With women of all walks in life;
Some I have left broken hearted,
One I made my wife.

Then they sent me to a prison cell,
Which turned my heart to stone.
To give up the one you love is hell,
Then I decided to leave women alone.

Oliver F. Jones

Mug Shots taken of "Derby" during prison stay 1924 through 1931
Idaho Historical Society Collection

XIV

A Short Life of Trouble

On June 5, 1926, I was out in the yard talking to some of the boys when I heard a voice behind me say, "Hey Derby, I thought you got your pardon, what are you doing here?" I turned around and there stood Clarence Rousch. They had captured him after one year and 344 days on the lam. He had been spending his time on the East Coast; they caught up with him in Pittsburgh, Pennsylvania.

Clarence and I started celling together. He had been a counterfeiter. We started enlarging one-dollar bills, making tens and twenties out of them. Every time a right guy would get out of prison, we would send them out, and he would pass them for us. They would shake you down when you left, so we figured a way to get by them. We would take the heels off the parolees' shoes; hollow them out and load them with bills. We never did get caught at it, but one of the boys who took out some of the bills got an outfit and started making them himself. He got pinched and got a jolt on McNeil Island.

The prison chuck was bum, and not much of it. It kept Clarence and me busy hustling something to eat. We would buy from the guy who ran the commissary. That is, when he could steal it. But almost everything he handled had to be cooked, and if you got caught cooking, that meant cake and wine. But when a guy is hungry, he will take a lot of chances. We stole some stuff out of the shirt factory and made us an electric plate. We got along fine for several months, but hard luck finally overtook us. Some guy blew out a fuse, and the warden had a general shakedown. Clarence and I got pinched, and it was the coldest day I ever saw. The warden decided to

165

make an example out of Clarence and me. He put us in the dungeon. The dungeon was a hole in the ground, about six feet wide, eight feet long, and seven foot deep, with a concrete floor and dirt walls. There were two metal doors that closed over it and a wooden stairway leading down. It was cold and dark. We had no blankets and had to keep pacing to keep warm. We only spent a couple of days down there, because there was big job in the shirt factory and we were needed to work, so the big boss sprung us and I wasn't a bit sorry.

While I was down in the dungeon, I got to thinking that twenty years is a mighty long time, and that it wasn't fair to Doris to ask her to wait on me. I had already been in solitary twice, and the way things were going I might not even make it out of the stir alive. The next time Doris came to visit, I told her I wanted her to try to get a divorce. She didn't want to, she said she would wait as long as it took, but I told her I didn't want her tied to me, that she was free and should be living her life. I finally talked her into trying for a divorce, but the Idaho courts turned her down. She tried again in Oregon, but they turned her down too. She later got one in Washington state.

In September of 1927 two new men were sent to the stir. They were in for bank robbery, having robbed the bank in Rathdrum, Idaho. They were Tom Surle and William Mahan. Tom was from Austria and only had one leg. He would take off his artificial leg and sit begging in front of the bank that he and Mahan were thinking about robbing to case it out. He would take the information to Mahan, put his leg back on and then they would rob the bank. This was not the first bank they had robbed. They had a halt put on them from Montesano, Washington, when they got out of the Idaho stir they were to be sent up there. This was not Bill's first time in a joint; he had done time in the Montana State Pen. He was a natural born leader and he, Clarence and I became close friends.

The three of us were always trying to figure out how to beat the stir. We wouldn't trust many of the others, for we had a big break planned. The few other cons that we trusted and had included on this break, Mike Donnely, Clint Allen, Charles Daniels, W. D. Mathews, R. J. "Spoons" Murphy, and John Toth. Bills girlfriend Nora Bergman would come out on visiting day and Bill would slip her notes to get to a couple of friends on the outside who helped smuggle in knives. We wanted guns but were not able to get any.

Darrell "Shep" Thurston, a boy who celled in another cell house who was serving a life term for murder, had a key made to the lock on his cell door. He was going to turn out the boys in the hole. The ten of us were of three different gangs, but we all respected and trusted each other. We had smuggled in a number of knives and we had fashioned a dagger to fit into a long pole used in the shirt factory. We were going to get the gun guards and grab a truck that came to the shirt factory each day. We planned on taking the driver as hostage and ram the front gate with the truck to make our getaway.

Shep had a rat in the cell with him, but we made sure he didn't know anything. On the morning of July 20th, 1928 the rat was in line to go into the factory. I got ahead of the rat, and Clarence got behind him and shoved him into me. I turned on the rat and began fighting him, thinking we would all three get pinched and put in the hole, then Shep could let us out, and leave the rat behind. It didn't work that way, because they stopped the fight, but didn't lock any one of us in the hole, so Shep was no better off than before. This was one time I was trying to break into the hole, but they wouldn't send me. That was only the first thing to go wrong that day. The truck that came to the shirt factory every day went to the storehouse instead. Still, Shep gave it a try. He came out of his cell that night, but there was a screw waiting for him with a rifle. The break was busted. It would have been one of Idaho's biggest breaks, but it didn't even really get started. That's when I resigned myself to the chance that I might have to do all of my time.

The next thing we knew, Bill, Mike, Shep, John, Mathews, Charlie, and Clint were all sent to the new dungeon, "Siberia". It turned out that the rat had gone to Warden Wheeler and told him that something was up. Wheeler then intercepted one of the notes Bill had sent out with Nora. Wheeler had been pretty rough on Nora and told her she had to leave the state or he would have her arrested. The screws knew what we had been planning, but they only knew for sure that the seven boys were in on it. In the paper the next morning Warden Wheeler was quoted as saying that he knew of at least three more men that were involved and that these ten men were the most desperate criminals in the Idaho State Penitentiary.

The warden had spent one hell of a lot of money to build another dungeon of concrete and steel. The boys called it Siberia. Two nights after the other boys went to Siberia the warden pinched Murphy, Clarence and I and threw us in Siberia. He felt we were his problem children. We all were in the hole without a trial, and the three of us didn't know why we'd been pinched. We soon found out that we were the other three desperate criminals that the warden suspected of being in on the break, but he had no proof.

They fed us two meals of cake and wine a day. It was dark in the hole; the only light came from the three-inch wide ventilator hole in the ceiling. There was only one man to a cell, with solid concrete floors and walls. We didn't have any beds, only thin cotton blankets to put under us when we slept at night. The only toilet was a drain in the floor. There was a small radiator in the corridor and that was the only warmth in the cell house. The doors to these cells were made of solid steel with a vertical opening about two feet high and three inches wide with a smaller steel door covering the opening. As in the old hole, the guards would only open the small door when it was time for a feed. What little food there was, was passed through to us on a three-inch wide tray. There were seven holes at the bottom of the door, about the size of my thumb and I have a very small thumb. They were for ventilation. The cells were three feet wide by seven feet deep by nine feet high, and very dark, you had to feel your way around them. They would turn the lights on in the corridor when they fed us, and keep them on for about ten minutes. That was it. Every two weeks, they'd move us into the corridor for a bath, and that was the only break.

For the first month we were in Siberia, all we had to eat was bread and water. Then we were allowed fried egg sandwiches. After we had been in there for some time, they would let us order other items from the kitchen. That is, the boys who had money on the books could order.

I had been in about six weeks when two screws came and got me. They gave me a shave and haircut and a bath. Then they put me back in. None of us could figure out what it meant, unless one of my mouthpieces was trying to get me out. The next day, they came and got me again. Instead of taking me to the office, they took me to a room inside the walls, and there was my mother, who didn't know me until I spoke to her. She was crying, and I felt like crying. I soon got her to stop. Then she told me that Warden Wheeler wasn't going to let her see me until she told him she was going to talk to the governor. Wheeler then consented to a ten-minute visit.

I got a pencil from the screw guarding me, and took a piece of paper, and gave my mother, my mouthpiece, Pete Cavaney's address downtown. I told her to see him because I thought he could help us get another visit.

Ten minutes is a very short time to talk to your mother when you haven't seen her for several years, and after she had traveled hundreds of miles. She went to see Pete, who came with her to the prison the next day. When they took me in to see her, she was crying again. I asked her what was wrong. She told me she didn't think she had done anything wrong by taking the address I had given her. I told her she hadn't. Then she told me how mad Warden Wheeler had been and that he had said some pretty nasty things to her. She also told me how close Pete had come to punching him. That sure was good news to me; I knew I could always count on Pete. They let us visit for fifteen minutes, and then they made her go. That was the most difficult and trying time of my life. When the bulls started taking me out of the room, a bull got in front of me and one got behind me. I heard my mother's voice saying, "Oh, I can't give up my son like that!" I turned around to take what I figured was the last look at my mother, which I would ever have. The bull behind me put his hand on my shoulder to push me along. I shook his hand off, and started to hit him, but then I realized they would beat me up, right there in front of my mother. They took me back to the dungeon and locked me up. I could still hear my mother's voice ringing in my ears.

The boys had told me that if Pete could spring us out of that damn hole, he could have all the money they had on the books and some besides. But Warden Wheeler wouldn't let Pete see me. We thought the warden was going to keep us in there the rest of our time, and some of the boys were doing life jolts. We decided if there was a way out, we would take it. As there was more than one gang of us, we elected a member of each gang to figure out some kind of a break, and the rest of us agreed to do the part assigned to us. Clarence represented Bill Mahan and me. Mike was one representative, and Spoons was another. They figured out a tough plan, but we were in a tough spot. We figured about half of us would get killed, but all of us were willing to take the chance, except for one guy, who had just been put in the hole a few days earlier. None of us trusted him; we figured he was Wheelers pet rat. Mike was to break the locks off his door and turn the rest of us out. We were going to make ladders out of our bunks. There were twenty-four locks. Three of the boys who were baseball players were going to throw the locks at the gun on the wall, while the rest of us would run with the ladders and try for the rifle when the bulls came to feed us.

Mike broke an angle iron loose from his bunk, and broke one lock on his door, but he couldn't make the other one. Six of the boys had broken their bunks loose from the wall. After we saw we couldn't make it, we just had to sit and wait for the pinch, which would be the next day. Turns out they only pinched five fellows and I wasn't one of them. The screws locked the little door on their cell, putting them on cake and wine for thirty days. The rest of us would feed them all we could. We took our tea towels, tore them in strips, and made a small rope out of threads from our blankets. We would wrap the dry chuck up in a roll, which would go through the holes at the bottom of the door. We would tie it on the rope. The boys who were locked up would take their bucket bails, tie them on a string, and stick them through the hole on their door. We would throw the rope. They would hook it and haul it in. We would eat soup and the chuck we couldn't get to them. We did this every day for thirty days.

Mike was one of the five that got pinched, and of course the warden decided he was the ringleader. He really had it in for Mike. He ordered the screws to "chain him up." We had all been chained up at one time or another, usually they would chain us to the iron ring in the wall and beat us with a rubber hose for breaking one of Wheelers precious rules. The screws would form a pool to buy moonshine for the one who could provoke us into breaking a rule. But this time it was worse.

They chained Mike to the wall and ran a cold stream of water over his naked body for about four hours. When they finally let him go it took days for him to stop shivering.

After they let us order, the first thing I ordered was a carton of smoking tobacco. The screws said sure, but when I got the tobacco they wouldn't let us have matches. When the screws who had been feeding us went on vacations, we happened to draw a good screw who brought us two small boxes of matches apiece, but we couldn't get any more. We would split them, and every time one guy would smoke, we would all smoke. By now my whiskers and hair were long enough to braid. Bill Mahan singed his whiskers one night during a smoke, and the next bath day, the bulls sure gave him the once over.

There had been quite a few boys who blew their tops and were sent to the nut house. We thought they were trying to get us to blow our tops, so they could send us away. One day, they unlocked my cell, and told me to come out. I went outside, instead of going toward the office; they took me to the hospital. I hadn't complained of being sick, so the first thought that struck my mind was that I was headed for the nut house. When I went to the doctor's office, he told me to take my shirt off. He wanted to look me over. I told him there wasn't a damn thing wrong with me. He seemed to read my thoughts, for he pulled a letter out of his pocket, and he said, "Derby, this is from your mother. She's worried about you." I pulled my shirt off, and told him to go ahead. While he was examining me, I asked him if he would answer mother's letter. He said he would, so I told him to tell her I never felt better in my life, than I did at present. Then they took me back to the hole. The boys wanted to know what the screws had done to me. I told them they had the Doc look me over. I still thought we were all headed for the nut house.

There was a colored boy who had beat up on a rat. They had him in the other hole, and we were feeding him. Then they brought him in where we were. We were sure pleased, for he gave us a lot of news; we had been isolated for a long time. Some years later, I had a fight in another prison with the same rat the colored boy had beaten.

Some welfare society from an eastern state was visiting all the prisons. They came through Boise. Warden Wheeler was with them when they saw the dungeon. They gave it a write-up. I didn't get to read it, of course, but I got part of the answer the warden wrote in reply to the welfare society. They would give us old newspapers to use for toilet paper. We would read them while the lights were on for us to eat. When they turned them off, we would then eat in the dark. I got a piece of newspaper with the warden's reply in it, and I read it to the boys. He said the reason he had built this dungeon was that we had broken out of every place he had in the prison. He also said we were the worst cutthroats and scoundrels that ever infested the Northwest.

When I read that part, the colored boy who was in for fighting, said, "Now, listen here, Derby, I ain't no cut-throat." I said, "Shut up, you scoundrel. Good Warden Wheeler can't be wrong! You have to be one or the other."

I went in the hole in July 1928, and came out in January 1930. I was locked up for eighteen months, even though there was a federal law that stated a prisoner could not be locked up for more than nineteen days. Bill Mahan came out two weeks ahead of me. Clarence came out two weeks after me. If we had been on bread and water the whole time, we would have starved to death, but it was "cake and wine" for us about as often as it was more normal chuck.

The day I came out of Siberia, there was snow on the ground and the sun was out. The second the glare off the snow hit my eyes, I felt like I had been hit with a sap. I had been in almost total darkness for eighteen months and the brightness hurt. I could barely see where I was going, and my eyes just didn't want to adjust. The captain asked me if I felt weak. I told him hell no, on the grounds that in prison you never want people thinking you're weak, but my knees were shaking. They took me to Warden Wheeler's office. He told me to sit down, then he laughed and remarked something about my whiskers. I didn't laugh, for I wasn't in a laughing mood. He asked me if I wanted out. I asked him if any sane person would want to stay in a place like that. He said he was going to turn me back out in the yard and restore all my privileges. I asked what I had been locked up for. He said I should let bygones be bygones. I told him I had a right to know. He said that he had thought I was part of the attempted prison break in July of 1928. Then he said he had investigated the break shortly after I was locked away in the hole, and had found out I had no part in it. He said I was exonerated from any blame. What that statement got me was a pardon, later, after Wheeler lost his job.

I saw a lot of new faces in the yard. There had been a number of prisoners who had come and done their time while I had been locked in the hole. I went to the barbershop and got a shave and haircut. That barber had himself a job where he could hear all sorts of things. The way the barber talked, I thought I might have a chance to get a pardon. Chet had been pardoned in April 1929, nine months after I went in the hole. I had my mouthpiece, Pete, come see me and the warden walked into the room we were in. He said there was no use for me to try to get paroled; that he didn't think I had enough time in. So I told the mouthpiece there was no use in trying, for I would do the time as long as Wheeler had his job. Pete said not to give up and to go ahead and try for the next board, which was to meet in October of 1930. I told Pete it would be a waste of time, but he said I had paid for my crime and it was time I got out. I filled out the paper work and appeared before the board, but just as I suspected they turned me down. Pete wouldn't let me give up; he pushed me until I put in for the April 1931 board. In February 1931 we found out that Wheeler was getting canned and the new warden, Richard Thomas, would be taking his place on April 1, 1931. I started thinking there might be some hope, so I filled out the paperwork and put in for the April board.

I had an interview with the board. There were two new members of the board, Governor Ross and attorney general Fred Babcock. They both seemed favorable, but one of the old members asked me a lot of questions about the jailbreak, and about the bank money they never got back. I told them it had been so long ago, and I had been in the hole so long, I had forgotten. Then they brought up my record in prison. I told them what Warden Wheeler had told me the day I got out of the hole, that he had no reason for putting me there or keeping me there. The board member didn't believe me, but the clerk, who had been there when Wheeler said it, was still on the job, and I proved what Wheeler had said by him. Still, the board denied me. The *Idaho Statesman* even reported in the paper that I was denied my parole. The article said "Oliver Jones, Eagle bank bandit, was among those denied a parole. He has served six years of a sentence of 10 to 20 years for his part in the most spectacular bank robbery in recent years." The article didn't give the names of the other twenty-two cons that were denied parole.

On May 4th, 1931, while I was still brooding about my parole being denied, Lydia Southard, Idaho's Lady Bluebeard, did what Mike, Clarence, Bill and I had been trying to do for years, she broke jail. She had been tending the roses in the yard around the women's ward. She had told Warden

Wheeler, before he left, that she needed some new trellises for her roses. A trusty, David Minton, volunteered to make them. The evening Minton was paroled, Lydia tore the roses off the two trellises, connected them were Minton had notched them and climbed over the wall on her personal made ladder. Minton was there waiting for her and no one knew she was gone until the next morning. I wonder if Wheeler would have allowed Minton to make those trellises had he had known that Minton had been climbing over the wall to the women's ward at night. It was really too bad that Thomas had to take the heat for this escape. He was really trying to clean things up in the stir.

I sent for Pete, and said I wanted to try the next board. When I paid his fee, I told Pete I would double it if he could spring me. He said he didn't want me to double it. He thought I had done enough time, and he would do everything he could to get me out. He was true to his word, he wrote to my mother and told her about my trying to get a parole, he told her I needed her help, that she needed to get as many people to write letters to the Parole Board as she could.

Well my mother was never one to do a half-baked job. She got J. S. Maples, an ex-circuit judge in Arkansas, and B. O. George, Vice President of the First National Bank in Berryville, Arkansas to write letters. She also got a third letter sent to the board. The letter read:

We, the undersigned citizens of Carroll County, Arkansas, respectfully represent state and petition your Honorable board the following:

We are personally well aquatinted with the said Oliver F. Jones, now a convict serving a sentence in the Idaho Prison, and we have known him practically all his life. He was born and raised in Carroll County, Arkansas, and lived here until he grew to manhood.

We know that he was a good citizen while he lived in Carroll County, Arkansas, and was never charged with a crime of the character of which he was convicted and was always a good working boy. It is our opinion, that if he has committed any crime, that he has been lured into it by some other person and was not his original thoughts or past character that prompted him into committing a crime. We can also state that while he lived in Carroll County, Arkansas, that he carried the U. S. Mail and was always honest and trustworthy in his duties.

We sincerely ask that if, consistent with your duties, you can show him any favor, or Executive Clemency that he is deserving, and would be an act that your Board or members thereof would not regret. Hoping that you can see your way clear to give Mr. Jones some relief (WHICH AS WE SEE IT SHOULD BE AN ABSOLUTE PARDON) we will ever ask for the same.

Respectfully Submitted,

One hundred forty five people signed the letter, which was just about the whole town of Urbanette, Arkansas.

The July board met, but I didn't get my parole, I got my Pardon. Sure enough, Pete and my mother had pulled it off. I couldn't believe it, in a few days, I was going to be a free man!

XV

Freedom

A number of the boys wanted me to deliver messages for them when I hit the bricks. I would have had a lifetime job if 1 had undertaken to deliver all of them. I promised a few of them that I would if I could. I thought at first that I had a conditional pardon and would have to be extra careful. I got permission from Warden Thomas to let a screw take me downtown to buy some clothes. I had been in the prison for six years and six months, and I had given all of my clothes away to other boys who were going out. The warden also made me buy a ticket to Kansas City. When I got back to the prison, Warden Thomas called me into the office, and told me when I got to Kansas City, and wrote him a letter; he would send my money to me. I told him that I was over twenty-one, and if I couldn't take care of my own money now, I never would be able to. Finally, he consented to let me have what money I had on the books.

On July 2, 1931, they dressed me out, and when they handed me my pardon and money, I thought the money was coupons of some kind. The government had changed the style of paper money while I was in prison, and I had never seen any of the new bills, which were smaller. There was a bull waiting to take me to the depot and put me on the train. When I looked at my pardon, I saw it had no conditions on it. I told the bull I was a free man, I didn't have to go with him. He said he had orders to put me on the Portland Rose for Kansas City, and it would be best for me to ride out the ticket and leave that part of the country. If some of those Boise bulls saw me in town, they would try to frame me back into the big house. I knew he was telling me right. I got in the car, and he drove me through

Boise. I hardly knew the town, for they had done a lot of building while I was locked up. There was a new motion picture theater with a real pipe organ, a new self-serve cafe that they were calling a cafeteria, and a new fourteen-story hotel. But the biggest change of all was the Inter Urban Loop Trolley system, it was gone. They had replaced it with buses.

On our way to the depot, the bull asked me if I didn't have some money planted close by. I told him I was supposed to have some. He said if it wasn't too far away, he would drive me to where it was, and let me get it. I asked him if he wanted to split it with me. He turned red in the face and said he didn't think I had that kind of opinion of him. I said, "You're a bull, what other opinion could I have?"

He waited at the depot with me until the Portland Rose pulled in. When I got aboard, I saw him drive off. As the train pulled out, I thought that would be the last time I would see Boise. I had a funny feeling. I felt like someone was watching me. I looked each passenger over in the coach, but I didn't recognize anyone. I didn't intend to ride out that ticket, for I had some unfinished business in Idaho. I wanted to get the money I had buried and paid for. I also wanted to look up my good friend Roy, and if he was holding anything, I intended to take it and beat his ears down.

Had I only been able to look into the future, I would have ridden that ticket, then bought another, and kept on going. But I wasn't thinking too clearly, I only had revenge on my mind.

At the first stop, I got off the train, intending to stay off, but as I unloaded, two men got off. I walked up toward the engine, and so did they. They looked like plain-clothes dicks to me. Just as the train pulled out, I got on again. So did the two men. I thought the warden had put them on my tail, thinking I would go to my plants. Then I thought of my old friend, Ed, and how scared he used to be of the prohibition agents. I decided I was getting the "bull horrors," just like him. At the next stop, which was Minidoka, Idaho, I unloaded. I went into the depot, and started talking to the telegraph operator, watching the train. No one else got off. When the train pulled out, I stayed in the depot. I felt free at last.

There was a branch line out of this town for Twin Falls, but I couldn't get a train until the next day. I looked for a taxi, but there wasn't any. I walked to a hotel. There was a long distance telephone office, where I put in a call to my mouthpiece. When the operator asked for a name, the first one I saw in the phone directory was Barnes, and that was the name I gave her. I got a room at the hotel and registered as Bill Barnes, of Kansas City. Later that evening, the hotel manager told me he was driving to another town and there was a bus line there. I told him I would be glad to pay him to go along. There was a Fourth of July celebration with a rodeo going on in the town we drove to. There was also a carnival. I found out what time the bus for Twin Falls was leaving. I had several hours to kill, so I went to the celebration, after walking for some time. I saw a boy I had done time with. He had a dancing show with the carnival. He gave me a wink to come inside the show. I bought a ticket and went inside. After he got through, he came over to me, and asked when I gotten out. I told him it was that day. He said he was moving out that night, and if I wanted, he would plant me in his outfit.

I laughed and told him I didn't need to hide, for I had a pardon. He wouldn't believe me until I showed him. He thought I had lammed. As he knew me only as a number, he asked my name. I told him "Barnes. He hadn't read my pardon to see my name. He had only glanced at it. He asked if I was related to the famous wild animal trainer and circus man, Al G. Barnes, and I said I was his brother. He then told me he

180

could get me on with the carnival if I wanted to work, but I told him I didn't want a job. He saw the boss, and called him over and introduced me as Al G. Barnes' brother. This made me a big shot, and after the show was over for the night, the mob of us threw a party, which lasted all night.

When I woke up the next morning and looked around the room, I was surprised not to see any bars. I didn't know where I was, but I did know I had a hell of a headache. After easing my headache, I went looking for a bootlegger. I finally found one. I had a little hair-of-the-dog and then got something to eat, and caught the next bus for Twin Falls. I had a cousin, Casey Jones, who ran a garage there. I went to Casey's garage, and when he didn't recognize me, I introduced myself as Bill Barnes, of Kansas City. I told him I was in need of a car, and I would buy a good used one. He led me in where the used cars were, and began to show me different cars. All the time he was telling me how good the cars were, and that he was selling them too cheap, but he was doing it because he was overstocked. I asked him if he ever sold life insurance. He looked at me and wanted to know who in the hell I was. Then I laughed and told him I was his long lost cousin, Derby Jones, whom they had buried alive. We shook hands, then he took me home to meet his wife and four kiddies, Doris who was ten, Eugene who was eight, Glen who was six, and a real flirt, Shirley, who was three.

He said he never would have known me, and wanted to know what all they had done to me while I was in the big house. Eighteen months in Siberia on near starvation rations had really aged me. I looked much older than my thirty-five years. I told him it would be easier for me to tell him what they hadn't done to me while I was there. They had done so much; I had no intention of going straight. This was not the way these things were supposed to work. All they had done to me was supposed to make me determined to never break the law again,

but it didn't work that way with me. I told my cousin I was
going to rest up, then I was going to do a little collecting for all
those shirts I'd made in prison. Casey had been in business for
a number of years, and he was a straight guy. He wanted me
to go straight. He also wanted me to buy a half interest in his
business. He said if I went into business and went straight, he
would pass my hot money for me, and while he was doing it, I
could go east and visit my mother. I told him I would think it
over, but I hadn't seen Roy yet.

One day, Casey and I had been out of town. We drove
up to his garage and parked. We were still in his car when
another man drove in behind us, and parked. He got out and
came over to our car. Casey introduced me as Bill Barnes, of
Kansas City. It was E. Forrest Prater, the sheriff of Twin Falls,
who was a good friend of Casey's. He had been on the
manhunt for me when I was a wanted man, but he didn't
recognize me.

I made the rounds of the games. Gambling was allowed
at this time, and I sat in two or three of the big games, but they
were too tough for me. When I was sent up, there was lots of
money in circulation. But now it was 1931, and times had
really changed.

I was throwing some wild parties and spending money
pretty freely. A gambler friend of mine told me I had better
slow down. Money wasn't so easy to get now. I told him there
was plenty more money where that came from.

I went to see the wife of Vern McBride, one of my fellow
inmates and gave her a message for him. I got a car from Casey
to make the drive, which was back to Boise. I knew I was
taking a chance, but I thought I could slip into town and slip
out again. I saw a number of bulls, but none of them seemed to
recognize me. I told Mrs. McBride what her husband wanted

her to do which was to go to Twin Falls and talk with some people there about writing recommendations for a pardon. She promised to come to Twin Falls, which was where her husband had been sent up from for grand larceny. The next day, July 14th, Vern's wife came to see me in Twin Falls. I drove her to see the people her husband wanted her to see. She had good luck. Every one of them offered to recommend him for a pardon. I drove her to the town where her folks lived. When we stopped at her home, she asked for her mother. A sister told her that their mother had got a long distance call from Boise, and had gone to the office to answer it.

We drove to the office to get her, but we missed her. Then we drove back to the home. I knew when her mother came out that there was bad news. She called me to one side, and told me that her son-in-law had hung himself in prison. The body was at the Summers and Krebs funeral home in Boise. She wasn't going to tell her daughter. I told her that Vern's wife had a right to know, and if she didn't tell her, I would. The mother seemed relieved and told me to go ahead. I told Mrs. McBride the easiest way I could, but the girl really took it hard and broke down sobbing. I was disgusted with Vern for killing himself, but part of me understood, I'd seen to many convicts that had been pushed to the end and could take no more and this was his third jolt in the Idaho stir. Vern's wife wanted me to drive her to Boise. On the way into Boise we stopped and picked up one of her girlfriends. Her girlfriend had a copy of the *Idaho Statesman* with the article about Vern hanging himself. The article really upset Vern's wife, it said that he had hung himself because his wife was planning on getting a divorce because she was disgraced that he was in prison. She said that she was not trying to get a divorce, that Vern had told her to because he didn't think he could get out and he wanted her and their daughter to have a good life. She had refused because she believed he would get out soon and they would have a good life as a family. After reading the article she didn't believe Vern had killed himself. When we got to the undertaker, I stayed in the car. She and her girlfriend went in to see him. I then drove them to where the girlfriend was staying.

Mrs. McBrides's landlady was a neighbor of the superintendent of the shirt factory. She told the young widow she couldn't understand why her husband had killed himself, for they had turned out one hundred and two men at the last board, and even that awful Oliver Jones was one of them.

I got a room at a hotel where I didn't know anyone. The next morning, the girl drove out to the prison. I cautioned her not to mention me in any way, and sure enough Warden Thomas asked her if she knew Derby Jones. She lied like a good fellow and said no. The warden then went on to explain that her husband and I were good friends, and some of the screws had noticed us talking quite a bit just before I left the prison.

When Mrs. McBride left the prison she came to the hotel where I was staying and told me about her visit with the warden. I had to laugh when she told me about her landlady's opinion of me.

Mrs. McBride made arrangements to have Vern's remains shipped to Twin Falls, where she had a doctor examine him to see if he really had killed himself. I knew he had done the job himself, for he was doing hard time when I left the prison. I got Casey to furnish a number of cars for the funeral. I am sure I left the young widow with a different opinion of me than her landlady had had.

XVI

Five To Fifteen

As for my old "friend," Roy Standlee, who ratted me to the bulls; I finally found him. He was bootlegging, but didn't have any real money. When we met again, I shook hands with him, never letting him know I was wise that he had collected the reward on me. He was very much in need of money, and he had a proposition. He said he would tell me about it later. Casey knew that I knew this guy had sold me out. He couldn't understand how I could treat him in a friendly way. He began to think I had changed. Then one day, Roy told me he wanted to help me rob a bank. I thought that here was a good way to even things up with him. I would take him in on a job, and when we split the take, I would take his split away from him, and tell him I knew about his getting the reward. Then I would beat his ears down.

I ran into Russell "Peewee" Cavendar, a boy I had done time with. He had been in the stir on a holdup charge. I told him about the proposition. He said he would like to go along to see the fun. Peewee and I decided to drive to Salt Lake City to see a couple of guy we had been in the stir with, while we were there we found a bank that looked like it would be easy to take.

When we got back to Twin Falls I told Roy about the bank Peewee and I had cased out. I told him we needed another guy. He said okay, that he would drive the car for us. I already had a bank in Utah cased. It was a perfect set-up. I could have pulled it alone, but I had to even the score. We got Peewee, and left for Utah. When we got to Salt Lake City and looked the bank over, everything seemed okay. We put on our disguises and drove up to the bank; Roy turned yellow and refused to get out of the car. We had no choice but to pass up the bank and drive out of Salt Lake City and we headed west. I accused him of being yellow, and he owned up that he didn't have the nerve to go through with the job.

We decided to go back to Twin Falls. We were headed to Nevada, so we decided to go on into Wells, Nevada and then head north to Twin Falls. On our way through Nevada, we stopped in Montello to get something to eat. It was July 30th and hot as a firecracker, so we decided to stay until later in the evening when it had cooled off, then to head on to Wells and Twin Falls. There was a gambling hall, the Guy Diaz Pool Hall and Gambling House, which seemed to be doing quite a good business. It looked like it might be good for two or three grand, so we decided to wait until later that evening and take it, to pay expenses.

After night had fallen we headed back to the pool hall. Roy, the yellow rat, wouldn't go in with us, so Peewee and I left him in the car. We burst in to the Guy Diaz Pool Hall and Gambling House with our rods drawn, just like a couple of real bandits. There were only a few customers in the joint at that time of night, and Diaz had already deposited the day's take. We forced him to open the safe, there was only eighty cents in the safe drawer, and there was only a few dollars in the cash register. We forced the owner to lie on the floor behind the bar and then lined the customers up against the wall and took what little money they had. All of a sudden the whole thing hit me as real funny. Two to three grand suddenly was looking like two to three ten spots, a real big haul. The same thought must have hit Peewee because we both started laughing. I told Peewee through choked laughter that we had better get the hell out of there. As we came out I told Peewee that the way things had been going we might just be afoot, that Roy was probably thirty miles from there by now. But, the only thing that did go right that night was Roy was still on the job.

On our way out of town, our rat of a driver took the wrong highway, and a carload of bulls overtook us. Roy got excited and killed the motor. I said I wasn't taking any pinch, and left the car. Peewee went with me. I was expecting a bullet any second, but Peewee and I made a safe getaway. The bulls pinched Roy, took him back to town, and threw him in jail, which is where I decided to leave him, let's see how he liked life behind bars.

Peewee and I walked for some distance, until we found a place to hide. We stayed there, in the heat, all the next day. We saw several carloads of bulls looking for us, but they didn't see us. We were very hungry and thirsty, but we stayed hidden until dark. Then we started back to Montello, where we had pulled the robbery. There wasn't anywhere else we could go out there. We could see the lights of Montello, but we found you can see lights a very long way in Nevada.

We walked all night, getting there about daylight. We found a cafe at the depot. I told Peewee to go in and buy us something to eat, and I would keep him covered. If the law pinched him, I would pinch them. He came out with an armload of chuck and some cigarettes. We went to the railroad yards and found a spot where we could eat, but our throats were so dry and raw we couldn't choke much down. We then hopped the first freight train for Ogden, Utah, where we had a run-in with a carload of bulls. We were able to hide in the shadows of the rail yard and got away. Later that night we hopped a train for Idaho. We got off the train in Burley, Idaho, where I wrote Casey to find out if we were hot. Instead of writing back, he drove over from Twin Falls and got us, telling us that Roy was back in Twin Falls, and we weren't wanted.

Roy had told the Nevada bulls that he didn't know we were going to hold up the pool hall. He said, we told him we were going in to play some pool, that he had left us there and come back later to pick us up. So they had released him.

A few nights later, Casey was with a girlfriend of mine and me. We went to a bootlegger's to get some booze. The bootlegger didn't have any in his room, but he did have some stashed out in the country. I told him to get in the car and we would drive him out to get some. We started out to where he had the booze stashed, for I was really needing a drink. It had been a rough week. We had driven about three blocks when a prowl car stopped us. They wanted to shake us down. Casey wouldn't get out of the car, but the rest of us did. Casey said they couldn't shake us down without a warrant. He really believed that the law was true and just. I told him that in the dealings I had had with bulls, I had found out they would do anything they could get away with.

On August 19th, I was sitting in a card house, reading a newspaper. I had been playing poker, and had quit to rest for a while. In came Sheriff Prater with a couple of bulls. They walked over to where I was sitting. Sheriff Prater asked me if my name was Jones. I told him it was, when I wasn't going by Barnes. The sheriff said he wanted to talk to me. He shook me down, and then told me I would have to go to the courthouse with him. On the way out, another bull pinched my good friend, that yellow rat, Roy. Then two more bulls pinched Peewee in another card house. At first, I thought the pinch was over some parties I had been in, but when they walked in with Peewee in tow, I began to think differently. When Sheriff Prater started questioning me, I found out it was a lot different.

Sheriff Prater told me he had orders to pick us up. There had been a robbery pulled over in Montello, Nevada, and some people were on their way to Twin Falls to see Peewee and me in a line-up. He said that if they didn't make me for the job, he would turn me loose.   He locked all three of us up, each in a different part of his jail. Later that night, a Nevada bull and a guy named Ed Kendrick who was the cashier from the Guy Diaz Pool Hall came to look us over. They picked out Peewee right away, but weren't too sure about me. The sheriff held me over, to give them time to identify me as one of the robbers. Kendrick finally said he was sure I was in on the robbery too. The Nevada bull wanted to take us back to his state right then and there, but we got a mouthpiece and told him we wanted to fight extradition. Within a couple of days we had lost out.

Casey heard of the pinch and came to the jail to see me. He was awfully sorry about it, and said he would spend every dollar he had before he would let me go up for another jolt. He also said he would give us an alibi, if he could. I told him not to get involved. He was a straight and decent guy, who really gave a shit about me. I didn't want him in any hot water on my account.

On August 26th, Sheriff Joe Harris, his son Harold, and a couple of bulls came to Twin Falls and took us down to Elko, Nevada. Montello was in Elko County and Elko, Nevada was the county seat. We got a court appointed mouthpiece, A. Clyde Stringham. He was a good mouthpiece, especially for a court appointed one, but he never would tell us what the "A" stood for, we just called him Clyde. He thought he could spring us if we stood pat and didn't do any talking.

We had been sitting around in that jail with nothing to do for about two weeks when I got a kite out to a girlfriend. She got some saws and slipped them to me in the jail. I cut all the bars in my cell, except one set, which was chilled steel. Roy had been talking to the sheriff and one-day Sheriff Harris came into my cell and shook it down. He found the bars I had cut and was really upset. He had a blacksmith come in and repair the cuts, swearing him to secrecy. No one was going to break out of his jail, or even attempt to. However he did tell the District Attorney, in case the D. A. thought he could use it against us.

It was September 24th before we finally had a preliminary hearing and the rat popped out in Roy. He turned states evidence. After we had our hearing, they turned Roy loose. He was to appear against us at our trial.

After we had left Twin Falls, Casey had gone to the sheriff and swore that Peewee and I were with him in Twin Falls the night of the robbery. He told the sheriff that Roy had turned me in for the reward, when I had lamed from the Boise jail. He said that Roy was afraid of me and was trying to frame me to get me put back in the stir. The sheriff of Twin Falls took his statement and contacted Sheriff Harris. As soon as Sheriff Harris heard the news, he called me out of my cell and tried to get me to plead guilty. I asked him what inducements he had to offer. He said "five to life." I told him he would have to find me guilty. I wasn't helping him in exchange for any sentence that had the word life in it. If I got convicted it would probably mean life. This would be my third time in a state pen and the lawmakers were all pushing for putting a three-time loser in for life.

Casey was going to come down to Elko to testify at my trial. On the evening of September 9th Casey and two of his friends, Ullin Kessinger and Lon White had gone to Filer to the fair. When they got ready to go back to Twin Falls, Casey, who was driving, went through a stop sign as he left the fairgrounds. Some bulls saw the violation and started chasing them. They started across a condemned bridge over the low line canal, when Casey lost control of the car. The car hurled through the bridge and plunged into the waters below. Both Casey and Kessinger were killed. The sheriff took great pleasure in showing me the newspaper a friend had brought from Twin Falls telling about Casey's death. The sheriff was still mad about my trying to break his jail.[11]

Our trial started on October 28, 1931. I had been out of the stir for one hundred seventeen days, during that time I had only seen forty-eight days of freedom. During the trial they tried to use the attempted jailbreak against us, but our mouthpiece ruled it out. They also threw out Casey's statement since they could not cross-examine him. The D.A. called a number of witnesses, Guy Diaz, the owner of the pool hall, Ed Kendrick, the pool hall cashier who had identified me in Twin Falls. Jim Griswold, W. L. Hargrave, and S. O. Guiliei, were all three customers that we had robbed. Finally the D.A. called Roy Standlee, and did he do a number on us, making us out to be real tough men, leading him astray. He said he was as much a victim as the men who had actually been robbed. I swore I would get that rat one day, not just beat his ears down, but put him six feet under ground. As the trial was ending I looked over the faces of the jurors. There were eleven men, Emile Mettetal, Bruce Westland, G. W. Welther, Phillip Sharp, Jasper Gregory, John Ritter, Dale Boil, Mark Scott, N. F. Stanovich, Harry Trott and M. H. Filzmorria and one woman, Mrs. Pearl McElory, who had been named jury foreman. The men looked like regular joes, most of them were ranchers from the surrounding county. But Mrs. McElory, well, there was a woman to contend with. I could just see her on Sundays, thumping a Bible, with that not to friendly look in her eye. I could also see her brow beating the male jurors into agreeing that I deserved a life sentence for twenty dollars. I asked my mouthpiece if he could get me off with ten years if I plead guilty. He asked why I asked and I told him I didn't feel the jurors looked very friendly. The judge had already turned the

[11] "Two Motorists of Twin Falls Drown In Low Line Canal" The Twin Falls Daily News September 10, 1931 (Newspaper Reprints page 332)

191

case over to the jury and the judge said we would just have to wait until the jury came back with their verdict. He dismissed court for the day and told the jurors to return the next day with their verdict. The next morning Mrs. McElory read the verdict to the courtroom. Guilty as charged. The judge said he would pronounce the sentence on November 2nd, and sent us back to the Elko jail. The next few nights Peewee and I tried real hard to figure out a way to beat that jail, it was the only chance we felt we had, but it was a tough jail to beat.

On the morning of November 2nd we went before Judge L. O. Hawkins to get our sentence. I thought we were facing twenty-five to life. I almost fell over when I heard Judge Hawkins say "five to fifteen years." It is strange when a five to fifteen sentence comes as good news, but still, it was for a lousy twenty dollars

XVII

The End of Fifteen Years in A Living Hell

On our way back to the jail after court, Sheriff Harris asked me what I thought of my sentence. I told him I could do it on my ear, and I almost wore my ear off before I got it done.

On the morning of November 12th, we saw the dog wagon, or as the sheriff called it "The Bad Man's Bus," parked in front of the jail. The dog wagon was a Buick sedan with a screened cage in it. The law had given me rides in almost every possible way, but this was my first time in a dog wagon. There were two more boys who made the trip from Elko with Peewee and me, a colored boy named Lee Roye James who had been pinched for doing a poolroom, and John Rucker, who had shot and killed a crap dealer in a gamblers war. Later they picked up another boy in some dust speck of a town on the way to Carson City, which is where Nevada had its big house. The scenery was just miles and miles of more of the same, and I did a lot more wondering what sort of hell was waiting for me than I did wondering how and why I had been stupid enough to get myself in this sort of fix again. I had read and heard quite a lot about Nevada's big house, and now I was going to see it from the inside.

About halfway across the state, the traveling guard stopped in another small town, and put us in a jail overnight. It was just like the Elko jail, and we had no way to beat it. We started out again in the morning, and late the next afternoon, we got to our destination. It was November 13, 1931. I have always been superstitious, and November 13 that year was a Friday, the third Friday the 13th that year. I couldn't help but wonder if this was the beginning of a worse living hell than in

Idaho. They fingerprinted and mugged us, and while this was going on, the warden, Matt Penrose, spoke to us, and asked which one was Jones. The sergeant pointed me out. Warden Penrose asked how much time I had, which I am sure he already knew. I told him fifteen years. He seemed to think the judge had handed me quite a jolt. I was already having a hunch that my record had beat me to the prison. They took us over to the commissary where we traded our clothes for a pair of denim overalls, a shirt and some underwear. There was no number stamped on the overalls. I knew my prison number was 3203, but so far everyone had called me Jones.

We got quite a surprise when they turned us into the yard. The screw pointed out a building to us, and said that it was the bullpen where cons loafed on holidays and during the morning hours. As it was cold and snowing, we walked over to it. Peewee and I wanted to see if there were any boys we knew in this stir. When we walked into the bullpen, we could hardly believe what we saw, for it was almost like walking into a gambling joint. There were seven tables running full blast, two of them stud poker, and the other five draw poker. There were a couple of tables off to the side that even had bridge games going, and they were being bet on. I knew Nevada was supposed to be wide open, but I didn't know they let prisoners gamble in the big house. I told Peewee I believed I was going to be able to do the fifteen years, which that judge had handed me.

We walked around and looked the games over. They were using brass tokens for money. The tokens were in nickel, dime. quarter, fifty cent, and dollar denominations. We found out that we could have as much "money" on us as we wanted. The tokens were good in the prison store, or we could "bank" it in the office. The money we banked would be returned to us "dollar" for legal dollar when we got out. We could even write "checks" at the prison store against our accounts. You could draw brass two days each week. That is, you could if you had money on the books.

We only found two boys we knew. We had done time with them in Idaho, but they were both considered phony. At that time, thanks to prohibition, the federal prisons were overcrowded. The Federal government had made a deal with Nevada to hold their overflow, the government paid Nevada one dollar and twenty-five cent per day per federal prisoner, so there were a number of federal prisoners in Nevada. When it came time to eat, we found the chuck was good, much better than in Idaho.

Nevada was building a two-story license plate factory in the prison. They put Peewee and me to work breaking rock. Neither one of us had ever done any of that kind of work before, but we liked it a lot better than making shirts, and there wasn't any task quota we had to meet, except to break the rock they pointed us at. This job didn't last long; we laid the last stone on November 18, 1931.

We got a look at the gashouse, where the boys paid with their lives for capital offenses. The original gas house at the Nevada State Penitentiary was built in 1921, and was the first of its kind in the world. In 1929 they had built a new gashouse and I soon met one of the first boys who had been sentenced to be gassed. He was a Chinaman, who was in for a tong killing. His partner, Gee Jon, was the first to be gassed in Nevada, and had been put to death some years earlier. The board changed this boy's sentence to life imprisonment on account of his youth. I don't know how old he was, but even when I met him, he still looked like just a kid. I found him to be a good coon can player, at least too good for me. He knew some of the Chinks I knew in Boise, and I got the idea he didn't like some of them, and liked some of the others.

After they got the factory running, they selected twenty of us and I was put to work making license plates. We started to work on December 2nd, and since Nevada didn't have many cars in those days, it didn't take us long to make all the plates the state needed. We had made a little over 39,100 sets of black plates with raised orange lettering by January 14th, 1932, with a week off for Christmas, and we got paid for it. The factory was then shut down until December of 1932.

There was no other work except the upkeep of the prison, and that which a con could find for himself. Many of the cons went into business for themselves. They made ashtrays, and lamps that rivaled the merchandise in the local art stores. Some worked with ivory that they would carve into cigarette holders. These were a true work of art, inlaid with real silver, offset in the barrel with abalone shell and tipped with a golden band. The cons would sell these pieces to other cons for our brass money, trade them for cigarettes or clothes, or even use them to bet with in the poker games. The boys could even sell them in the prison store to people visiting the jail. Some were so good that local merchants would sell them on consignment in their establishments.

One of the boys who had charge of one of the poker tables had made his board, and I bought his layout, which I kept until I left the prison. I ran a poker and blackjack game for over five years. We were not allowed to use a real deck of cards, they were too easily marked. The "cards" were made of domino blanks with the suit and value painted on them. The poker chips were cut from old phonograph records. The racks that held the chips were hand made from blocks of wood and were quite elaborate. As I gave my trade as cook and waiter, they put me in the kitchen cooking, but I only had to work every other day. I hired another boy to run my game the days I had to work. As a game owner I would take a "rake" off each good pot. That money was used to pay the boy for running my game, and to pay the dealers. A number of the boys hired out as dealers, they were paid fifteen cents per hour.

The guy who ran the library, Neb Hulk, was the oldest prisoner there. That is he had the most time in, about seventeen years. He had been sentenced to death, and had got his sentence commuted to life. He was in for stagecoach robbery and murder. One day, I was talking to him. We were listening to the radio. I said that when I was a kid, I used to read about the great train robbers and stagecoach robbers, and I never thought at that time that I would grow up and do time with one of them. He said that I was lucky, and I asked how was that. He laughed and said he guessed he was the only one that was still alive and in captivity. He then told me his story.

During the early winter of 1916 the stage carrying three thousand dollars, pay for the miners in Jarbridge, Nevada, was found partially concealed in a clump of willows on the outskirts of town. The driver was sitting in his normal seat, but he was dead, with a gunshot wound to the back of his head. The three thousand dollars was gone. A posse was formed and following tracks left in the snow, they soon found bloodstained clothing, a money sack with one hundred eighty two dollars in coin and an envelope with a palm print in blood on it. A further search turned up a long black over-coat, and a shirt with the letter "H" marked in ink below the collar. The over coat was identified as belonging to one Neb Hulk. He was found at his cabin, which was near Jarbridge. When they shook down his cabin they found a bloodstained bone handled Colt 45. The gun did not belong to Hulk, but he, the owner of the gun and another fellow were charged with the robbery. Hulk's trial was held September 18, 1917. During the trial a finger print expert testified that the bloody palm print found on the envelope with the money was identical to Hulk's palm print. He was sentenced to hang. Since there was no precedent for identifying a palm print, the appeals went clear to the

Supreme Court. The conviction was nonetheless upheld. Hundreds of letters were written by Hulk's relatives in an effort to have his sentenced commuted to life. One week before he was to hang, he appeared before the Board of Pardons to plea for the commutation. Through out his trial and appeals he had held fast to his denial of guilt. While in front of the board he decided he had nothing to lose, so he finally admitted his guilt. He told the board that he and the stagecoach driver had made a plan to rob the stage. Hulk was to hold up the stage, the driver would make a pretense of resisting, but would finally give up the money. Hulk told how he had borrowed the gun, and that when the driver turned yellow and did not hold up his end of the bargain, Hulk became fearful that the driver was going to kill him, so he killed the driver in self-defense. He told them a friend had dug up the stage money where he had buried it and had turned it over to his mouthpiece. Hulk later learned that the "friend" had not turned the money over to the mouthpiece, but had lammed with it and went on a yearlong tour of the United States. The board commuted his sentence to life. Since 1918 he had applied for a pardon twenty seven times, and was turned down each time. He was fifty when I met him.

He was also an old-time gambler. Any time I had a good game with lots of money in it, I would let him sit in, and make sure he ended up with a share of winnings. He soon had a nice bankroll, and since he didn't have much hope of ever getting out with it, he could use it to gamble on his own.

Time began to drag. I had looked the prison over for a spot I could beat, but it was a pretty tough stir. The head cook had a halt on him, because Oregon wanted him when his sentence in Nevada was up. As we became good friends, we decided we could beat the kitchen. Two other boys wanted to go along. We made a hacksaw; the frame was made from a piece of reinforced steel rod we had taken from a window frame. We had notched one end so we could put a blade in it, and at the other end we had an eyebolt to tighten the blade. We had pinched a meat saw and attached another small tin saw with a phonograph spring. It was mid-summer and the weather was real nice. Every Sunday the warden brought an outside baseball team in to play our prison team. Our team was pretty good and usually gave the visiting team a real dubbing. The betting was real heavy on these games, so they were real popular. No one hardly ever missed a game. The only time we could saw the bars was on Sunday during the ball game, when all the other cons left the kitchen to watch the game and each morning during recreation period when no one was around. Butch and I would stay in the kitchen and do the cooking. He would watch for screws while I sawed the bars. We had two sets of bars to go through. Everything was going fine. We had only two more bars to go when Warden Penrose called Butch on the carpet and Butch owned up to everything. Then Warden Penrose called me out. Butch had told me he had copped, so there wasn't anything else for me to do. When the warden asked me about the cut bars, I told him I had cut them. He accused the two other boys of helping me and I told him I had done all the cutting myself, that the other two boys were at the ball game and couldn't have helped me. He told me all of us had been cutting the bars and he told me about it in such detail I figured that one of the two boys had turned rat and told the warden everything. I could do nothing but agree with him. It was real strange when he called both of the other two boys in, I figured I could find out who the rat was, by seeing who was not called in. But everyone was called in, so I didn't know who the rat was.

I thought I'd have about six months to a year in the hole, but Warden Penrose surprised me by saying "Derby, I haven't decided just what I am going to do with you yet, I will call you out again. Now, go on back to the kitchen and get to work." That night he had the screws give the kitchen a general shake down. They found our shives, a blackjack we had made from a piece of garden hose, files we had pinched from the machine shop, and our hacksaw.

The next day he called me out again. He had me sit down and began to talk to me. He wanted to know how much time I had done before I came to Carson City, and what I was in for, and what started me on the road to crime. I knew he knew about my previous time, and why I was in there, but I wondered about his questions about what got me started in this way of life. Then he told me he wasn't going to put me in the hole, but he was going to take Butch and me out of the kitchen.

When the warden dismissed me, he had me report to the cell house screw to be moved. After we finished the move, two screws got all four of us and took us out to the shop. They made us pull an acetylene-welding machine across the yard and into the kitchen. Then we had to weld the bars we had cut. I would have rather done a year in the hole than that welding job, for every con in the prison was giving us the "ha, ha."

We found out later just who the rat was. It was the warden himself. The first Sunday that we didn't show up at the ball game he became suspicious. He came strolling by the kitchen and heard a strange noise. He knew that if he walked in on us he would see nothing, so he went to his office and got a periscope he had been given for Christmas. Using the periscope he was actually able to watch us saw those bars without us seeing him. He watched us everyday, and every night he had the guards check the cuts we were making. He finally decided we were far enough along and that's when he called Butch on the carpet.

Years later, in a book Warden Penrose wrote called "Pots of Gold," he mentioned our break, along with a number of others.

Of all the wardens I had had dealings with, I respected Warden Penrose the most. He treated us like men; he knew every con in the stir by name, not by number. He encouraged us to think for ourselves and he let us know we always had direct access to him. He would often come down into the yard just to chat with a few of the prisoners. He was the only warden I knew who actually cared about our futures. Maybe that is why seventy-five percent of the cons who were paroled during his term stayed on the outside. One thing that Warden Penrose would not tolerate though was drugs or liquor of any kind. In 1934, shortly before warden Penrose left the prison, he let me know just how little tolerance he had for booze.

There was a guy from Kentucky doing time, and he sure knew how to make moonshine. Three of us got drunk during a ball game. That was the first time I made the hole in Nevada. Warden Penrose put me there for four days. One of the other fellows that got drunk with me, had been in the pen for some time, made a board, gotten out, and was back in prison again. It was his first day back, so his first night back was spent in the hole.

Just before sunrise one July morning in 1934, a stream of cars came into the prison compound. The people in those cars were to be witnesses to the gas execution of Joe Behiter. Joe had killed a dance hall girl with a miner's pick down in the small southern Nevada town of Las Vegas. We watched with a heavy silence as they walked Joe across the yard to the gashouse. Not one con spoke; it hardly seemed that some were even breathing. All of us were thinking the same thing, "When I get out, if I don't go straight, will that be me someday?" The rest of the day everyone was unusually quiet. The games were almost empty, the recreation hall subdued. It was a real gloomy place. I ran into Peewee late in the afternoon. He said "Hey Jones, you might just be right about being superstitious." I asked him why he said that, he replied "Hell, don't you know what day this is, it's Friday the 13th." Several of the boys paid with their lives by inhaling gas while I was at Carson.

Shortly after the execution, a group of men showed up to see Warden Penrose. Word had it that they were from the newly rebuilt federal stir, Alcatraz. They were looking the Nevada State Penitentiary over to see what methods Penrose used in preventing escapes. Rumor had it that the Feds were going to put the most notorious cons there. We also heard that some of the Federal Prisoners that were still in Nevada were going to be sent to Alcatraz.

On May 15th, 1935 we got a new warden. Warden William L. Lewis was an ex-fighter, and an all-around sport. The first thing he did was to build a gymnasium where he could put in a fight ring. Then we began to have fight cards. We also had shows. I think he brought in almost every good show that was in Reno.

Good as all this was, we also had several fights in the bullpen that the warden didn't schedule and referee. There were some hard losers in the Nevada big house, and if you ran a game, you had your share of dealing with them. The first fight I had was with a con who was somewhat larger than I was, and I didn't have a shiv. Fortunately, neither did he. I took a good beating that time. But the next time, I evened things up. I had some fights, and some of them tough, but I never made the hole for them, and I never had to kill or really hurt anyone. And no one really hurt or killed me.

On May 26, 1935 the head lines in the newspapers read "Weyerhaeuser Family Pleads With Kidnapers To Return

Young Son." Nine year old George Weyerhaeuser had been grabbed on his way home from school, Friday, May 24th in Tacoma, Washington. A ransom note demanding $200,000 in five days had been sent to the boys' parents and was signed by the "Egoist". There were fifteen G-men on the case and they figured that some "big shot" gangsters from the east were the kidnappers.

For the next six days, the kidnapping was front-page news. The G-men had no idea who had the boy or where they were. The number one suspect in the case seemed to be Alvin Karpis who was involved in another kidnapping that had gotten a $200,000 haul and had never been caught. Karpis was the current "public enemy number one" in the country. Before long all the big boys were being investigated. The G-men questioned Paul Chase, henchman of Baby Face Nelson and the recently killed Dillinger. Even members of "Machine Gun" Kelly's gang were questioned. The Weyerhaeuser's even asked the Feds to back off, for fear their interference would cause the death of their son. The five-day deadline came and went with no word from the kidnappers. The story had us all waiting for the next newspaper. Of course, we were betting on the kidnappers.

On June 2nd the headlines read "Desperate Kidnapers Release Ransomed Weyerhaeuser Lad; Law Army Hunts Karpis Gang." The story told that George had been released unharmed and the kidnappers had gotten all $200,000 in ransom. Little George said the names he heard the kidnapers use were "Harry, Bill, and Allen. This just made the G-men more sure that the Karpis gang were who they were after. After talking to George they had him convinced that the name "Allen" that he had heard was really "Alvin". Two known members of the Karpis gang were Harry Campbell and Bill Weaver.

For the next seven days the papers were full of stories about the G-men chasing the kidnappers. On June 5th a man bought a ticket on the Union Pacific from Portland to Salt Lake City with a twenty-dollar bill that was part of the ransom. After that the G-men backed off the theory that the Karpis gang was involved, one of the Karpis gang had been arrested in St. Paul the day after the kidnapping, so there was no possibility of his being involved. They started saying it was a "local" gang, which they chased across four states, Washington, Oregon, Idaho, and Utah.

Finally on June 10th the headlines read "Weyerhaeuser Kidnapers Captured." Two people had been arrested in Salt Lake City passing some of the ransom money. The two arrested were a man and his wife, and to my surprise I knew the man. He was Harmon Waley, a guy I had done time in Idaho with. He had been sent to the Idaho stir for burglary shortly before I got out. He was a youngster without too much smarts, so it wasn't surprising when I read that the leader of their gang was my old pal Bill Mahan. I also read that Bill had almost been captured in Butte, Montana when a bull saw him standing beside a car and recognized him. Bill went over a fence and out ran the bull across a rooftop and got away.

Now the G-men knew who they were looking for. A G-man came to the prison to see me. He kept me on the carpet for over one hour, trying to get me to tell something that would help them catch Bill. I didn't know anything, and I told the G-man so. I wouldn't have told if I did have anything to tell, and I told the G-man that, too. He said it was about what he expected. I told him I was due out of prison soon, and he could rap me if he wanted, but I hadn't lied to him. All I knew was what I read in the newspapers. He told me Bill's job was one of the smoothest ever pulled.

That was after Pretty Boy Floyd was killed, and for awhile there, Bill was "public enemy number one." Bill beat them for a year or more, and when they caught him in San Francisco, there wasn't a shot fired. I read that Bill got sixty-five years and was sent to McNeil Island. After about a year they transferred him to Alcatraz. While he was in Alcatraz he was caught planning an escape attempt. He had made two guns. They were muzzle-loaders, with copper tubing for barrels and rubber bands for triggers. He even made ammunition using match heads for powder and little pellets of lead. The warden found Bill's guns under a mattress in an empty cell next to his after another con had ratted him out. I heard later that he blew his top while he was in Alcatraz, and they transferred him to a government mental hospital. I thought of what I had told Bill when he had talked the snatch racket to me. My words had come true. He had got more time than he could do.

One day, Peewee and I were called out to the office and they mugged us and printed us once again. We didn't know what it was all about at the time, but we later learned that a bank had been robbed in Idaho, and the Idaho bulls thought we had pulled the job. We sure had a laugh on them. They couldn't hang the job on us, for we had an ironclad alibi.

Peewee and I were on every board, trying to get a parole. Since he hadn't got caught trying to make a break, I knew he would get out before me. The board met every six months, and Peewee finally made it. When he was released they made him buy a ticket to San Francisco and told him never to come back to Nevada. When two guys are in on the same rap, and one makes parole, the other one was almost sure to make the next board, and if that happened in my case, it seemed almost too good to be true. I had come in under a five to fifteen sentence. I was past five, with only one trip to the hole, and it looked like I was facing just six months more in prison. Time can go very slowly, but it is surprising sometimes how much can happen in just six months.

There was a load of "fish" that came in, and one of them was the con whom the colored boy had beaten up in Idaho. He had a lot of news for me, as he lived in Idaho. He told me of a number of the guys I knew, who had got bumped off. This fish had the name of being phony in the Idaho stir. As I had decided to shake my time and get out on the up and up, when he propositioned me to make a break with him, I told him my partner had gone out on parole, and I expected to make the next board. There were a few of the boys trying to lam, but I made a point of knowing as little as I could about it. This fellow was the last person I wanted to hear talk about a break.

While I was waiting the next board, they transferred the last of the federal prisoners to McNeil Island to finish their time. There were some who say federal time is easy time, but none of these boys seemed too happy to be leaving Nevada.

We had a route to get booze inside. One of the truck drivers would get it downtown, and pass it to the commissary. It would then pass on to the hospital, and then be bootlegged to the cons in the yard. Everything had been rosy for some time, but then a number of the boys threw a big drunk that reminded me of that guardhouse party in France, and the lot of them got pinched and thrown in the hole. Then they tore our playhouse down, so no more bonded booze.

On January 26, 1937 another one of the boys was sent to the gashouse. This particular execution really made me do a lot of thinking. His name was Luther Jones, and I couldn't help but think that it could have been another Jones, me. All I wanted to do was, do my time and get out of there, so I decided to play it easy so I could get my parole.

Time was going slowly for me. I began to see boys who were just in their teens come in from almost every reform school in the United States. Some of these boys wanted to gamble, but not too many of them were as good at it as they thought they were. I was down to my last month before the board met, and I had some of my bankroll out among those youngsters, who had lost in my game and borrowed from me. As I still hoped to make the board, I offered a number of them a fifty-percent discount if they would pay off. If they weren't holding, I canceled what they owed me. This was a square deal, but the boy from Idaho, whom my colored friend had beat up in the Boise stir, got tough when I asked him for a settlement.

I was trying to ride my remaining time smoothly, but this Idaho boy made it impossible. Even though I didn't like him and didn't trust him, I had dealt him square and tried to be generous. Now he was returning my favor by trying to worm out on his debts. I told him I wasn't about to let him get away with spitting in my face when I held out such a good deal to him, and he cussed me, then came up with a shiv. As I had a shiv available too, we had us a battle, which ended with me chasing him down the aisle between the bunks; cutting on him and cursing him for dealing me dirty when I tried to deal him straight. There is not much that used to make me angrier than when I did a man a favor, and he does me dirt in return. You might say that I was angry enough to kill him, which is just about what I did. I put that boy in the hospital, which put me in the hole. I thought for a while that they were going to try me again. The rumor was out that the doctor said he had no chance to live, and I could see myself taking gas, even though he was the one who had been looking to fight. That was the toughest time I ever served, not knowing what I was facing when I came out. I was sure that I had blown whatever chance I had of making the next board.

They brought me out of the hole in time for the board, but it didn't seem to go good for me. When a screw came and told me the returns were in, and I had made it, I thought he was kidding me. But it was true. And when I knew it was true, I felt like I was the luckiest con in the world.

Mug Shot Oliver "Derby" F. Jones 1931 - Nevada State
Penitentiary Collection

Kindness During Life

I would rather have one little rose,
From the garden of a friend.
Than to have the choicest flowers
When my stay on earth must end.

I would rather have one pleasant word
Of kindness said to me,
Than flattery when my heart is still
And life has ceased to be.

I would rather have a loving smile
From friends I know are true,
Than tears shed round my casket,
When this world I bid adieu.

Bring me all your flowers today,
Whether pink, white or red.
I 'd rather have one blossom now,
Than a truck load when I'm dead.
                    Oliver F. Jones

XVIII

Crime Doesn't Pay!

On the morning of November 13, 1937, exactly six years to the day that I had been put behind the walls of the Nevada State Penitentiary, they came to dress me out. I had to wait around two hours. That was the longest two hours of my life. A screw drove three other boys and me to Reno, where he bought me a ticket to Salt Lake City, out of my own money. He wouldn't give me my money until I was ready to get on the bus. He left us at the bus station while he drove over to Sparks to get a boy who had also made parole out of the nut house. He told us not to leave the bus station until he got back.

I was sitting there waiting, when a gambler friend of mine came into the station. I hadn't seen him for a number of years. We shook hands, and he asked when I got to town, and how long I was going to stay. He didn't know I had just got out of the big house, and I didn't tell him for some time. He suggested we go get a drink, and I couldn't turn him down. After we had a few drinks, he told me he could get me a deal on a dice table where he was working. Then I told him I had just got out of stir, and I was being exiled out of Nevada. We had another drink, and I thought the screw had had time to drive to Sparks and back. We had just got back to the bus station, when in came the screw with the boy who had blown his top several months before. I shook hands with the boy. He didn't seem so crazy to me. He had blown his top over religion, which was a common thing for cons to blow their tops over.

As time for my bus drew near, I asked the screw if I could stop in Elko. He gave me a dirty look, and said that I had to leave the state. I asked if I could go to work in a gambling joint, and again he said no, I had to leave the state. I asked him what the hell I was going to do to make an honest living, but he had nothing to say except that I had to leave the state. When he gave me my ticket and money, I stepped up to the conductor and said I wanted a stopover in Elko. The screw gave me a dirty look, but didn't say anything.

I made some acquaintances on the bus. We had some drinks at a stop, and I bought a bottle. While buying the bottle, my bus left, and I didn't get on the next bus. My bag and overcoat were gone, and I was getting drunk. Not wanting to get pinched, I got a hotel room, and the next day got back on a bus. I found my bag at Elko, and my overcoat in Salt Lake. At Salt Lake, I bought a ticket for Ogden, where I had some friends. They told me I should go straight, but I had no intentions of going straight. I stayed in Ogden a few days, and while there, I had a doctor give me the once over, because I wasn't feeling too strong. The doctor told me I was in worse shape than I had thought. He said I would be lucky if I lived six months. I told him I was a gambling man and I bet him ten to one that I would live a lot longer than any six months. I felt my luck had changed, and from now on I was going to be damn lucky. He got real serious and suggested I go east, and check into the Mayo Brothers Hospital, as I was the worst physical wreck he'd ever examined. I paid him his fee, and walked out, feeling worse than I had when I come in.

I caught a train for Twin Falls, thinking I might find Roy, the yellow rat, but a gambler told me he had left for California as soon as he heard I had made my board. The gambler said he was real scared when he left. Twin Falls didn't seem right to me. With my cousin, Casey gone, it just wasn't the same. I made the rounds, seeing a lot of the boys I had known. None of them recognized me, for I looked like a walking corpse. I had no idea how bad I looked, but now I knew. That doctor hadn't told me exactly all the things that were wrong with me, just that I was a wreck, and I guess he must've known his business. I ran into Smith, a boy I'd done time with. He wanted to know what had wrecked me so, and I told him I guessed I had done too much damn time. He told me I had better rest and watch my step, for I couldn't shake another jolt. I knew he was telling me right. He had been out almost seven years. He wasn't going straight, but he was being damned careful.

Smith and I decided to go to Odgen. While we were there we met an ex-con who had been doing life in Idaho while I was there. He had been released because of his health. He was a worse wreck than I was and didn't have long to go. He needed some dough and wanted us to help him with a job. Smith and I didn't like the looks of the job so we passed it up. Smith suggested I go home to see my mother, but I wanted to get some color back into my face first, so I decided to bum for a while, stay out of jail, and when I decided to pull another job, pick one I could do alone.

I bought a quart of booze before I went to the yards to catch a freight for the east. I was dressed fairly warm, but I wasn't used to being outdoors. I ran into a blizzard in Wyoming, and Old John Barleycorn saved my life. I really believe I would have frozen to death if I hadn't bought that bottle of booze. When I unloaded off that train, I was so numb I could hardly walk. I left my bag when I unloaded, and went looking for a fire. After I thawed out, I went back to look for my bag, not really expecting to find it, but it was still where I left it. I stayed overnight, and the next day I was warmer. I decided I had better travel while I could, so I headed south. I met a number of ex-cons who had made the same board as me. They were just like me, no place to go, just going. It wasn't just ex-cons on the bum, though. There were all sorts of guys out bumming, looking for work. The country was still in a

213

depression, and on the trains and in the jungles; there was a new class of bums. I even met a number of boys who had been to college, and were almost as well read as the better class of ex-con.

Before long, I washed up in Denver, Colorado, and the next day I read the *Denver Post*. All I could see was holdups and burglaries. I knew that was no place for me. If some bull caught me and made my record, I would have gotten a trip to jail or back to Carson City, even if I hadn't pulled a job.

The train I left Denver on was loaded with bums, but I didn't know any of them. I wondered how many had just got out of some big house, and how many of them had never thought they would be on the bum with guys, who like me, had just come out of prison. Almost everybody was broke. One fellow told me that if I got to Kansas City, I could go to the courthouse, where they had funds for the stranded. I wasn't broke, but I was close to it. It was too cold for most of these boys to go out and bum something to eat. When we got to Kansas City, I got the five bums I was traveling with, and took them off to get something to eat. We went to the courthouse, and I had them wait outside while I went in the office. The clerk handed me a big form to fill out. A man who was real hungry could have starved to death before filling that form out. I finally answered all the questions and handed the papers back to the clerk. He looked me over, and made out another form, then asked how many of us there were. I told him there were six of us. He had me sign some more forms, then handed me some papers, and told me to take them to another office and give them to the woman there. Then he asked me if I needed gas. I told him no, we had come in on a freight train. That clerk turned red, and I believe he would have snatched back the papers if he thought he could get away with it. The woman in the next office gave me a three-dollar order on one of the stores. Three dollars for six bums wasn't a lot of money, but it was enough for one feed.

I got the other bums, and we went to the store. While two of us were trading out that order, the other four did a little boosting. When we got to the jungles, we had enough chuck for twenty bums. I told them about the clerk offering us gas, and one of the bums wanted to get it, and sell it. I told him to go ahead, but I had had enough of Kansas City.

I caught the next freight east, and at the next stop, I sent in a report to my parole officer, as I was to do every month. Heading south to Oklahoma, I ran into another blizzard, and at my next stop, I had a run-in with some bulls. That was my first run-in with the law, since rejoining the free world, and I managed to get by without a pinch, but it caused me to do a little thinking. I had done fifteen years hard time, not counting the time I had spent in all those jails. I had met all kinds of crooks. I considered Bill Mahan the smartest one I had met. He had got away with more money than any gangster I knew, but now he was paying off in full. I thought of all the boys who had been bumped off, the boys who weren't famous, and the famous ones like Pretty Boy Floyd, Baby Face Nelson, Bonnie and Clyde, and John Dillinger, who had all been killed in 1934 while I was gambling in the pen. There was a number of things we had in common, the most important of which was that for all of us, good luck was more than balanced off by our bad luck. That was the day I really started thinking about going straight. I might never make something big of myself, but at least I could have a long peaceful life.

On the twenty-third of December 1937, 1 stepped off the train in my old hometown of Urbanette, Arkansas. When I met my mother, she didn't recognize me. I thought of the last time I had seen her, when I was in prison, and she didn't recognize me then, either. I intended to stay only until after the holidays.

I told mother I would have to move on, as my past would catch up with me.

A few days later, I took sick, and almost cashed in my chips. It took some while to get better, and this delayed my leaving. One day, I was sitting near the window, and I saw two cars coming. I told my nephew those cars were loaded with bulls. He asked how I knew, and I told him I had been hunted so much in my life, I could almost feel the bulls coming. Sure enough, I was right. The bulls unloaded and surrounded the house. The sheriff and another man came in. The sheriff shook hands with me, and introduced the other man, who was a G-man. Then my mother walked into the room. She turned pale, not knowing what it was all about. I felt relieved when the sheriff told mother that some of the boys thought they might find Ted Cole there.

Ted Cole was one of the cons who lammed from Alcatraz Island. On December 16, 1937 there had been a dense fog over Alcatraz. Ted Cole and Ralph Roe had been working in the mat shop. As soon as the screws had left after making their count of the mat shop, the two had run to a window where they had already cut two bars. They bent the bars, broke the window glass, sawed a sash and slipped out. They moved through the fog, came to a fence where they smashed the gate lock with a wrench they had brought from the mat shop, groped there way to the edge of a twenty foot cliff and jumped down onto a mound of discarded casings from the mat shop. Then they plunged into the bay, never to be seen again. A lot of people thought they had drowned, but not the G-men who were in my mothers' living room.

As they left the room, the G-man handed me a photo of Ted Cole, and asked if I knew him. I told him I didn't. I knew the G-man didn't believe me, but I was telling the truth. It was probably the only time in my life I told a bull the truth. After they had searched all the rooms and didn't find Ted Cole, the G-man talked to me for some time. He was friendly enough, but I was glad when they left.

A few days later, there was a liquor store robbery, and several cases of liquor stolen. Another car stopped at mothers, and a bull got out and came in. He wanted to shake the place down again. I told him he could, if he had a warrant, otherwise, he couldn't. The bull left. Thinking they were going to get a warrant and come back, I got in a car, and went down to the sheriff's office for a talk. When I mentioned the first shake, the sheriff said that the order had come from Washington, D. C. I told him I didn't have to stay in that part of the country, and if every time there was a job pulled, they intended to shake my mother's house down, I would leave the country. Here I was home, and my old record was causing my poor mother a lot of grief.

Then I met Tot Davis, a boy I had palled with when I was just a kid. I told him of my intention of leaving the country, and why. He said I didn't have to leave. He said I should stay home with my mother, and show them I could come back and go straight. I said I had thought I was hidden from the outside world, down in the Ozark hills. I wasn't wanted, and I was going to go straight, if they let me. Tot told me it wasn't up to them to let me go straight, it was up to me. What he said caused me to do some serious thinking. With the experience I had had with the law, I knew I wasn't smart enough to beat them. I knew I hadn't been smart to even try.

Then and there is where I quit the racket. I had paid my debt to society, and I was still paying with my health, I had been all over the United States, and the Army had taken me to Europe. I had gambled all over, and I had gambled in almost every game a man could play. I had gambled for high stakes, and I had gambled with my life. Sure, I knew the world hates a quitter, but it takes a smart man to know when he is beaten. I don't claim to be smart, but I was smart enough to know that I was beaten. I had gambled, and I had lost. I thought I was smart, but all the time I was a fool. There is an old saying that everyone knows, and I could see now that it was true. Criminals pay for their crimes, and so do their victims. But I could see now that crime itself just doesn't pay.

You might say that I was a very slow learner.

WHEN I DIE

When I die, please cremate me;
Then I will feel that I am free.
Just toss my ashes for the wind to blow;
Then I will decide where I want to go.

I have heard all about their heaven and hell;
What I have heard doesn't suit me so well.
I want to look around for someplace new;
If it happens to be good, I will send for you.

Oliver F. Jones

EPILOGUE

My father did stay in Urbanette for a while. In the spring of 1938 he went to a dance in Blueeye, a short distance from Urbanette. There he met a young woman of 18 named Jesse Lilly Hopper. Oliver called her "Billie".

Dad fell in love with Billie and they moved halfway between Urbanette and Berryville so he could be close to his mother. He worked in the woods making pine poles for fences. They even tried their luck at raising chickens. During this time they had two daughters, Betty "Bets" June, and Billie Juanita "Neat". After a while, his "itchy" foot started to get to him and he got to thinking about moving his family to the golden state of California to try and better their lives. When a tornado blew through Berryville, blowing half the town away, including his front porch, Dad decided it was definitely time to go.

In 1943 the Jones family arrived in Sanger, California. Dad got a job running a couple of ranches that belonged to Japanese families who had been placed in internment camps. During this time he ran into a nephew of his, Faye Spencer, who helped him buy a Model A Ford that he truly treasured. Faye was very special to him and when his third child, and only son, was born; he named me Derby Faye Jones. My name was a combination of the name my father had carried for so many years, and the name of his favorite nephew. When Faye Spencer decided to become a preacher, Dad was furious and would not have any more to do with him. Faye founded a church in Compton, California, The Revival Tabernacle, which is still in existence today. The church had a monthly Magazine called "The Old Fashioned Healing Magazine," and a twice-weekly radio broadcast "The Old Fashioned Healing

Broadcast" heard on Saturday mornings and Sunday afternoons.

In 1945 we moved to a place between Sanger and Clovis, and Dad and Mom started running poker and crap games. Then in 1947 they decided to go home for a visit, they sold the Model A, bought a 1939 Chevrolet and left for Arkansas. We got as far as Needles when the radiator went out on the car. We spent three very hot days in Needles while the car was being fixed. We left Needles and went on toward Arkansas, but our car broke down a number of times on the way. When we arrived, we were tired and broke. Dad did odd jobs around Urbanette, until one day a couple approached him, and offered to pay him to take them to California. He did just that, and after he was paid, he had the money to come back to Arkansas and get his family. We headed back to California.

In 1948, we landed in Fresno, California, and Dad went to work at a railroad camp. That is where we lived, amidst the grime and noise. In 1948 Dad had had enough and moved the family to Del Rey. He went back to his love, gambling, but because times had changed and gambling was becoming a pasttime, he had to roam further and further away from home to find a good game that had relatively high stakes. He was gone for long periods of time and we missed him. During one of his trips he ended up in Northern California in the giant redwood country. It was the most beautiful place he had ever seen, and he vowed to return one day. When he returned home Mom was tried of him being gone all the time and told him "Either get a real job and stay home, or I am going to take the kids and leave."

He did not want to lose his family, so in 1949 he got a job running a ranch in the Del Rey area. He ran ranches during the winter months and during the summer he would contract out peach drying sheds, and the whole family would go to work drying peaches. We would also hire out and pick cotton and every kind of fruit California could grow. The whole family worked, even little four-year-old Derby. Dad taught his children, at a very young age, that you give a full day's work for a day's pay. He instilled in us a work ethic that stays with us to this day.

In 1952 Dad was picking grapes and stuck his head in wasps' nest and was badly stung. He was very ill and so swollen he was barely recognizable. While he was convalescing he got to thinking about those giant redwoods he had seen in Northern California and decided he had had enough of the fruit business. So in 1952 he moved the family to Humbolt county, and started working at a lumber mill.

The lumber mill was a large camp with a crooked boss who cheated Dad out of his wages. He just wouldn't pay, so Dad decided to try another lumber mill because he had a family to feed.

Over the next few years we moved several times, living all over Humbolt County. Then in 1958 we moved again, this time to Redway. Dad rented a piece of property that had a small four-room house on it. In July 1960 the house burned to the ground. The landlord sold the property to my father, and the lumber mill donated studs and we rebuilt the house. The house was made entirely of studs, both walls and floor.

Dad worked at the Munski Stud Mill until it shut down in 1961; it was then that he decided to retire. However he had never given up his gambling. He would have mill workers over to his house and play poker or shoot craps with them. He still used marked cards and loaded dice. One evening he had beat a fellow mill worker out of about $500 shooting dice, and of course the dice were loaded. The fellow gave Dad the pink slip to his 1956 Ford, to play just one more roll of the dice. Dad told him "You don't want to do that, you will lose." The man insisted, and as Dad had said, the man lost. Dad just could not take everything from the man so he returned his pink slip.

In 1962 Dad was in a car wreck and his hip was broken. It never healed; he would remain in a wheel chair for the rest of his life. In 1963 he finally ventured back into Nevada to gamble legally. But he never stayed long only making occasional weekend trips. In 1964 Dad moved to Ukiah where he lived peacefully until he passed away in 1968 at the age of 72.

Dad spoke often of his early life, he was always up front and honest about who he had been and what he had done. He told us of Bill Mahan, Clarence Rousch, Chet Langer and Dora Douglass. Dad had truly loved and respected Dora, and spoke of her often during our childhood. While doing the research for this book we found that after Dora Douglas got divorced from Dad she remarried a miner in Washington State. The marriage did not last long, and she moved back to Star, Idaho. She spent the rest of her life living with her oldest son, Gilbert, in Star. Her youngest son, Luther, became a pilot when he grew up and flew twenty-nine successful bombing missions over Germany during World War II. When he returned to Boise he met a young man, named Ernest Hemingway, and they became best of friends.

Dad did spend more time in jail. In 1946 we went to Clovis, California for the day. On our way to Clovis a black cat crossed the road in front of us. Dad wanted to go back home, but Mom told him his superstitious nature was silly. Later that evening Mom, my sisters and I had gone to the theater, when the show finished Dad walked up the street to get us. As we were walking back to the car a man came up and confronted Dad and a fight ensued. Dad was arrested on disorderly conduct and spent one final night in jail. He also remained superstitious the rest of his life.

My father had a profound impact on my life. He was a quiet disciplinarian, who rarely raised his voice or hand to any of us. But his looks could be more painful than any whipping. He never hid his past from us, teaching us that you learn from your mistakes. Dad also taught us that you never judge anyone from the way they look, but you judge from their mannerisms, and they way they treat you. He would often say "Nothing in this world comes free, if you want something you have to work hard for it." I remember my sister working one whole summer picking grapes for a pair of roller skates. Dad always told us that life was to be lived. He had spent fifteen hard years locked away from life, and he always let us know how important living free and living life to its fullest was.

It was hard sometimes; having a father who was the same age as my friends' grandparents. We did not do a lot of the things that the other boys did with their fathers, like go hunting or fishing. However we did go fishing one time, I was about eight years old and Dad and his friend Frank Cooper took me fishing. Dad caught a fish, and I have always wondered if it was the first fish he had ever caught, you should have heard him giggle and laugh as though nothing had made him happier in his entire life. We may not have done normal father and son things, but I always knew he cared deeply about my sisters and me. We never had much money, so toys were scarce, but those we did have were all the more special because Dad made them. I remember a handcrafted logging truck he made out of redwood for me. I spent hours playing with; it was so special because Dad made it just for me.

My father touched a lot of people during his life. When he passed away there was standing room only at his funeral. He had some very close friends while we were growing up, Jim

Moore and George "Pineapple" Centenio. They were both nondescript men, Pineapple spent a lot of his life working in the Saudi Arabian oil fields, and Jim Moore spent much of his time in Alaska as a carpenter. Dad could always count on these men to be there if he needed them. He often said that he would be proud to ride the rails with either one of these men. As a friend Dad was outgoing and friendly with all he knew. Pineapple had worked as a bartender for years and he told me he didn't know any bad side of Dad. He said that when Dad would come into the bar it was hello to everyone and that if you saw Derb, you saw Billie. Pineapple also played cards with Dad, and of his card playing Pineapple said "Let's put it straight, Derb was in the game to make it. But he wasn't a sore loser. If he lost, he lost, if he won, he won."

Dad left behind three children who would make him proud. We all married and gave him a total of seven grandchildren, whom he delighted in. Both Betty and Juanita worked outside the home, and because of the work ethic instilled in them by our father, they would become highly valued employees. I started working by my fathers' side in the lumber mills at age fifteen. I started pulling green chain, one of the hardest jobs in a lumber mill. I was small for my age and pulling green chain takes a lot of strength. Dad was always there encouraging me, telling me I could do the job if I put my mind to it. In 1965 I enlisted in the Army. I became a paratrooper serving in the 101st, 82nd, and 509th, serving three tours in Vietnam and coming home with a Silver Star. I spent four years in Italy, and while there, won one of the highest awards a soldier can receive while serving overseas, the Sergeant Moralas Award. I spent twenty-one years in the military and retired as a sergeant major, making that rank in only nineteen years. I am now working for the United States Post Office in Boise, Idaho. I feel that what I have achieved in my life can be directly attributed to the man who raised me. He instilled his values deep into my soul, values that he learned the hard way. All three of his children were very proud to say that Oliver Jones was their father.

Dad had one dream that went unfulfilled. He wanted to go down the full length of the Mississippi, with me, on a riverboat. I would like to think that, that is where his spirit is now, floating down the Mississippi, gambling with those spirits that had the same dream.

"Derby" and "Billie" October 1943

The Jones Family - 1944 (from left) children Derby,   Billie
Juanita, Betty, adults Oliver, Jessie "Billie"

Oliver and Derby 1958

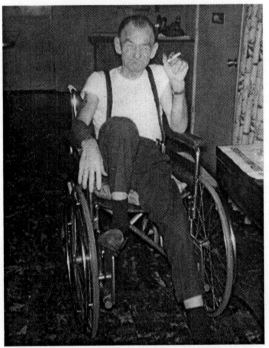

Derby" Jones - May 1967

Derby Jones and Lester Summers - August 1996

Derby Jones and Margaret Fikkan Gilliam - June 1996

GLOSSARY

A. E. F.   Armed Expeditionary Force - American troops sent to France and Germany during World War I.

Back on the Bricks   Released from jail. City streets were at one time made of brick. The expression "back on the bricks" refers to a prisoner being released from jail and free to walk on the city streets again.

Big House   Penitentiary.

Blinds of a Passenger Train   The area between two passenger cars. Canvas or leather covered the area. There was a walkway between the two cars used by passengers to move between the cars. The blinds was the canvas covering. From the outside of the canvas to the edge of the car was a space about 24 inches wide. The bums would ride; hanging on to the ladder that went up the side of the car. Sometimes there was a small metal plate at the base of the ladder they could stand on. It was a very dangerous place to ride. If the train was taking a sharp curve, or had to stop suddenly, the cars could come together, cutting the person riding in the blinds in half. Another area on passenger trains that bums would ride would be the "Rods". Two long parallel metal rods ran the length of the underneath side of a passenger car. The bums would but a pad between the rods and lay on the pads. They definitely had an interesting ride.

Bughouse   Solitary confinement.

Bulls   Policeman.

Bullpen   Common area where a group of prisoners were brought for exercise and fresh air.

Cased   watched, or looked over to determine if a robbery was possible.

C. C. Pills   Cascara, A laxative very popular in the early 1900s.

Celling   Prisoners sharing a cell.

C-Note   One Hundred Dollar Bill.

Cold-decked In a card game a cold-deck is a deck of cards that have been stacked as a losing hand by a dishonest dealer. When a person is cold-decked circumstances in his life have caused hardship.

Coon Player A person who participated in playing Coon was an old card game.

Flatfoot   Police Officer who walks a beat.

Free Labor   Employees who are paid by the business they work for, not by the government.

Green Chain   Stacking lumber freshly cut in the saw mill.

Grujo   Marijuana.

Hasher   Waitress.

**Header
Barge**   Wagon that followed a columbine during the
wheat harvests. Workers picked up the wheat
that had been cut by the columbine and loaded it
on the wagon.

Hokum   Exaggeration of the truth.

Hop   Opium.

Hypos   A person addicted to Morphine. A hypodermic
needle was used to inject the morphine.
Hypodermic was shortened to Hypo.

**John Doe
Warrant**   A warrant made out on a minor charge used to
hold a person while investigation of a more
serious crime takes place.

Kangarooed The court has determined a person is guilty
before the trial and only has a hearing as a
formality.

Kite   A note or message.

K. P.   Kitchen Police - A term used in the military for
someone assigned to work in the kitchen as
punishment for an infraction of the rules.

Lam   To escape or run from the law.

Mouthpiece A Lawyer.

Plants   Where an item has been hidden, in the story Oliver "Planted" both liquor and money.

Rank   A problem.

Rod   A gun.

Sawbuck   A five dollar bill, a double sawbuck would be a ten dollar bill.

Screws   Prison guards.

Section Gang   Workers who laid and repaired the railroad lines.

Slacker   A draft dodger. Someone not willing to serve his country in the military due to cowardice.

Shack   Engineer or Conductor on a train.

Shiv   A homemade knife, this could be made out of metal, glass, or wood, anything a convict could sharpen and use as a stabbing weapon.

Snitch   An informant.

Stir   Penitentiary.

Stove Lifter   A metal rod used to lift a hot lid off a wood-burning stove.

Tank   Where prisoners charged with major offenses are confined.

Take-Off   A percentage of the winnings in a poker game taken by the dealer or owner of the game.

Tong   Chinese gangs who often reported directly back to mainland China , often know as the Chinese Mafia.

Wobblies   Members of the International Workers of the World Union.

Wye   A track shaped like the letter "Y", but with a connector between the two arms of the "Y".

Reference

Newspapers

The Boise Evening Capital News

"Masked Automobile Bandits Hold Up The Bank Of Eagle and After Locking Cashier Fikkan and his Daughter in Vault at Point of Gun, Make Away With $2600 in Cash" - August 11, 1924 - page 1

"Three Men and Woman in Law's Clutches, Held by Authorities for Sensational Robbery at Eagle Monday and Part of the Loot Recovered." - August 12, 1924 - page 1

"Confessor of Holdup Refuses to Give Officers Additional Information Concerning Case." - August 13, 1924 - page 1

"Officers Believe Another Bandit May Be Involved." - August 14, 1924 - page 1

"Alleged Bank Robbers Saw Their Way Out Of Ada County Jail Early Thursday Morning, and Overpowering Watchman Make Escape." - October 16, 1924 - page 1

"No Trace Yet Found of Two Prisoners Who Made Getaway" – October 17, 1924 - page 1

"Jury Selection in Murder Trial Moving Slowly" - November 13, 1924 - page 1

Justice Defeated When Alleged Bank Robber and Star Witness For State Against Him Wed in Ceremony in Jail" - January 6, 1925 - page 1

"Langer Pleads Guilty to Charge of Robbing Eagle Bank; Oliver Jones Last of Accused Four, May Follow" - January 17, 1925 - page 1

"EAGLE BANK ROBBERS CONFESS ON EVE OF TRIAL - Oliver Jones Follows Lead of Langer and Pleads Guilty to Robber Eagle Bank; Langer is Sentenced 6 - 15 Years" - January 18, 1925 - (Headlines) page 1

"Penitentiary Term of 10 to 20 Years Given Oliver Jones." - January 19, 1925 - page 1

"Antiquated Prison Should Be Razed, Modern One Built" - January 31, 1927 - page 1

"Prison Like Keg of Powder Ready For Fatal Blast" - February 1, 1927 - page 1

"Prison Houses Youths" - February 2, 1927 - page 1

"Prison's Factory Godsend" - February 3, 1927 - page 1

"They Put Unruly Convicts In Den Called 'Siberia'" - February 4, 1927 - page 1

Elko Daily Free Press
"Montello Pool Hall Robbed." - August 4, 1931

"Three Men Held For Robbery of Montello Store" - August 20, 1931

"Sheriff Returns With Prisoners" - August 27, 1931

"Youths Bound Over To District Court On Robbery Charges Today" - September 25, 1931

"Youths Plead Not Guilty to Charge" - October 1, 1931

"Two Face Hold-up Charge In District Court Today" - October 28, 1931

"Fate of Two Men Held By Jury Today" - October 29, 1931

"Sentence to Be Passed Monday" - October 30, 1931

"Cavender, Jones Sentenced 5 - 15" - November 2, 1931

Elko Independent
"Ex-Convict 'Vamped' By Lady Bluebeard Missing With Her After She Flees Pen" - August 31, 1931

"Two Held on Charges of Robbing Pool Hall" - September 25, 1931

"Holdup Men Found Guilty" - October 30, 1931

"Prison Van is Due Thursday" - November 11, 1931

"Beware - Today is Friday the 13th, Third During '31" - November 13, 1931

The Idaho Statesman

"Allumbaugh is Named Sheriff of Ada County" - March 8, 1923 - page1

"Allumbaugh Now County Sheriff" - March 9, 1923 - page 8

"Five Prisoners Escape From Penitentiary" - June 21, 1923 - page 1

"Convicts Still at Large; 7 New Guards Named" - June 22, 1923 - page 1

"William L. Cuddy Prison Warden, Critically Ill" - January 5, 1924 – page 5

"Stories That Men Entered Women Prisoners' Cells at Night, Termed Inconsistent" - January 22, 1924 - page 7

"Cuddy Resigns; Snook Named Prison Warden" - January 24, 1924 - page 5

"Snook Assumes Duties at Prison." - January 25, 1924 - page 4

"Snook Will Make Changes at Prison" - January 26, 1924 - page 10

"Sheriffs Scour Country For Three Bandits Who Looted Eagle Bank" - August 12, 1924 - (Headlines) page 1

"Charges of Robbery Filed Against Four In Eagle Bank Case" - August 13, 1924 -page 1

"Sheriff Seeking Robbers' Loot" - August 14, 1924 - page 2

"Robbers' Cache Still Unfound" - August 15, 1924 - page 3

"Bandits Still Free After Jail Break" - October 17, 1924 - (Headlines) page 1

"Clues Fail to Give Results" - October 18, 1924 - page 1

"Search Fails to Locate Bandits" - October 19, 1924 - page 2

"Alleged Motor Bandits Try to Regain Liberty" - October 21, 1924 - page 8

"Bandits Rob Bench Store" - October 29, 1924 - page 1

"Officers Fail to Find Traces of Grocery Bandits" - October 30, 1924 - page 12

"Escaped Bandits Bound for Coast, Officers Believe" - October 31, 1924 - page 2

"L. E. Allumbaugh" (political advertisement describing Allumbaugh as sheriff) - November 2, 1924 - Features Section - page 3

"G. O. P. Majority Carries Elam Through Storm" - November 6, 1924 - page 1

"Board of Doctors Probe Into Sanity of Hoagland" - November 9, 1924 - page 1

"Loop Carmen Rout Bandits" - November 13, 1924 - page 1

"Sheriff's Posse Combing County for Two Escapes" - November 19, 1924 - page 1

" 'LET'S KILL HIM," JONES PLEADS WHEN TRUSTY IS TAKEN; LANGER IS AFRAID" Article 1. *"Sheriff Blames Loss of Bandits to State Deputies"* Article 2. *"Dykeman Escapes After Being Held Bandit Prisoner"* - November 20, 1924 - (Headlines) page 1

"Sheriff Thinks Eagle Holdups Out of County" - November 21, 1924 - page 8

"Men Captured at American Falls Not Bank Bandits" - November 22, 1924 - page 2

"Woman Bandit Charged With Bank Robbery" - December 4, 1924 - page 2

"Twin Falls Police Catch Jones; Admits Identity" - December 9, 1924 - page 1

"Jones Held Under Double Guard in Ada County Jail" - December 10, 1924 - page 2

"Arraignment of Bandit Delayed" - December 11, 1924 - page 2

"Jones to Plead Saturday" - December 12, 1924 - page 2

"Bandit Suspects Deny Guilt at Hearing Saturday" - December 14, 1924 - page 2

"Sheriff Expects Langer's Arrest In Los Angles" - December 15, 1924 - page 2

"Langer Nabbed in California, Sheriff Hears" - December 16, 1924 - page 1

"Woman to Turn State's Evidence, Says Prosecution" - December 18, 1924 - page 2

"Douglass Woman Freed By Court" - December 19, 1924 - page 8

"Endsley Admits Being Accessory to Eagle Holdup" - December 21, 1924 - Page 6

"Langer Back in Ada County Jail" - December 22, 1924 - page 2

"Bobbed Hair Bandit Gets 10 Year Sentence" - December 22, 1924 - page 1

"Court Paroles Bandit Driver" - December 23, 1924 - page 10

"Langer Enters Not Guilty Plea" - December 27, 1924 - page 2

"Date Fixed For Bandits' Trial" - December 28, 1924 - page 2

"Progress Marks Year At Prison" - January 4, 1925 - Sports Section - page 4

"Dora Douglass Marries Alleged Bank Bandit" - January 6, 1925 - page 1

"Elam Probing Bandit Wedding" - January 7, 1925 - page 2

"State Opposes Venue Change in Bandit Case" - January 16, 1925 - page 12

"Bandits Write Final Chapter in Bank Drama" - January 18, 1925 - page 1

"Jones Goes to State Prison" - January 20, 1925 - page 1

"Jurko is Hanged at State Prison" - July 9, 1926 - page 1

"Fail in Break at Idaho Pen" - August 4, 1926 - page 1

"Prison's Tragedy Pathetic" - February 5, 1927 - page 1

"Warden Foils Prison Break" - July 22, 1928 - page 1

"124 Idaho Prisoners Petition Pardon Board" - July 2, 1930 - page 12

"Boise Pastor Hurls Attack at Idaho Prison Injustices" - February 23, 1931 - page 5

"Thomas Gets Prison Post" - February 25, 1931 - page 1

"Penitentiary Guards Fear Little Danger of Outbreak Similar to Illinois" - March 19, 1931 - page 1

"Prison Needs Drastic Rule" - April 1, 1931 - page 3

"Pardon Releases 18" - April 4, 1931 - page 1

"Prison Warden Details Plans for Convicts" - April 12, 1931 – page 9

"Warden Details Convicts' Needs" - April 24, 1931 - page 5

"Work Shirts In Vivid Hue" - June 4, 1931 - page 1

"Warden Flays Welfare Chief" - June 4, 1931 - page 1

"Warden Thomas Reveals Plan For Penitentiary Cleanup; Lukens Scores Past System" - May 13, 1931 - page 1

"Lydia Battles Against Odds" - May 13, 1931 - page 1

"Ross Against Probe at Pen" - June 12, 1931 - page2

"Thomas Prepares Code of Convicts In State Prison" - June 20, 1931 - page 1

"Pen Completes Interior Work" - June 27, 1931 - page 2

"Many Prisoners Demand Pardons" - June 30, 1931 - page 5

"Convict Hangs Self at Prison" - July 14, 1931 - page 1

"Twin Falls Nab Suspect Trio In Holdup Case" - August 20, 1931 - page 6

"Idaho Penitentiary Has Yet to Experience It's First Big Prison Break" - November 15, 1931 - page 1

"Weyerhaeuser Family Pleads With Kidnapers To Return Young Son" - May 26, 1935 - page 1

"Silence Shrouds Dread Fate of Kidnaped Tacoma Child; Guns Blaze In Pasadena Plot" - May 27, 1935 - page 1

"Kidnapers of Child Believed Contacted; Federals Seek Trio" - May 28,1935 - page 1

"Weyerhaeuser Lad's Parents Anxiously Await His Return" - May 29, 1935 - page 1

"Deadline Fails to Bring Word of Boys Fate" - May 30, 1935 – page 1

"Police Reveal Kidnap Gang to Return Boy" - May 31, 1935 – page 1

"Desperate Kidnapers Release Ransomed Weyerhaeuser Lad; Law Army Hunts Karpis Gang" - June 2, 1935 - page 1

"Suspected Kidnapers Escape Guarded Trap in Oregon Area; Great Manhunt Spreads Wider" - June 3, 1935 - page 1

"Abandoned Kidnap Auto Found On Seattle Street; New Outlaw Gang Sought" - June 4, 1935 - page 1

"Kidnap Ransom Bill Spent For Train Fare In Oregon; Trail of Gang Warming Up" - June 5, 1935 - page 1

"Kidnap Victim Joins In Hunt For Criminals" - June 6, 1935 – page 1

"Agents Seek 'Gray House' in Gang Hunt" - June 7, 1935 - page 1

"False Report Brings Kidnap Hunt to Idaho" - June 8, 1935 - page 1

"Weyerhaeuser Ransom Bills Found in Utah" - June 9, 1935 – page 1

"KIDNAPERS CAPTURED IN SALT LAKE" article 1. *"Kidnap Arrest Follows Week of Excitement"* article 2. *"Man and Wife Make Confession of Weyerhaeuser Child Abduction; Former Idaho Prisoners Involved"* - (Headlines) June 10, 1935 - page 1

"Law Moves Swiftly To Nab Remainder of Kidnap Band; Montana Draws Net Closer" - June 11, 1935 - page 1

"Mahan Set Free In Idaho Despite Order For Arrest; Mrs. Waley's Trial July 5" - June 25, 1935 - page 1

"Idaho Prison Once Dungeon" - April 22, 1937 - page 1

"Wise Convict Wins Rewards" - April 23, 1937 - page 1

"Laws Provide Pardon Power" - April 24, 1937 - page 1

"Politics Rule Pardon Board" - April 25, 1937 - page 1

"Convicts Fear Dark Dungeon" - April 26, 1937 - page 1

"Idle Convicts Cause Trouble" - April 27, 1937 - page 1

"Low Pay Hurts Prison System" - April 28, 1937 - page 1

Twin Falls Daily
"Wrecked Automobile Blazes Trail To Booze Cache Near City Limits--Auto's Driver in Hospital--Slim Bush on Guard" - September 16, 1920 - page1

"Harrison Loses in Booze Trade" - October 12, 1920 - page 1

"Jones and Gonzales Released From Jail" - December 13, 1920 - page 1

"Bandits Hold Up Jerome Eating House, Report" - January 21, 1921 - page1

"Gun used With Deadly Effect" - January 22, 1921 - page 1

"Slagle Holds Reticent Mien" - February 7, 1921 - page 8

"Murder Against Slagle" - February 5, 1921 - page 1

"Bank Official is Sought by Authorities" - June?? 1921 - page 2

"Prisoner Escapes At Portal of His Prison" - June 21, 1921 - page 1

"Banker Ordered to Serve Penal Term in Prison" - July 2, 1921 - page 8

"Officers Find Slim Kendrick Hiding at Buhl" - July 14, 1921 – page 1

"Three Hold up Bank at Eagle and Get $2700" - August 12, 1924 - page 1

"Boise Robbers in Jailbreak" - October 16, 1924 - page 1

"Police Arrest Bandit Suspect in Twin Falls" - December 9, 1924 - page 1

"Officers Nab 3 For Robbery of Montello Store" - August 20, 1931 – page 1

"Montello Bandit Suspects Return to Face Charges" - August 27, 1931 - page 2

"Two Motorists of Twin Falls Drown In Low Line Canal" - September 10, 1931 - page 1

Books

"Dillinger - The Untold Story" - by G. Russell Girardin with
William J. Helmer
William J. Helmer and Suzanne Girardin (pages 16, 82 - 102)

"A Farewell to the Rock ESCAPE FROM ALCATRAZ' - by J.
Campbell Bruce McGraw-Hill Book Company (pages 23, 61, 62,
64-69)

"Idaho Chinese Lore" - by Sister M. Alfreda Elsensohn O. S. B.,
M. S (Ed.)
Idaho Corporation of Benedictine Sisters (Chapter Thirteen -
Chinese in the Boise Area)

"Lady Bluebeard" - by William C. Anderson
Fred Pruitt Books

"Pots 'O Gold" - by Matt R. Penrose
A. Carlisle & Co. of Nevada (pages IX - XIII, 112, 113, 125 - 139,
197 - 233)

Miscellaneous

"Old Idaho Penitentiary 1870-1973 -A Walking Tour Guide" - by Jil
M. Sevy

"The Oregon Boot" - by Gene K. - Shadow Newspaper
Centennial Issue 1959

"The Biennial Reports of the Idaho State Penitentiary"
Fiscal Years 1921 - 1922, 1923 - 1924, 1925 - 1926, 1927 - 1928,
1929 - 1930, 1931 - 1932, 1933 - 1934

"The Biennial Reports of the Supt. Nevada State Police and Warden State Penitentiary"
Fiscal Years 1929 - 1930, 1931 - 1932, 1932 - 1934, 1934 - 1936, 1936 - 1938

Newspaper Reprints

SHERIFFS SCOUR COUNTRY FOR THREE BANDITS WHO LOOTED EAGLE BANK

Masked Men Get $2700 and Escape in Touring Car After Locking Cashier and Daughter in Vault; Boise Taxi Driver Says He Was Forced at Point of Gun to Drive Robber Car; "Drive Like Hell," He Says Were His Orders.

Sheriffs of two states were Monday night scouring the country for three bandits who raided the bank of Eagle Monday morning in broad daylight, took $2700 from the strong box, locked E. H. Fikkan, cashier of the bank, and his 18-year-old daughter, Margaret, in the vault and escaped in a Boise taxicab.

Meanwhile H. F. (Hank) Endsley, taxicab man and driver of the bandit car, is held by the Ada county sheriff for investigation. He said he had been held by the robbers all night in a deserted shack and was forced to drive the car to the scene of the robbery and then to "drive like hell" to a point beyond Middleton, where the hold-up men had cached a dust-covered Hudson roadster in which they made their escape.

Three persons in addition to Endsley, were held early this morning for investigation by L. E. Allumbaugh, Ada county sheriff. After several hours of questioning, the persons were locked up and the sheriff was unable to give a statement as to whether he was following a warm clue. The persons held, two men and a woman, are E. L. Jones, Dora Douglas and Chet

Langer. All three were arrested in Boise and gave their addresses as Boise.

Scuttling under the low plate glass windows of the bank, two of the bandits, masked with black handkerchiefs, appeared in the bank door suddenly at about 9:15 Monday morning.

Cashier Fikkan had just opened the vault and its strong box preparatory to starting business and was at the moment sitting at his desk in the front of the bank. Margaret Fikkan, his daughter and assistant, was at an adding machine back of the teller's window,

When one of the masked men, covering Fikkan with a gun, commanded him to throw up his hands, the girl ran into the open vault. The bandits crashed through the low swinging door in front of the banker's desk, backed him into the main room back of the grill and out of sight of the street and ordered the girl out of the vault.

She came but refused to put up her hands.

While one of the men was rifling the strong box and the other covering the man and girl, Fikkan endeavored to get a view of the bandit's car parked in the street east of the bank building. He saw a shiny big Cadillac with a driver unmasked and a crouching figure in the rear seat which he thought to be a woman.

But the man with the gun, seeing the direction of his gaze, growled, "you're looking around too much," and faced him to the wall, meanwhile calling to his confederate in the vault, "Make it snappy."

The other dashed out, his arms loaded with currency and coin.

Lock Bankers In Vault.

Then both banker and daughter were marched into the vault. The door clanged shut. The heavy bolts were shot home with a twist of the door handle. Fikkan and his daughter were prisoners.

Meanwhile the bandits stuffed their plunder into a sack and rushed for the door.

The screen must have caught shut, for it developed after the robbery that in their haste to get away they had broken the frame of the door and ripped two of the hinges from their fastenings.

The robbers scrambled into the big car. A quick order was given the driver and in a few seconds the car was going at high speed on the pavement leading toward Star, Middleton and Caldwell.

While all this was happening, Mrs. Reta Moretson, whose house commands a view of the bank and who saw the masked men enter, was pounding on the door of a store near the bank. There was no answer to her pounding so she rushed to the nearby house of Mrs. George Witte crying "The bank's being robbed." Mrs. Witte immediately called the Boise police and so it happened that the police knew of the robbery in the very moments when it was taking place.

Others, too, had see the car. One of them, Miss Dorthy Perkins, daughter of the proprietor of a filling station near the bank, was sure that the crouched figure in the back seat of the car was a woman.

Fikkan Releases Self.

While the bandit car was speeding toward Star and the sheriff's car was on the way from Boise, Banker Fikkan, in the stifling vault dimly lighted by a single electric bulb, was attacking the mechanism of the lock with a screwdriver. It required only the removal of a few screws to release the catch which held the heavy system of bolts in place. This done, the banker succeeded by tugging at the bolts in getting them out of their sockets and the door swung open into fresh air and daylight.

Miss Fikkan, in a nervous and distraught condition, was turned over to women in the crowd which quickly collected. The banker turned to appraisal of the damage.

To inquirers he said:

"I kept a screwdriver and some pliers in the vault in case such an emergency should occur.

Thought Time Had Come.

"It was my first experience with a bank robbery in spite of many years in this business. But just as soon as I saw those masked faces, I said to myself, "My time has come."

"A check-up shows the robbers got away with $2700. This was in currency and coin. No securities were touched. After the robbery we found rolls of coin and gold which had dropped in the road when the robbers got into the car. The value of this was $175.

"The losses are fully covered by insurance."

The pretty bob-headed daughter said;

"I saw the heads of the robbers as they sneaked past the window. I was not alarmed. I thought it was children playing in the street.

"I really was not afraid for myself, but I thought they were going to shoot father.

"I don't know why I didn't put up my hands.

"One such experience is enough for me."

Immediately after the robbery Eagle business men offered to the bank such amounts of cash and currency as they could spare. Business went on, but not as usual. The bank was never so overrun with visitors as it was Monday.

Approximately six hours after the robbery of the bank, "Hank" Endsley, Boise, driver of the Cadillac car which carried the robbers and which had been in their possession, according to Endsley, since about 10 o'clock Sunday night, reported to the Ada county sheriff's office. He had been searching with deputy sheriffs from Canyon county for the holdups since they alighted from his car about a mile north of Middleton and ordered him to turn back.

Endsley Covered With Gun.

Endsley who is employed as chauffeur by the Central livery, in his statement to the sheriff and a Statesman representative, said that Sunday night he received a call from Twenty-first and Jefferson streets about 10 o'clock and when he arrived there three masked men rushed to the car, and covering him with revolvers, ordered him to drive to State street and out the Valley road to eagle. From Eagle they went west several miles, then south

across the Boise river and up a hill, then west about four or five miles, after which they turned north to Star, then went back up the highway to Darling station and turned north again, reaching a vacant house and what looked like a barn. Here Endsley said he was ordered to stop.

"One man held me there," said Endsley, "and with a warning, 'Eyes ahead and no moves,' he kept me covered with his gun while the other two men went towards the house.

"In a short time the tow men returned and marched me into the house. They locked me in a closet, where I remained until they called me out to go to Eagle."

When they drove back to Eagle Monday morning, Endsley claims, the masked bandits still had him covered, and when the man riding with him in the front seat alighted to go into the bank with one of those in the rear seat, the remaining bandit, Endsley said, kept him covered with a gun.

"When the robbers came out of the bank," Endsley said, "they carried something that looked like a flour sack. It contained the money."

Drive Like Hell.

"Drive like hell!" was Endsley's order then, and he drove to a point west of Middleton to the top of a hill, where a dust-covered Hudson speedster was standing in the road. According to Endsley, the masked men got out of the car and into the speedster, and started north towards New Plymouth.

Endsley says he drove quickly to Caldwell, where he gave the alarm to the sheriff's office. Deputies boarded the car with him and drove north on the highway toward New

Plymouth. About a mile out they met a tourist car, and a woman passenger told them they had been there, fixing a puncture, since 8 o'clock in the morning, and that no such car as the officers descried had passed them.

The searching party then returned to Caldwell, Endsley says, and getting another deputy, drove out to the Pickle Butte bridge and walked there a while, making an investigation. Then he returned to Caldwell, left the Canyon county officers, and drove on into Boise.

Endsley could give but a meager description of the bandits. He says one was clad in khaki trousers and shirt, another was dressed in khaki trousers and blue shirt, and the third had on overalls and a blue shirt. The men, Endsley says, were of medium build, the stature of two of them being about five feet seven inches and the other man about five feet ten inches. He could not describe their facial appearance or color of their hair.

Following Endsley's arrival at the county jail, he was subjected to nearly an hour's questioning by Sheriff Allumbaugh and Police Captains Swanholm and Stoops. His story to the officers and that given to The Statesman reporter practically coincided.

Sheriff Allumbaugh and city detectives say they are skeptical of the story of Endsley. Captain Stoops of the police force says he saw Endsley in his car a short while before midnight and Elmer Overholser, plain clothes officer, says that he saw Endsley in his car with two passengers at Eleventh and Grove streets at 12:10 o'clock Monday morning.

Clues From Horseshoe Bend.

Shortly after 3 o'clock Monday afternoon Sheriff Allumbaugh returned from Horseshoe Bend after following clues to that section. Information had been given to the sheriff soon after his arrival at the scene of the robbery that the holdups were headed towards Horseshoe Bend, and that country was scoured by sheriff and deputies.

Sheriffs of surrounding counties were informed of the robbery within a short time after receipt of the news in Boise by Sheriff Allumbaugh.

Monday afternoon the sheriff at Baker Ore. telephoned he had intercepted a touring car coming into Baker from Idaho, and was holding the passengers, as they could not give a straight account of their drive from Pocetello Sunday evening and their whereabouts early Monday morning. After getting a description of the occupants and checking up on the car, Sheriff Allumbaugh decided that it would be useless to hold the parties.

Endsley is a son of Thomas Endsley of Boise and has resided in this city for 14 years. He is married, has a wife and two children, and lives at 1708 North Fourteenth Street.

There were no women in the bandit gang, in the opinion of W. B. Rainey of Boise, who was spending the night in Eagle, and passed the robbers twice.

"I first observed the party at 9 o'clock Monday morning," Mr. Rainey said. "I was at the Eagle service station when a machine, driven by Endsley, whom I recognized, drove slowly into eagle from the west, apparently bound for Boise. There were two men in the back seat and a third man, beside the driver, on the front seat. I just throught Endsley had a bunch of drunks, whom he was sobering up. The faces of all were carefully muffled. They slowed down, almost stopping, In front of the bank, then drove east.

"When I was on the east edge of Eagle, headed for Boise, the party passed us again, this time headed west. It was 20 minutes later, and I judge they had driven to Edgewood and back. That was just before the robbery. The way all had their faces covered gave me the same suspicion, that they were drunks trying to sober up. The next I noticed was when the sheriff's car passed us at Pierce Park, going at a terrific speed.

"The man sitting in the front seat with Endsley had on a brown coat, the collar of which had been turned up around his face, and a light cloth summer hat. Of the two in the rear, I noticed nothing save that one wore a light suit and the other a dark one. They also were curiously muffled up and did not seem to want to attract any attention."

Reprinted from The Idaho Statesman, August 12, 1924

CHARGES OF ROBBERY FILED AGAINST FOUR IN EAGLE BANK CASE

Former Convict, Waitress, Driver and Rancher Held
Chet Langer, One of Those Accused, Confesses to His Part in Affair and Implicates Others; Cashier Identifies Two Men in Party.

Six hours after charges of robbery had been files Tuesday afternoon against four suspects held by Ada county authorities in connection with the robbing of the Bank of Eagle Monday morning, Chet Langer, son of a Boise valley rancher and one of the suspects, confessed to Laurel E. Elam, Ada county prosecuting attorney, to his part in the theft and Ada county peace officers were confident Tuesday night that they held a correct solution to the robbery.

Charges of robbery were filed by Mr. Elam against "Hank" Endsley, driver of the Cadillac automobile that figured in the robbery of $2772 from the bank. Dora Douglass, bobbed haired waitress, in whose trunk at the farm home of Orrin Summers, south of Star, where the two Douglass children were being cared for, was found $29.50 in pennies, thought to have been taken from the bank; Langer and Oliver Jones, former convict at the Idaho state prison. Carl Norris, justice of the peace, held a preliminary hearing at the jail. The prisoners were committed to the custody of the sheriff under $20,000 property bond or cash bail in the sum of $10,000.

Langer in his confession states that Monday shortly after midnight the party went to a shack north of Eagle on the Pearl road and stayed there until almost 9 o'clock Monday morning when they drove to Eagle and he and Jones went into the bank. Both had guns, Langer said, and they picked up the money and getting into the car they drove west to a point where the woman and Jones got out near the Summers home and he walked up the road a short distance, then boarded a car, went around the loop and got back home. The Douglass woman and Jones carried the bank loot to the Summers' home, Langer said in his confession.

Tuesday night at 10 o'clock the sheriff's office had recovered all but $7.75 of the plunder of the bank robbery at Eagle Monday morning. Shortly after 10 o'clock Tuesday night $1947 was found in another trunk in the Summers' home, south of Star, where $29.50 was found earlier in the day among belongings of the Douglass woman on the second floor of the house where Mrs. Douglass had her trunks.

The money was found in the denominations of currency in the sum of $1502 and the remainder in silver and small coins.

Sheriff's officers were continuing the search at midnight Tuesday.

Keeping ceaseless vigil over the maneuvers of a Cadillac car which had been reported to police headquarters as parking in front of the Kurrie flats at 401 South Tenth Street near midnight Sunday with the occupants acting suspiciously, city detectives of Boise, in conjunction with Sheriff L. E. Allumbaugh and deputies, were able Tuesday afternoon, they asserted, to unravel the mystery of the bank robbery at Eagle Monday morning.

Discovery Clinches Case.

Following the arrest by the city police department and the sheriff's forces late Monday night and with Endsley already held incommunicado in the county jail, the solving of the robbery shortly after 9 o'clock Monday morning when E. H. Fikkan, cashier, and his daughter, Margaret, were marched into a vault while the robbers looted the bank of $2722, was approaching a crisis. At 2 o'clock Tuesday afternoon, when Carl Burke, assistant county attorney, who has been active in the search for the robbers with Deputy Sheriff H. W. Brown, reported recovery of $29.50 in pennies found in a sack in the Summers' home, it was asserted by officers that the mystery was solved.

Developments came thick and fast after this discovery.

First, Dora Douglass, who has been employed as a waitress at a Boise restaurant, and had been release earlier Tuesday morning by the sheriff on her own recognizance, was brought to the county jail, and then Chet Langer, who had been held in the city jail, was taken to the county bastille. Oliver Jones, former convict, had been in the county prison since Monday night. Endsley at this time was in the detention ward with orders to deputies that no one should see him.

Cashier Identifies Two Men.

E. H. Fikkan, cashier of the Eagle bank, had been telephoned to come to town at once when the officers were convinced there was no doubt of the guilt of those under arrest.

When Oliver Jones, released from the penitentiary April 12 of this year, after serving an indeterminate sentence of one to 15 years for burglary from Jerome county, was brought from the jail and escorted into the yard, Cashier Fikkan, after a close survey of the prisoner, asserted;

"This is the man that covered my daughter and me with the gun. I can tell from his actions and his movements, and he has a way of crouching just as he did when he placed the revolver close to my body."

Called to the city jail to identify another suspect, Mr. Fikkan, when he saw Langer being photographed, exclaimed, "this is the bird that looted the vault and carried out the money. I am positive of his identification."

255

A Bandit Called Derby

When a money sack marked $500 was brought in by the deputies it was thought that the bag contained $500 in silver, but on being counted by Mr. Fikkan in the presence of sheriff's officers and The Statesman's representatives, it was found that the sack contained $29.50 in pennies

According to bank officials, the money taken Monday by the robbers was $1600 in currency from the safe $700 in currency from the counter in the bank and about $400 in small stuff, or a total of $2722

Reprinted from The Idaho Statesman, August 13, 1924

BANDITS STILL FREE AFTER JAIL BREAK

Chet Langer and Oliver Jones Saw Way from Cell, Overpower Watchman in Ada County Jail, and Makes Escape; Jailer, Locked In, Liberates Self and Gives Alarm.

Oliver Jones and Chet Langer, alleged to have robbed the Bank of Eagle August 11, were still at large early Friday morning following their daring escape Thursday at 2 a. m. from the Ada county jail after sawing their way from their cell and overpowering Charles R. Stahl, night watchman.

The night watchman had answered a call from Charles Smith, serving a sentence for violation of the narcotics act. Smith was locked in the section of the jail known as the "strong room" or "tank," where prisoners charged with major offenses are confined. The jailer conducted Smith to the lavatory, and was about to lock him in again, when Jones, according to Stahl, leaped at him with full force, struck him a stunning blow on the right side of the face, and knocked him against the door post. Langer then struck the helpless watchman over the left eye with a stove lifter. With threats and curses, Stahl says, they dragged him to the cell which they but a few minutes before had occupied, and after pinioning his arms behind him with part of an old shirt, they threw him into the cell with Smith, Jones shouting, as Stahl afterwards related, "Hit him a crack and knock him out, so he'll keep quiet."

The two had made their escape from their cell in the tank by picking the inner spring lock with a screw driver or knife and sawing off the staple holding the outer protective lock with a hacksaw made from an old case knife.

Once out of their cell into the space leading to the jail corridor, the robbers waited until the night watchman had returned from the lavatory with the prisoner, Smith. As Stahl opened the outer door, the two made their assault.

Take Three Revolvers.

When the bandits reached the sheriff's office the gun case was pried open, three revolvers and 100 rounds of ammunition taken and the telephone on the office desk torn from its connection. Drawers in the desk were found open but nothing had been removed.

When a trusty, awakened by Stahl, rushed to the rescue and recovered the key to the outer jail door left by Jones and Langer in their flight, he released the night watchman, who was bleeding profusely from the nose, caused by Jones fist. The blow on the left forehead delivered by Langer with the stove lift shattered the glasses that Stahl was wearing and caused quite a lump on his head.

Stahl was able to report for duty Thursday night and gave The Statesman the following story of the occurrence;

"I was called to the door to the corridor leading into what is known as the 'strong room' or 'tank' about 2 o'clock Thursday morning by Charles Smith, a prisoner serving sentence under the state narcotic law, who had been sleeping in the corridor of this section of the jail, due to crowed conditions in the other

257

part of the prison. Smith said that he wished to go to the lavatory. As a fair light shines in upon the cells from the window in the garage adjoining, I looked in without turning on the lights in the jail proper, and the doors of all the cells seemed to be in perfect condition. I let Smith out into the main hall of the jail building, and not hearing any noise at all from the 'strong room,' I waited for his return.

"When I opened the door to let Smith pass back to his cot, Jones jumped at me with full force and struck me on the right cheekbone, probably with some concealed instrument in his clenched fist, knocked me back against the door jamb, which stunned me, then dragged me in, when Langer reached over and struck me with a stove lifter over the left eye and grabbed both arms.

Arms Tied.

"Langer then pinned my arms and tied them behind me with cloth torn from a shirt, and pushed me back to the cell out of which a short while before they had sawed their way, with a threat of 'knocking me out.' I grabbed at the edge of the door, which closes with a spring lock, as best I could, endeavoring to put the door between myself and my assailants so they could not hit me again.

"Then Jones said 'Hit him a crack and knock him out, so he will keep quiet,' but I pulled the door, and it locked them out from me.

"Both men cursed at both me and Smith, and yelled 'If either of you make any noise for 20 minutes we will kill you both as soon as we get our guns.' "

By working his arms and hands, Mr. Stahl says, he was enabled to stretch the cloth that bound him and get loose. Then he took out his pocket knife and started to work on the spring lock, as the protective lock had been sawed off.

"As soon as I heard the screen door at the entrance of the sheriff's office slam, I yelled to a trusty who does janitor work and who sleeps in the boiler room. I had trouble awakening him, but finally I aroused him and told him to hunt for the keys, as Langer and Jones had escaped.

"The trusty found the key where the prisoners had dropped it, opened the door, and I rushed to the telephone and found that it had been torn out. Then I went to the courtroom upstairs and telephoned the sheriff and notified the police department, then returned to the jail, looked at the clock, and it was 2:25 a. m."

Pursuit Starts.

Within 30 minutes after the alarm was given by the jailer, Sheriff Allumbaugh and all his deputies were at the county jail and early Thursday morning the news of the escape of the bandits was 'broadcast' throughout Idaho and all towns in surrounding states.

The county commissioners authorized a reward of $500 for the capture of the two men or $250 for either of them.

Accompanying the notices of the reward which were rushed to print early Thursday morning were the following descriptions;

Oliver Jones - Age 28 years, height 5 feet 8 inches, weight 130 pounds, complexion pallid, thin face, small blue eyes, light brown hair worn long pompadour, Gold teeth in front. Has several tattoos on his body including one of naked woman on right upper forearm. Finger print classification,

1 Rr 16
1 A 16

Chet Langer - Age 27 years, height 5 feet 7 inches, weight 150 pounds, is well built, Hair dark and wavy, eyes dark brown, small and very keen; will not look you in the eye; scar over right eye about one inch long. Features very sharp and nose pointed.

Caviness "Heard Noise"

A. E. Caviness, under sentence of life imprisonment for the murder of his wife, but held at the county jail pending the outcome of his appeal to the supreme court, occupies a cell in the same section where the jail break occurred and told a reporter for The Statesman Thursday afternoon that he was awakened by the noise and when he looked out thought they were bring in a "drunk."

"I heard Jones say 'get on in, we don't want to have to hurt you.' They repeated this two or three times," said Caviness. "Then Langer lunged through the door and struck the night watchman with his fist and said '_____ get in there, you d_mn fool, we don't want to hurt or kill you.'

"They took the watchman into the cell they got out of," said Caviness. "Jones, telling Langer to keep watch over the jailer, then rushed out to the office. I could hear him opening the desk drawers and breaking open the gun case in the sheriff's office."

Other prisoners confined in the "strong room" are Nick Watkins, awaiting trial for the murder of David F. Jennings; Charles Smith, and Edgar Crane, serving sentence for violation of the narcotics law, and three men sentenced on liquor charges. Outside of Caviness and Smith, who called the jailer to the door, none of the other inmates heard anything of the assault, according to their story to the sheriff Thursday.

Blames Congestion.

"Congested conditions at the county jail are responsible for this affair, and not the sheriff," said Herbert Lemp, county commissioner, Thursday, "and if it had not been necessary to put one of the prisoners held for a minor offense into this section of the jail, with a cot to sleep on in the corridor, the jailer would not have been called to let him out to go to a lavatory in another part of the building."

"Jones has been troublesome to all the officers since his incarceration," said Sheriff Allumbaugh, when discussing the escape, "and he was almost hated by all the other prisoners."

The sheriff said that he and his deputies were well aware that Jones was a desperate character, and took all precautions possible to prevent his escape.

"No changes of any kind were ever made in the cell occupied by Jones and Langer," said the sheriff, "unless two officers were present, and even when serving meals the trusty would usually be accompanied by two of my deputies."

Explains Locks.

Explaining the kind of locks used on the doors or cells in the "strong room" where the escape took place, the sheriff said that the outside door leading to the jail corridor has what is called a present door lock; the main door to cells has a separate lock to each cell, the one in which Langer and Jones were confined had double locks, while the other cells have only one.

Sheriff Allumbaugh also said Thursday that some time ago he had endeavored to have both Jones and Langer removed to the penitentiary for safe keeping, but that Ivan L. Hiller, attorney for the two men, had threatened to institute habeas corpus proceedings in such an event.

When asked about the matter Thursday, Mr. Hiler said that it had been his intention to proceed in the matter as indicated by the sheriff, had his clients been removed to the penitentiary, and he still expressed the opinion that the sheriff had no right to remove the men to the state institution until they were tried.

County officers are still mystified as to just when the sawing of the lock occurred. Experts who were called to the jail early Thursday to investigate conditions and examine the locks, declared that the present locks were easy to saw through and should be replaced at once. The old case knife converted into a hacksaw, they said, could accomplish the work in a short time.

Jones Has Record.

Oliver Jones, considered the arch conspirator in the plot to rob the bank of Eagle who probably planned the jail break, was released from the penitentiary April 12 of this year, on parole, after being sent up from Jerome county, July 27, 1921, to serve an indeterminate sentence of 1 to 15 years for burglary.

According to Sheriff Allumbaugh, Langer has been involved in some petty cases about town but as far as the sheriff can ascertain he has never been in serious trouble until his alleged connection with the Eagle bank robbery.

Ever since the holdup at Eagle the Burns detective agency has been trying to recover the missing loot of $775, working in co-operation with local officers, and it is said that delayed reports from the agency in this matter had caused the county authorities to proceed slowly in regard to bringing the alleged participants to trial.

Robbery August 11.

The Bank of Eagle was robbed Monday morning, August 11, just after it had been opened for business. F. H. Fikkan, cashier, and his daughter, Margaret, were held up at the point of a gun by a masked bandit while another looted the vault and picked up all the money in the cash trays in the office, finally locking the cashier and bookkeeper in the vault and escaping in a waiting automobile. When Mr. Fikkan released himself and daughter from the vault and made a check of all money on hand it was found that the bandits had stolen $2722.

Reprinted from The Idaho Statesman, October 17, 1924

"LET'S KILL HIM," JONES PLEADS WHEN TRUSTY IS TAKEN; LANGER IS AFRAID

Sheriff Blames Loss of Bandits to State Deputies
Independent Posse, Deputized by Order of Governor Moore, Incenses Allumbaugh; Badges Ordered Revoked; Special Deputies Explain Position.

"I want their badges recalled or mine goes in to the county commissioners tonight."

Thus did L. E. Allumbaugh sheriff, declare himself to F. A. Jeter, commissioner of law enforcement. Wednesday night about 5 o'clock upon learning for the first time that the four men had been commissioned as deputies of the state department of law enforcement to aid in the man hunt for Oliver Jones and Chet Langer, Eagle bank robbers who escaped from the Ada county jail October 16.

Within three Hours after Sheriff Allumbaugh made his complaint to Mr. Jeter the four men deputized Tuesday afternoon in Mr. Jeter's absence on authority of Governor C. C. Moore, were ordered to turn in their badges. Mr. Jeter immediately sent a long distance telephone message to the governor who was visiting on a ranch near Eliss. The commissioner's message was:

"The four men deputized yesterday are working independently of Sheriff Allumbaugh. He didn't know they were out until tonight. I think the badges should be called in at once. Can I have your permission?" The governor's answer was, "Yes."

Their message had to be taken to the governor by messenger and it was shortly after 8 o'clock when Mr. Jeter received a reply.

The sheriff got in from the chase about 4 o'clock in the after noon having been out almost constantly since 11 o'clock Tuesday morning, he said.

"These men have been a hindrance in the work of running down these criminals and it was only a miracle that some, if not all four of them, were not shot last night," he said. "I did not know they were deputized until 4 o'clock this afternoon."

The badges were not issued by Mr. Jeter as he was out of his office practically all day Tuesday. The four men commissioned were:

Emmit Pfost, sheriff-elect, Henry Swanholm, Boise detective captain, Oliver Day, Boise police captain, and Thomas Bowler. Their badges were issued by F. E. Lukens, chief clerk to Mr. Jeter, on the authority of the governor.

The four men went voluntarily to Mr. Jeter's office

Tuesday afternoon and asked to be deputized, but in Mr. Jeters absence Mr. Lukens did not want to act himself and asked Governor Moore and A. H. Conner, attorney general, to consider the matter. Both the governor and attorney general said they wanted to see the bandits caught and finally the governor authorized Mr. Lukens to issue the commissions.

It seems that the governor thought they were to work in connection with the sheriff's office, although the sheriff's office was not called even after Mr. Pfost suggested, at the conference of the four men with the governor, that Mr. Allumbaugh be notified, Mr. Luken said.

Blames Independents.

"I consider, " Sheriff Allumbaugh told Mr. Jeter, "that these four men caused my forces to lose those two criminals because we lost several hours in acquiring additional men and rifles to surround a house in which we were positive the refugees were hiding only to find that the men we had thought were the bandits were the independent deputies of the department of law enforcement. And if the men I sent to the penitentiary to get long range rifles had returned 10 minutes sooner one or more of those deputies would have been killed because I gave orders to bring the bandits dead or alive and the distance was too great to distinguish."

The sheriff says he is practically convinced that Langer and Jones boarded a freight train near Orchard at about 9:30 o'clock Tuesday night and that if he hadn't wasted so much time on the false trail caused by the four independent deputies, he would have had an even chance to capture the bandits.

Both Mr. Pfost and Mr. Bowler called The Statesman Wednesday night to give their side of the affair. Mr. Bowler, when called by The Statesman, would not tell whether he was deputized or not, but later admitted that he was.

Mr. Pfost said that the deputies were sworn at about 3:30 o'clock Tuesday afternoon and would have gotten the bandits except that the sheriff's men got there first and as he said "scared them away."

He said the fact that the bandits were in the cabin had been reported to the sheriff on Saturday. Sunday and Monday and no action had been taken. When the governor was told of this, Mr. Pfost said, he communicated that he wanted to see the bandits taken.

"I wanted to notify the sheriff that we had been appointed deputies," he continued, "but the man who was to give us the information about where the bandits were refused to tell us if the sheriff was in any way connected with the matter. He also refused to tell us unless he was promised the full reward. I was asked to go by Mr. Bowler and of course none of us was to get any salary or any part of the reward."

Reprinted from The Idaho Statesman, November 20, 1924

Dykeman Escapes After Being Held Bandit Prisoner

Tied to Bed in Deserted Farm House, But Cuts Off Bonds; Eagle Bank Bandits Out of Country, Came Back to Pull Job, They Told Him

Threatened with instant death after his capture, and driven at the point of a gun, Jack Dykeman, trusty in the Ada county jail, escaped Wednesday morning form Chet Langer and Oliver Jones, Eagle bank bandits, who broke jail October 16 and set in motion machinery of justice in all of south Idaho for their recapture. Guards Wednesday afternoon were watching strategic points in an endeavor to cut off their escape, and descriptions had been wired to every town along Union Pacific railroad.

"Let's kill him," Dykeman declared Jones said, when they had dragged him into the cabin they were occupying. Langer, Dykeman said, dissuaded his partner only after an argument.

Dykeman was taken prisoner by the bandits Tuesday afternoon. H. W. Brown, deputy sheriff, and Dykeman started out on tips from ranchers in the Orchard neighborhood that two men had been staying in a deserted cabin near the main line tunnel. They were strangers and their actions aroused suspicion.

Reaching the cabin, two miles west of the main line tunnel on the road to Orchard where the highway turns into Isaacs gulch, Brown and Dykeman cut off from the road, approaching the cabin from the south or rear side.

Dykeman Went Ahead.

"Go on ahead; they don't know you, and if there is anyone in the cabin, ask the road to Orchard," Brown instructed the trusty. Dykeman circled the house, approaching from the opposite side, or north, and was shut off from Brown by the house.

"They grabbed me and took my gun away," Dykeman told a Statesman reporter Wednesday. "I recognized them right away in spite of their new beards and general disreputable appearance.

"Jones wanted to kill me at once; said it would save trouble and teach other to look out for them; but Langer interfered. He said they were in hot water enough, without adding any more to their troubles. So, after they had argued awhile, Jones gave in.

Saw Posse Passing.

"They put a gun on me and marched me out of the cabin and to the southeast, along a little draw, where we lay in hiding while the posse was hunting. The posse went up the draw instead of coming down.

"Then about dusk, we went over the hills and came to a ranch building (identified by officers as the T. R. Wilson ranch), where they broke in, looking for food. The place was deserted, so they took me upstairs and tied me to a bed, and lit an oil lamp, while they went clear through the place.

"One of them, I don't remember which, saw a light flickering in the distance, and they began to untie me and then put out the light, ready to move. When I got my hands free I reached into my side overall pocket, got out my knife and put it under me on the bed."

The two waited for some time, Dykeman said, then decided to tie him up and leave him in the Wilson home. They went off after extinguishing the light.

Cut Off Ropes.

"I worked my hands around under me, got the knife I had hidden, worked it open and began to saw on the ropes with which I was tied." Dykeman continued. "I cut my hand, and the blood hindered me some, but finally I got loose."

He did not know what time it was, he said, but estimated it from later events as shortly after midnight. Going out of the house he walked around it to get his bearings, then locating the lights of Orchard in the distance he started in that direction. Arrived at the station, he wired at once to Boise, telling of his safety and giving a complete description of the bandits.

Jones, according to a description furnished officers by Dykeman, has grown sideburns half way down his face. He is wearing a light cap, blue overalls, black shoes and a brown mackinaw. Langer has a mustache, a light cap, a brown lumberjack shirt, blue bib overalls and black shoes.

In the meantime Deputy Brown, hidden behind the brow of a small hill about a quarter of a mile from the house, had seen Dykeman go around the corner and disappear. Shortly after three men came out and started drown the draw mentioned.

Too far away to shoot, Brown turned back to the road, a half mile away, and started toward Boise. On the way he met L. E. Allumbaugh, Ada county sheriff, and a posse, and they took up the search, looking, as Dykeman said, at the wrong end of the draw.

The posse returned to Boise, and reorganized, leaving shortly after midnight Tuesday. Fruitless search all the morning convinced them that the two had resorted to a ruse practiced once before when the chase grew too warm, and had "hopped" a freight to get out of the neighborhood temporarily.

The station agent at Orchard, Wednesday morning found on his door a piece of envelope, evidently taken from the Wilson home, as it was addressed to Wilson and on the back was printed;

"You will find Jack Dykeman at Tom Wilson ranch tied up in the house. Send someone to turn him loose."

In formation gleaned by Dykeman from the men's conversation led to the arrest Wednesday of Jerry Firestone, 40, Nampa, as one of the bandits confederates, but authorities declared after a through questioning that evidence was so slight they might be forced to release Firestone. Carl A. Burke, assistant prosecuting attorney, went to Nampa to conduct the examination.

Firestone, authorities said, denied any connection with the case, and declared he was in Bowmont at the time of the bank robbery. He was arrested at 5 o'clock, Tuesday morning and has been in the Napa jail since.

The bandits' food supply was running short, authorities said Dykeman told them, but they were expecting a fresh shipment Tuesday afternoon. Apparently their confederates in Boise were warned of the impending raid, sheriff's deputies said, since Dykeman declared the two were seriously concerned over failure of the food to arrive. Outside of food he declared they were well supplied. They each have a revolver in addition to the shotgun they took from Dykeman.

For ammunition they have five shells in the shotgun, deputies said, as well as what cartridges they stole from the sheriff's office the night of their escape. Some of these have been used, apparently, killing rabbits for food, and a box of shells was left behind in their haste, but deputies estimated each had a box of cartridges with his revolver.

Jones and Langer, Dykeman said, had assumed less of a "hard boiled" attitude in their recent exploits to turn suspicion away from them. Knowing they were regarded generally as desperate characters, the trusty said they told him, they had striven to make their later holdups committed mostly for the bare necessities of life, appear the work of much less dangerous persons.

"We aren't going to leave this neighborhood for awhile," Dykeman declares they told him; "We have one more job to pull off in Boise before we pull our freight."

They gave no hint as to just what this job was, Dykeman said, but repeated the remark as if to impress it on him. They were safely away once before, they told the trusty, but came back for this job. They were referring, officers think, to the time when they were reported to have ridden as far as Huntington on train No. 28.

Though they conversed freely before him, Dykeman said they did not refer to any of their "jobs" and merely addressed him occasionally, ignoring him most of the time.

Lived On Rabbits.

The cabin, Dykeman says, is about 10 by 20 feet, and is divided into two rooms, one a kitchen, barely large enough to get into, and the other a living room. In the front room was a double bed, fitted with army blankets, a stove, a few dishes and pans, some groceries, rice, jam, flapjack flour and a few cans. The house itself stands on the brow of a slight eminence. Behind it is a smaller shed.

Rabbits have been added to the fare of the fugitives, Dykeman says, some skeletons and some half-eaten portions still remaining in the room while he was there. That both were getting short on rations, he declare, was proved by the way they grabbed at and downed two raw onions, the only food found in the Wilson house.

Dykeman returned to Boise with members of the sheriff's posse, who went to Orchard by automobile after him.

A Bandit Called Derby

"The big mistake," members of the posse declared on their return from the man hunt Wednesday noon, "came at the very first when we refused to be much impressed by stories that Jones and Langer were in the shack. Had we really felt there was a chance of finding them in the cabin we would never have sent the two men alone after them, but it was more a matter of form to check up on every angle that they were sent out. we have received so many false alarms on these two that we were not properly impressed by this story."

Anonymous letters by the score purporting to tell where the jail breakers could be found, have been investigated, without result, it was said, and this has induced "more or less a careless attitude" on the part of the searchers

Reprinted from The Idaho Statesman, November 20, 1924

POLICE ARREST BANDIT SUSPECT IN TWIN FALLS

Man Wanted In Connection With Bank Robbery at Eagle Captured; May Also Have Held Up Street Car.

A watch corresponding in description and number to the one taken from the conductor when an interurban car was robbed near Boise recently, has been traced by P. O. Herriman, Twin Falls chief of police, to the possession of Oliver J. Jones, 27, one of the alleged robbers of the Eagle, Idaho bank on August 11 last, who escaped October 16, last from the Ada county jail at Boise, and who was captured here Monday by a police squad led by Chief Herriman. Jones was Monday afternoon delivered into the custody of Sheriff L. E. Allumbaugh of Ada county, who hurried here by motor on being advised that Jones had been captured.

Jones readily admitted his identity. He declined to tell anything of the whereabouts of Chet Langer, who is alleged to have participated in the Eagle bank robbery and who escaped with Jones from the Ada county jail. In reply to inquiry as to Langer he countered with a laugh and question. "The chief hasn't caught him yet, has he?"

Found In Bed

The police at 8:30 o'clock Monday morning arrested Jones in a dwelling on Second avenue south occupied by Roy Standlee, where Jones said, he had stayed since last Friday, although, he said he had been in Twin Falls for about 10 days. Jones was in bed when the police, weapons in hand, entered the room. His right hand was under his pillow where the officers found a 32-20 caliber revolver that was later identified as one taken from the Ada county jail at the time of the escape of Jones and Langer.

"We got you now, Jones." Chief of Police Herriman said, covering the fugitive with his Winchester rifle while Patrolman Del Kennlson stood in the doorway with drawn revolver. "I guess that's right," Jones replied with a laugh.

Over Confident

When interviewed at the city jail while awaiting the arrival of the officers to take him back to Boise, Jones expressed the belief that his capture has been the result of over-confidence on his own part. He characterized as "bunk" published stories that a "trusty" prisoner seeking to effect capture of Jones and Langer had been kidnapped by them and threatened with death.

"That fellow was playing for a pardon" Jones said. "We never saw him after we left the jail."

Jones denied that any lock was sawed by himself or Langer when they escaped from the Ada county jail, and exhibited amusement over published pictures of the broken lock.

"We got out of jail," Jones said, "after we 'stuck up' the night watchman with a dummy *gun that I had whittled out of a piece of wood and covered with tinfoil cigar wrappers so that it glistened like a gun."*

Jones stated that after the escape he had written to Sheriff Allumbaugh a letter telling how the escape was accomplished and that he sent a copy of the letter to the Idaho Statesman, but that no reference to it had been published.

Jones told of staying in Boise and vicinity for several days after breaking jail. He indicated familiarity with newspaper accounts of the jail break and pursuit.

Saw Sheriff Go By

"We stood one evening on the street in Boise and saw the sheriff and two deputies carrying rifles drive by in a car," he said. On another occasion he said, he had hidden behind a sagebrush "like an ostrich" when members of the sheriff's posse passed within a short distance of him.

He referred to this circumstance when Sheriff Allumbaugh snapped handcuffs on his wrist Monday afternoon preparatory to the return trip to Boise.

"I'm not going to try and get away," he said. "You fellows are too willing to shoot me; that's why I held my breath when you passed so close while I hid behind that sagebrush."

Puts Name On Gun

When the revolver that was taken from under Jones' pillow was returned to Sheriff Allumbaugh, Jones remarked to Allumbaugh, "I rubbed your initials off of it and put my own on instead. I didn't think you'd be using it again."

Desire for revenge upon Sheriff Allumbaugh by causing him embarrassment during his campaign for re-election, Jones said was the motive back of the jail break.

"They have nothing on us and can't convict us of the Eagle robbery," Jones said. He told of the circumstances surrounding the arrest of himself and Dora Douglass, a waitress, and Langer, all of whom are charged with committing the Eagle bank robbery in which $2722 is reported to have been taken, all but $775 having since been recovered by the authorities.

Trouble With Sheriff

Trouble between himself and Sheriff Allumbaugh, Jones said, was of several years standing, dating back to the time Jones was released under parole from the state prison where he was serving a term for burglary committed at Jerome to which he and four other confessed, Jones receiving a prison sentence and the others lighter sentences.

"Allumbaugh tried for a long time to catch me in a violation of my parole so that I would be sent back to the 'big house,'" Jones stated. "When we were arrested and charged with the Eagle robbery he tried to get confessions. About two weeks before we left jail, Allumbaugh made good his threat to beat me up. I just folded my arms and took it. I knew that if I showed fight it would help Allumbaugh in his campaign for re-election and I began to plan to get away. I figured that I would put Allumbaugh in bad, and probably cost him his job. The election returns were good news to me."

Standlee Not to Blame

Jones indicated concern that Standlee, in whose room he was arrested, might be involved in the affair. He mentioned that his acquaintance with Standlee's parents was of several years standing, dating back to his arrival in Twin Falls from his former home in Oklahoma.

"Standlee knew nothing of my trouble," Jones declared. "I met him here and told him I was broke and hungry and he took me in."

The fact that Jones was in Twin Falls had been know since last Friday to the police; Chief Herriman stated Monday. Since that time Jones has been under close surveillance while the officers entertained hopes that he would be joined here by Langer so that Jones and Langer might both be captured at the same time.

Make Decision

Decision to wait no longer but to spring the trap for Jones was reached early this morning. Officers William Taylor II, H. U. Butz and Kennison were instructed by the police chief as to their part in the capture.

"It worked out like a motion picture play," Chief Herriman stated.

From previously designated vantage points the officers saw Standlee leave the house with a bucket going for water. Timing their entrance so that Jones would be expecting Standlee's return, Chief Herriman and Patrolman Kennison entered the room, the other officers remaining outside to guard avenues of possible escape.

Escape of Jones and Langer from the Ada county jail was made about 2 o'clock in the morning. According to accounts at the time, the prisoners had sawed the locks off their cell with a hacksaw and knocked the night watchman on the head with an iron bar. The night watchman had been called to the jail section where prisoners charged with more serious offenses were confined to let one of the prisoners who was ill, into the corridor. When he opened the outer door he was struck on the head. He recovered from the effects of the blow sufficiently to give the alarm after about 20 minutes.

Take Three Guns

The escaping prisoners broke open the gun case in the sheriff's office and took three revolvers and 100 rounds of ammunition and left the building.

Jones and Langer were the alleged principals in the robbery of the Eagle bank, the former being alleged to have covered the cashier and his daughter with a gun while the latter looted the vaults and cash trays in the office of $2722.

Within 24 hours after the arrest of Jones and Langer and the other alleged accomplices, Dora Douglass and "Hank" Endsley, driver of an automobile which is believed to have been in the control of the robbers during the robbery, sheriff's officers and Boise police recovered $1947 of the missing plunder.

Informations have been filed in the district court of Ada county charging the four suspects with robbery, but they had not been brought to trial when the jail break took place.

Reward of $500 for the capture of Jones and Langer has been offered.

Reprinted from Twin Falls Daily News, December 9, 1924

JONES HELD UNDER DOUBLE GUARD IN ADA COUNTY JAIL

Special Precautions Taken to Prevent Repetition of Eagle Bank Robber Suspect's Recent Escape; Talks Freely.

Double guard was placed over Oliver Jones, returned prisoner, in the Ada County jail Tuesday night and will be continued so long as Jones remains there, it was said by L. E. Allubmaugh, sheriff, who, with Henry Black, deputy, arrived late Monday night from Twin Falls with the prisoner. Jones was arrested Monday morning in a rooming house in Twin Falls following his escape from the Ada county jail October 16 with Chet Langer, who is still at large. Information filed against Jones, Langer, Dora Douglas and Hank Endsley by Laurel E. Elam, prosecuting attorney for Ada county, charges the quartet with robbing E. H. Fikkan, cashier of the Bank of Eagle, in a hold up of the bank August 11 last.

Jones was communicative enough following his arrest until the prosecuting attorney's office announced Tuesday afternoon it would not permit reporters to talk to the prisoner nor allow visitors to see him.

According to the story of the escape told by Jones to Sheriff Allumbaugh Tuesday morning, a "big car" figured in the getaway of the two prisoners, and what Jones designated as a "Main street gang" assisted in the plan. When the two left the jail, Jones is quoted as saying, they headed southeast towards the river bridge on Broadway. As soon as they saw the "big car," Jones is reported as saying, they knew they were safe.

Had Visited Boise

Jones said he had been in Boise after the escape and that twice he had "rubbed shoulders" with Ira Emory of the Boise police force.

The prisoner was quoted as saying that "he had been treated well" by the "Main street gang" and that now that he was recaptured they ought to see that he has a good attorney.

Efforts of the sheriff's office Tuesday to have Jones transferred to the penitentiary were unsuccessful, as state officers said, according to the sheriff, the penitentiary already is crowded and they could not see how they could make room for Jones. Sheriff Allumbaugh said he had obtained permission from the county commissioners to employ an extra night guard who will work with the regular watchman at the jail in guarding the prisoner.

The prosecuting attorney said Tuesday that Jones probably would be arraigned this morning, following the appearance in court at 10 o'clock of Dora Douglas to enter her plea. Mr. Elam said that so far as he knew the three alleged robbers in custody will be tried at one time. This will be some time at the January term, Mr. Elam said. No intimation has been received from attorneys of the prisoners that separate trials will be sought.

No Other Charge

No additional charge would be placed against Jones, said Mr. Elam, relative to the escape from jail. Under the statue, an escape from a county jail is a misdemeanor, punishable by a jail sentence.

H. W. Brown, deputy sheriff, Jack Dykeman, trusty, and a force of men returned Tuesday afternoon from near the T. R. Wilson ranch, Orchard, bring with them the gun Jones and Langer are said to have taken from Dykeman when the trusty was held prisoner by them November 18. Jones has denied the story as told by Dykeman, maintaining he never saw the trusty since leaving the jail. According to the sheriff, Jones said that the men who were in the shack where Dykeman was captured had told him where they threw the gun. The sheriff said he doubted Jones' story, and thinks the finding of the gun corroborates the story told by Dykeman. A lamp chimney, said to have finger prints on it, was brought back from the Wilson ranch and the prints will be examined to see if they correspond with either Jones' or Langer's.

The gun, a single barrel shotgun, the property of George Hardin, deputy sheriff, was broken off where the stock joins the metal, and the barrel was rusty from exposure. It was found in the sage brush half a mile east of the Wilson ranch, where, according to Dykeman, he was tied up by Jones and Langer, and later was able to release himself and make his way back to Boise.

Reprinted from the Idaho Statesman, December 10, 1924

DORA DOUGLASS MARRIES ALLEGED BANK BANDIT

Ceremony Performed Through Iron Bars of County Jail, State's Chief Witness in Eagle Robbery Cannot Be Complied to Testify Against Husband.

Dora Douglass, alleged member of the quartet that held up and robbed the Bank of Eagle August 11 last, and Oliver Jones, another of the alleged band, who is facing a charge of robbery, were married in the county jail Monday afternoon at shortly before 4 o'clock by Lawrence Johnson, justice of the peace. The ceremony was performed through the bars of the door leading to the cell room where Jones is confined. Marriage license was obtained at the county recorder's office earlier in the afternoon by Mrs. Douglass, who had with her as witness Frances L. Fitzpatric. The ceremony was witnessed by Miss Fitzpatrick and Ivan Hiller, attorney for Jones.

Mrs. Douglass was freed by the court, when the charge of robbery against her was dismissed on condition that she become a state's witness. According to Laurel E. Elam, Ada county prosecuting attorney, Mrs. Douglass consented to testify. As the law will not permit a wife to testify against her husband or a husband against his wife, unless the permission of both is obtained, the present circumstances, according to the prosecuting attorney's office, has temporarily embarrassed the states position.

According to Ben Paine, deputy, who was the only one in the sheriff's office at the time, Mr. Hiller came in the front entrance while Mrs. Douglass and Miss Fitzpatrick came in the rear door. A few minutes later Mr. Johnson arrived. The ceremony occupied but a few minutes. Several prisoners who were in the room adjoining the cell stood about while the ceremony took place. Mr. Paine said he was unaware of what was going on until after everything was over.

L. E. Allumbaugh, sheriff of Ada county, who was in Caldwell Monday on business in connection with his office, said that had he been present he would have forbidden the ceremony to take place in the jail.

Members of the Ada county board of commissioners said Monday that the mothers' pension which Dora Douglass has been drawing for her two minor children, totalling approximately $20 a month, would automatically cease now that she is married.

Jones is scheduled to go on trial before Judge Clinton H. Hartson in district court January 19, along with Chet Langer; another of the alleged band. The fourth alleged member, Henery Endsley, who pleaded guilty to a charge of accessory after the fact, was paroled by the court December 22.

Langer and Jones escaped from the county jail October 16, following their arrest on the robbery charges, and Jones was recaptured December 8 at Twin Falls and Langer at Taft, Cal., December 15.

Reprinted from The Idaho Statesman, January 6, 1925

JUSTICE DEFEATED WHEN ALLEGED BANK ROBBER AND STAR WITNESS FOR STATE AGAINST HIM WED IN CEREMONY IN JAIL

Marriage Is Well Planned and Executed --- County Peace Officers Ignorant of Proceedings Till Too Late.

"We have postponed our honeymoon indefinitely," was the comment of Oliver Jones, jailbreaker and alleged bank robber, when he was congradulated on his marriage to Dora Douglas, shortly after the ceremony in the county jail, Monday afternoon.

The former Mrs. Douglas was the alleged accomplice of Jones and two others - Chet Langer and Hank Endsley - in the hold-up and robbery of the bank of Eagle, Aug. 11, 1924. Charges against her were dismissed on agreement of counsel when she agreed to turn state's witness against Langer and Jones. As a result of the marriage, however, the woman will not now be required to testify against her husband, according to the rules of the law.

Well-Planned

That the marriage was well planned and executed is evidenced by the speed and facility with which it was carried through. At 3 p. m. Monday Mrs. Douglass appeared at the county recorder's office and with Frances Fitzpatrick as witness obtained a marriage license. At 3:05 she stood at the bars of the cell occupied by Jones, having slipped into jail, unobserved, through a rear entrance. Lawrence Johnson,

justice of the peace, was conveniently at hand, ready to perform the ceremony. Ivan Hiler, counsel for Jones, was another witness.

The woman reached her arms through the iron bars, clasped the hand of her lover, and by 3:15 Oliver Jones and Dora Douglass were man and wife.

Prisoners Watch

In the detention ward across from Jones' cell the prisoners pressed their gaunt faces against the heavy bars of a small aperture - interested but silent spectators of the unusual proceedings.

But one member of the sheriff's force was in the building at the time. Ben Paine, deputy, who occupied the front office, declares he knew nothing of the happenings until the ceremony had been performed. Sheriff L. E. Allumbaugh, however, is emphatic in his contention that had he been present he would have done everything in his power to prevent the marriage.

Jones and Langer will go on trial for bank robbery in Judge Clinton H. Hartson's district court, Jan. 19. It is now a question as to the extent the case of the state will be weakened by the marriage of its star witness.

"The marriage will in no way affect the outcome of the trial," said Laurel E. Elam, prosecuting attorney. *"The two are just making things worse for themselves."*

Different Opinion

Other lawyers, however, are of the opinion that the case of the state against Jones has suffered a complete collapse as a result of the wedding. As one attorney put it:

"The marriage of Jones and Mrs. Douglass has not only weakened the case against the former, but has also materially weakened the case against Langer, for much testimonyy that involves Langer can now be held back on the grounds that it is prejudicial to Jones."

Another lawyer laid blame for the entire affair on the state.

Says State Outwitted

"The state," he said, "Has been outwitted all the way through. Charges against Mrs. Douglass should have never been dismissed until she was ready to ascend the witness stand. The wheels of justice have moved to slowly in this case and the unnecessary delays have resulted in disaster."

Although a statement of damaging testimony against Jones and Langer is alleged to have been obtained from Mrs. Jones by the prosecuting attorney, it is considered unlikely that introduction of this as evidence in the trial will be permitted by the court. It is felt in some quarters, however, that if it can be shown that the marriage was brough about with the deliberate intentions of defeating the ends of justice that introduction of the statement will be allowed.

In Prospect Three Years

According to Jones, his betrothal to Mrs. Douglass had been in prospect some three years.

"I am a very happy man," he said at the close of the ceremony, Monday afternoon.

Jones escaped from the Ada county jail with Chet Langer, Oct. 16. He was recaptured in Twin Falls, however, Dec. 8, and Langer was nabbed in California a week later. Both pleaded not guilty. Hank Endsley, who pleaded guilty as an accessory after the fact to the robbery was paroled by Judge Raymond Givens after he had been sentenced to from one to two years in the state penitentiary.

Reprinted from The Evening Capital News, January 6, 1925

BANDITS WRITE FINAL CHAPTER IN BANK DRAMA

Jones and Langer end Sensational Case by Pleading Guilty to Holdup at Eagle; Langer Given 6 to 15 Years

Oliver Jones wrote finis Saturday to the Eagle bank robbery drama, when he pleaded guilty to robbery before Judge Clinton H. Hartson. In the dingy little Ada county court room where Moyer, Haywood and Pettibone stood trial for the murder of Governor Frank Steuneberg, and before a little gathering of court attaches, sheriff's deputies and newspapermen, the reported leader of the band signified his desire to change his former plea of not guilty, and asked the court to set Monday afternoon at 2 o'clock for pronouncing sentence.

The prisoner dressed in a pair of overalls and a khaki shirt, confined his discourse to repetition of "yes sir," as the court asked him if he desired to change his plea, and further queries if the time for fixing sentence was acceptable.

Earlier in the afternoon Chet Langer, Jones' partner had appeared in the same court room, changed his plea of not guilty to guilty, and had been sentenced to serve from six to 15 years in the state penitentiary. While Jones was in court attaches from the penitentiary were conveying Langer to the state prison to begin his term.

Woman Granted Immunity.

Henry Endsley, driver of the taxicab in which the bandit gang traveled, is on parole following his plea of guilty as accessory, while Dora Douglass-Jones wife of the central figure, who turned state's evidence has been granted immunity.

It was early in the morning of August 11 that an auto bearing three masked persons besides the driver, stopped in front of the bank of Eagle. The three masked bandits, a woman and two men, descended. The woman stayed by the machine while the men entered and held up the cashier, E. H. Fikkan, and his daughter, Margaret, forced them to stand to one side while one looted the vault, and then locked them in the vault. They drove away to the west.

They were captured the following night in Boise and charges of robbery filed against them.

The quartet was next heard from when in the early morning hours of October 16 Jones and Langer sawed their way from jail, hit the jailer, locked him in, and decamped with guns and ammunition, leaving Endsley and the Douglass woman to face the music.

A series of small holdups, culminating with the robbery of an interurban car, marked October. The offensive on the car was not so successful as some of the others, for the doughty train crew fought back and worsted the assailants, who however, escaped with a watch.

It was just a month later that Sheriff L. E. Allumbaugh was tipped off that the two were in the neighborhood of Orchard. A posse started out after them, and the robbers distinguished themselves again by kidnapping a member of it, Jack Dykeman, a trusty at the county jail, taking his gun away from him and taking him to a vacant ranch house, where he was tied and left, as he told the searchers later.

Watch Led to Undoing.

The watch led to Jones' undoing, however. It appeared in a Twin Falls pawnshop, and shortly after, in the closing week of November, he was arrested and brought to Boise. Langer was captured the next week in Bakersfield, Cal., and also returned here.

Their next contribution to the gaiety of Boise came after the Douglass woman had been promised immunity in return for her testimony against the other three. Jones was arraigned December 8, and 10 days later pleaded not guilty. A few days following Boise awoke to the fact that the Douglass woman had entered the jail and become the wife of Jones, the ceremony being performed by Lawrence Johnston, justice of the peace. Those who had watched the case immediately recalled that a wife cannot testify against her husband except with his consent.

Meantime Endsley pleaded guilty to a charge of accessory after the fact and was paroled.

The closing act of the drama came as a surprise. Jones and Langer were to have gone on trial Monday morning and 50 jurors had been summoned. Last minute preparations were complete, when at 2:30 o'clock Saturday afternoon defense counsel asked Judge Hartson to hear them in regard to the case. Langer appeared and pleaded guilty, his sentence being pronounced at 3:30 o'clock.

Jones held out longer, and seemed undecided, but just as the courthouse clock struck five he entered the courtroom and admitted his guilt.

Witnesses who had known Chet Langer during his life in Boise appeared before the court and asked leniency. Defense counsel intimated Saturday that witnesses to seek similar consideration for Jones would appear Monday afternoon.

Reprinted from The Idaho Statesman, January 18, 1925

EAGLE BANK ROBBERS CONFESS ON EVE OF TRIAL

OLIVER JONES FOLLOWS LEAD OF LANGER AND PLEADS GUILTY TO ROBBERY EAGLE BANK; LANGER IS SENTENCED 6-15 YEARS

Last of Alleged Robber Band Changes Plea at Eleventh Hour__Many Witnesses Are Called for Langer

Deserted by his alleged accomplices and blocked by an apparently insurmountable wall of damaging evidence, Oliver Jones, last of the quartet charged with the robbery, Aug. 11, of the Bank of Eagle, late Saturday afternoon entered a plea of guilty. Earlier in the afternoon, Chet Langer, another member of the alleged rober band, had also changed his plea to guilty.

Langer was sentenced by Judge Clinton H. Hartson, of the district court, to not less than six nor more than 15 years in the state penitentiary. Commitment papers were issued immediately, and Langer was removed to the penitentiary Saturday afternoon by Warden Joseph W. Wheeler, to begin sentence.

Jones' Sentence Monday

Pronouncement of sentence on Jones was deferred to Monday afternoon at 2 o'clock, on motion of Ivan Hiler, attorney for the defendant. Speculation is rife as to whether Jones will receive a heavier sentence than Langer. As yet, no mitigating circumstances have been introduced in Jones' case, as was done for his fellow prisoner.

Laurel Elam, prosecuting attorney, expressed satisfaction with the action taken by the two men.

"Considering the strength of the evidence," he said, "I don't see what else they could have done."

Venire Drawn

The trial of the two alleged bank robbers was to have begun Monday morning with the selection of a jury. A venire list of 50 prospective jurors had been drawn up. Judge Hartson ordered Saturday that no official action toward dismissal of the ventremen be taken until Monday.

Decision of Jones to plead guilty came only after a series of conferences with his attorney Saturday afternoon. Jones was stubborn to the last. Several times during the afternoon he had announced emphatically his intentions of fighting the charges to the "bitter end." He was finally persuaded, however, to pursue a different course, and at 5:30 o'clock made it known that he would enter a plea of guilty.

Heavier Than Expected

Langer was apparently dissatisfied with the penalty imposed. He is reported to have said that the sentence was considerably heavier than he had expected.

Twelve witnesses took the stand on Langer's behalf to testify as to his past life and habits. The witnesses were Lafe Boone, C. H. Packenham, Rev. E. N. Murphy, Fire Chief W. A. Foster, W. E. Curtis, K. E. Way. Mr. Chester, Ed M. McGuffin, Mrs. Susan Roberts, Mrs. Hansen, Mrs. Elizabeth Mathews, and Mrs. Cluster. All professed to be acquainted with the defendant and his family and testified that Langer's record previous to the Bank of Eagle affair had be unmarred. P. E. Cavaney, in his final plea for the defendant, requested leniency in view of mitigating circumstances described by the witnesses.

Jail Break Stressed

Mr. Elam closed the argument for the state by outlining the facts of the robbery and laying emphasis on the subsequent jail break. He stoutly refused to make any recommendation of leniency for Langer.

Judge Hartson in pronouncing sentence, pointed out that he had taken into consideration the previous record of the defendant and had given it due weight. "However," he continued "we must also consider the rights of the state and of the people." Judge Hartson alluded to the jail break as a matter of some weight in determining the severity of punishment.

Mr. And Mrs. Frank Langer, parents of the confessed robber, were present in the court room. The latter went freely throughout the proceedings.

Sigh of Relief

Hearing of Oliver Jones was in marked contrast to that of Langer. No friends, save his attorneys were there to plead for him. Jones appeared slightly nervous during his arraignment, but at it's conclusion heaved a sigh of relief and was conducted back to his quarters in the county jail. Monday afternoon, after sentence is pronounced, Jones will follow Langer to the "big house," there to spend the best years of his life.

Sentencing of Jones Monday will bring to a close one of the most sensational criminal cases in the annals of Ada county. Beginning with the daring holdup and robbery of the Bank of Eagle, Aug. 11, the affair has been fraught with the startling and unexpected.

First There Were Four

Originally there were four defendants to the robbery charge. "Hank" Endsley, Dora Douglas, Langer, and Jones. All were housed in the county jail until the escape of Jones and Langer therefrom. The latter two were recaptured, however, after about two months of "absence without leave."

"Hank" Endsley was released on parole after he had pleaded guilty to being an accessory after the fact to the robbery. Dora Douglas was even more fortunate. Charges against her were dismissed, when she agreed to turn state's witness against Langer and Jones, both of whom had pleaded not guilty.

But that was not the end, Mrs. Douglas took everyone by surprise by becoming the wife of Jones in a quiet jail ceremony. This it was expected would wreck the case of the state against Jones, since the former Mrs. Douglas would not be required to testify against her husband. The change of plea by Jones, indicates, however, that Mrs. Douglas was not the only trump in the hand of the state.

Reprinted from The Evening Capital News, January 18, 1925
(Front page Headlines)

JONES GOES TO STATE PRISON

Confessed Eagle Bandit Given 10 to 20 Year Sentence by Judge Hartson.

Oliver Jones confessed bank robber, will spend not less than 10 and not more than 20 years in the state penitentiary for his part in the holdup of the Bank of Eagle August 11 last. This was the sentence pronounced Monday afternoon at 2 o'clock by Judge Clinton H. Hartson in district court. Chet Langer, alleged accomplish, was sentenced Saturday to not less than six nor more than 15 years in the penitentiary. Both men changed their pleas Saturday to guilty, after arrangements had been made for trial which was scheduled to start Monday morning. All but 20 of the venire of 50 men summoned were dismissed Monday by Judge Hartson. The 20 will report again next Monday to the court.

Dora Douglass-Jones, wife of Oliver, whose wedding in the county jail January 5 was one of the several sensational features of the case since the arrest of the quartet alleged to have taken part in the bank robbery, was a spectator in the court room when sentence was pronounced. She received immunity December 18 when the charge of robbery against her was dismissed on condition that she would be a state's witness. She stood in the rear of the court room, near the entrance, and made no sign of emotion when she heard the sentence. They left the court room together, his arm about her, and walked to the county jail accompanied by a deputy.

Goes to Prison.

The commitment papers were signed by Judge Hartson later in the afternoon and Jones went to the penitentiary at 5:45 o'clock. Langer was taken to the prison Saturday. The one other member of the alleged robber band, Henry Endsley, was paroled December 22, after a sentence of not less than one year and not more than two years was pronounced.

Ivan Hiler, attorney for Jones, plead for leniency, and referred to the disposition of the charges against the other defendants. Mr. Hiler said there was no doubt but that by pleading guilty the county had been saved much expense, as a trial of the case would have been long, and many witnesses brought to testify. This matter, he said, should be taken into consideration. S. L. Tipton and Thomas J. Jones, Boise attorneys, spoke for Jones, interceding for the court's clemency. Laurel E. Elam, Ada county prosecuting attorney, reviewed the story of the robbery, and gave the court a statement of what had been learned of Jones' past record.

Judge Hartson's comments were brief. He held that Jones had been given a chance and had failed to take advantage of it.

Reprinted from The Idaho Statesman, January 20, 1925

TWO MOTORISTS OF TWIN FALLS DROWN IN LOW LINE CANAL

N. E. (Casey) Jones, 30, and Ullin (Casey) Kessinger, 23, Drown When Car Breaks Through Span

The bodies of N. E. (Casey) Jones, 30, Van Buren street, and Ullin (Casey) Kessinger, 23, Twin Falls, were recovered late last night, after the car in which they were riding hurtled through a condemned bridge into the waters of the low line canal two miles west and one mile south of Flier about 9:15 last night.

Lon White, 217 Third Avenue East, a third member of the party, released himself from the submerged car and swam to the shore, escaping without injury.

Shortly before the fatal plunge, the car in which the three men were riding had left Flier, with two state traffic officers in pursuit. It was asserted that traffic officers sought to overtake the car on account of traffic violation charged against the driver when it passed through traffic at the entrance to the county fairgrounds about 8 P. M.

The three men had been on the fairgrounds during the afternoon and earlier evening. They were traveling in Jone's car, a big sedan.

Lead in Rescue Efforts

Pursuing officers arrived at the canal bank almost immediately after the car disappeared under the water, and led in the efforts to rescue the doomed men

There were bruises about the head and face of each of the drown men indicating possibility that they had been hurt and so rendered unable to extricate themselves from the car after it plunged into the water.

White suffered from severe shock and was unable to give any coherrent account of the occurrences.

Dr. H. N. Lette, county coroner, following an investigation last night at the scene of the accident, said no inquest would be held.

N. E. Jones, one of the drowned men, had been a resident of Twin Falls for about 12 years, coming here from Arkansas with his mother, Mrs. Elizabeth McIntyre, 233 Quincy street, and a number of brothers and sister. He had been engaged for some months past in business here as a dealer in used automobiles. He was married and is survived by his widow and four children, Doris 10; Eugene 8; Olen 6, and Shirley 3. He also leaves eight brothers and three sisters.

Ullin Kessinger had been a Twin Falls resident for about three years and was employeed as a clerk at Dell's Cigar store. He came here from Springfield, Missouri, where relatives reside. He was not married.

Lon White is an employee of the Standard Furniture Company.

Reprinted from Twin Falls Daily News, September 10, 1931

TWO HELD ON CHARGE OF ROBBING POOL HALL

Russell Cavendar and Oliver Jones charged with robbery of Guido Daz at Montello during the summer, were today bound over to the district court on $3000 bail which they were unable to furnish and their trials will probably be held during the fall term of the court.

At the preliminary in the justice court this morning, the state had two witnesses, Daz who was robbed and Ray Standlee, who was arrested at the time of the robbery and who was released upon motion of the district attorney who stated that after full investigation he believed that there was insufficient evidence to connect him with the crime.

Daz stated that the two men entered his pool hall, held him up at the point of a gun and after removing approximately $25 from the cash register, forced him to open the safe. There being but eighty cents in the safe drawer, they did not disturb it.

The two robbers then forced Daz to lie on the floor back of the bar while they made their escape. As soon as they were gone Daz notified the officers and the men were later picked up in Twin Falls.

Judge M. W. Johnson of Montello heard the case. District Attorney J. L. Clark and Deputy District Attorney Lester Foley represented the stat and the defendants were represented by attorney A. Clyde Stringham.

Reprinted from The Elko Independent, September 25, 1931

HOLDUP MEN FOUND GUILTY

Attempted Jail Break by Cavendar and Jones is Foiled

Again a jury in Elko District Court found evidence of guilt sufficient to convict defendants charged with crimes against the peace and dignity of the State of Nevada, when eleven men and one woman brought in a verdict of guilty to a charge of holding up and robbing the poolroom of Guido Daz at Montello, last July 30 against Russell Cavendar and Oliver Jones Thursday afternoon. The conviction carries with it a minimum of six years imprisonment in the state penitentiary, at Carson City.

Judge L. O. Hawkins presiding in the absence of Judge Carville, announced he would pass judgment and sentence upon the convicted men Monday morning at 10 o'clock.

Nothing like so much interest has been manifested in this trial and in that of the state against Ernesto Hess, convicted of burglary in the second degree last week, as was shown in the trail of Reta Thurman but the court room has been about half full at nearly every session.

The state's case against Jones and Cavendar was all on direct evidence and the defendants were forced to offer weak alibi, which was exploded Thursday morning by two witnesses who came here from Twin Falls Idaho. Jones has served sentences for burglary and bank robbery prior to his present conviction and Cavendar has been in prison once, on conviction on a holdup charge.

During the trail evidence was adduced showing that the defendants had tried to escape from the Elko county jail and that they had sawed the locks on their cells partly through when discovered by the jailor.

According to Sheriff Harris, the saws were passed to the defendants through an outside window presumably by a person who had served six months in jail on a bad check charge. There are screens on all the windows, but one was easily cut and the saws received by the inmates.

District Attorney Clark made an effort to have this testimony brought out before the jury but Judge Hawkins ruled that it was inadmissible. The purpose of the testimony, according to the District Attorney was to show the defendants guilt inasmuch as they desired to escape before their case came to trail.

There has never been a jailbreak in the Elko county jail although it has held some desperate criminals who have been accused of almost every know crime.

Reprinted from Elko Independent, October 30, 1931

A Bandit Called Derby

PRISON VAN IS DUE THURSDAY

Four Convicted At Present Court Term Go To Carson

The State's "Bad Men's Bus" otherwise know as the prison van which transports prisoners from county seats to the Nevada Penitentiary at Carson City, is expected here Thursday some time, Sheriff Harris said today, and four prisoners convicted and sentenced at the present term of court here will make the journey to the capitol to start serving their terms.

Oliver Jones and Russell Cavendar, who were convicted of robbery in connection with the holdup of a poolroom, at Wendover, were sentenced to serve one to five years.

John Rucker, convicted yesterday of shooting E. G. "slim" Davis in a gambling place at Wells, will be sentenced Thursday in time to make the trip with the others. His term will be one to fourteen years.

Le Roye James, Negro, who pleas guilty to a charge of burglarizing Rupe's poolroom, and was sentenced to serve one to five years, completes the quartette that will go from Elko on this trip of the bus.

Reprinted from Elko Independent, November 11, 1931